SEIZE THE TIME

SEIZE THE TIME

Vladimir Keremidschieff

With an Afterword by Jamie Reid

Vancouver | New Star Books | 2013

NEW STAR BOOKS LTD.

107 – 3477 Commercial Street | Vancouver, BC V5N 4E8 CANADA
1574 Gulf Road, #1517 | Point Roberts, WA 98281 USA
www.NewStarBooks.com | info@NewStarBooks.com

The publisher acknowledges the financial support of the Canada Council for the Arts and the Government of Canada through the Canada Book Fund, and the Province of British Columbia through the British Columbia Arts Council and the Book Publishing Tax Credit.

Cataloguing information for this book is available from
Library and Archives Canada, www.collectionscanada.gc.ca.

Cover and book design and layout by Rayola Creative
Cover photo by Vladimir Keremidschieff
Printed and bound in Canada by Friesens Printing, Altona, MB
First printing, October 2013

SEIZE
THE
TIME

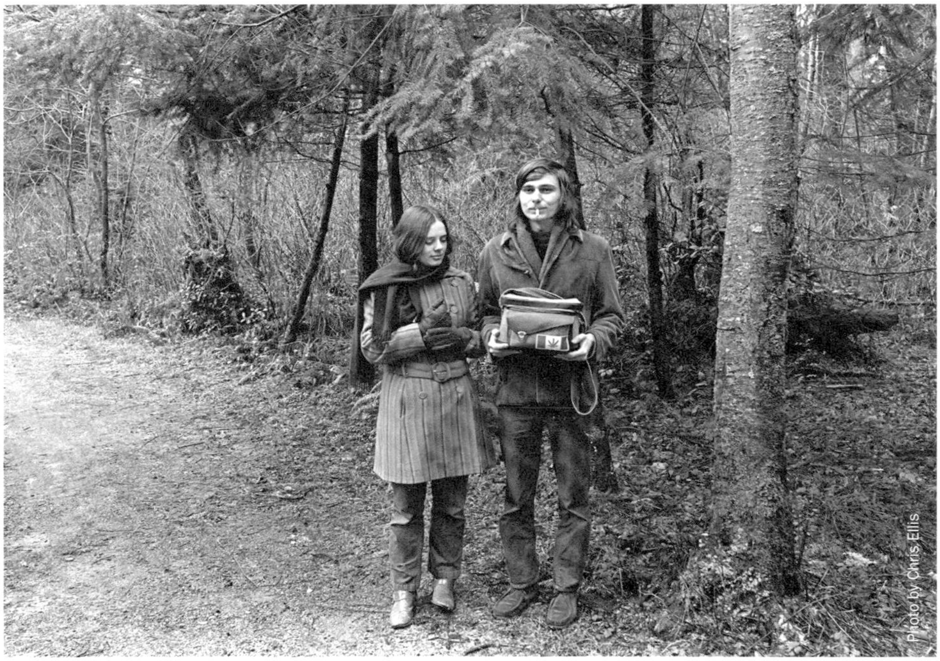

To Lindsay, who was there then and is here now.

IF MY FRIEND CHRIS HAD GONE TO JAIL after being arrested for smoking marijuana in Los Angeles, I might never have become interested in photography. As it turned out, he was never charged and was free to return to Vancouver, his hometown. He had gone to L.A., met a woman and decided to stay there (love does that). However, after his arrest he returned to Vancouver for Christmas. He brought with him a new Honeywell Pentax Spotmatic 35mm camera (outside of the U.S. it was known as the Asahi Pentax). We took pictures of each other walking along Denman Street in the West End, sitting in trees, fooling around on the beaches in the cold, cloudy winter. We photographed everything we saw — shop windows, statues, peeling paint, birds and squirrels and seagulls, boats, gutters full of debris, cobwebs and trees — it didn't matter what, we were having fun. So much so that when Chris realized he had made a mistake coming back to Vancouver and returned to L.A and his woman, I went out and bought my own Pentax and, through trial and error, learned how to use it.

When I bought my Pentax in 1967, I wasn't even 21 and was already married. (I no longer have the camera but my wife is still with me.) The following year we drove our lumbering dark-green Dodge Fargo flower-delivery van, Ours is a Blooming Business, to Banff for a summer school course in photography. It was at the Banff School of Fine Arts, in the magnificent Rocky Mountains, that I fell in love with the darkroom.

We were surrounded by the breathtaking beauty of the mountains, the glories of incredibly clear blue mountain lakes, an exuberant mother nature showing off what it can do — a setting that could make you believe in God. But I found the most joy in the weird darkness of the photographic darkroom. I loved the smell of the chemicals, the eerie glow of the red light, the solitude of working in that dull twilight, seeing my photograph slowly emerge from the chemical bath. This was the most satisfying thing I had ever done; photography was no longer just a hobby or a plaything. I had a need and a desire to learn more. I felt I had to take photographs, I had to be in a darkroom making prints, I had to be good at it. This would be no small thing.

Photography is not all that complicated. There are a few basic rules and firstly you get good at them, learn to really understand them, and then you break them. I used up many rolls of 35mm film, gallons of chemicals and probably thousands of sheets of photographic paper that ended up in the garbage to learn how to control the medium, to understand the technology and make it do what I wanted. Of course, it's not just technique that makes a good photograph. Some technically excellent photographs are boring while some remarkable photographs may lack good technique but have that undefinable quality that reaches out and touches the viewer.

The mid-to-late sixties were boisterous times. God wasn't in the mountains and streams but in marijuana, LSD and music. The music came from England, from New York, from San Francisco and Los Angeles and drifted up like smoke into Vancouver, turning everyone on. Led Zeppelin came in 1969 and played at the PNE Agrodome. They weren't yet famous enough for the larger Pacific Coliseum where the Monkees had played a few months earlier. I photographed Phil Ochs playing a free concert at Second Beach in 1970. He did a lot of that, he was always available to help out. He suffered mental problems later, became an alcoholic and lived on the streets for a while. Just six years after his wonderful free concert in Stanley Park he hung himself. Acts such as Frank Zappa, Peter, Paul and Mary, Jefferson Airplane, Jimi Hendrix, Cream and Blind Faith, Ike and Tina Turner, Paul Butterfield, the Velvet Underground, James Brown and the Rolling Stones put Vancouver on the music map. Van Morrison played at the War Memorial Gym at UBC. Ella Fitzgerald played at the Cave Supper Club. Blues artists, folk singers, hard rock acts, jazz masters — all visited and opened minds and doors.

In 1965 Bob Dylan played the Queen Elizabeth Theatre. You could buy tickets for $2 — or $4 if you wanted premium seats. He'd already released five albums by then. When we discovered his first album in 1962, we were blown away. Dylan wrote in his autobiography, *Chronicles: Volume One*, that listening to Roy Orbison "made you want to drive your car over a cliff." Listening to those early Dylan recordings was like having a dump truck explode in your head. He could make the blind see, the deaf hear and the righteous weep. I didn't get a chance to photograph him until 1974, in Seattle. It was the last photo I had printed in the *Vancouver Sun*.

Besides dope and music, the other defining event of this era was the Vietnam War and all that went with it. Although Canada was not sending soldiers to the jungles of Vietnam, there were constant protests against Canada's complicity in the war. Canadian companies made fortunes selling war materiel to America. Some 2.5 billion dollars of napalm, explosives and ammunition was sold to the Pentagon by approximately five hundred Canadian companies. Supplementary material such as boots, berets and food brought in another ten billion dollars. Canada also aided the war effort by providing training grounds for the U.S. military — American bomber pilots practised carpet-bombing techniques in Alberta. While about ten thousand Canadians joined the U.S. military, approximately thirty-two thousand

American draft dodgers and deserters fled to Canada. These Americans helped to radicalize Canadian youth. University, college, and even high school students were at the forefront of the anti-war demonstrations.

In October, 1968, Vancouverites participated in the International Day of Protest against the war. Protest marches with signs, banners and music gradually became larger and larger as more and more Vietnamese and Americans died in the paddy fields and jungles and cities of Vietnam. The Tet offensive in Vietnam exposed the weakness of the American position and the lies the American military had been feeding the public. Even middle-class Canadians, moms and dads, turned against the war. It wasn't until 1995 that the then Secretary of Defense, Robert McNamara, finally admitted that the whole thing was a terrible mistake. We knew that long before he did.

Nineteen sixty-eight was one of the most turbulent years of the era. Martin Luther King was murdered in April and some 110 American cities went up in flames, resulting in the deaths of at least thirty-six people. Students rioted in Paris, and in May a general strike by eleven million workers across France paralysed the nation. In June, Robert Kennedy was assassinated. On August 21, Russian and Warsaw Pact tanks rolled into Czechoslovakia to suppress the "Prague Spring." A few days later the infamous Democratic Convention took place in Chicago, resulting in over 100 demonstrators being sent to hospital and even more arrested. Richard Nixon became president in November. The year ended with the three astronauts of Apollo 8 circling the moon for the first time, in preparation for next year's Apollo 11 moon landing.

Two years later, in October, 1970, there was another round of massive protests when Prime Minister Pierre Trudeau invoked the War Measures Act of 1914 in response to the kidnappings of British High Commissioner James Cross and the Quebec Minister of Labour, Pierre Laporte. A week after kidnapping Laporte, the FLQ (Front de libération du Québec) announced that he had been killed. Heavily armed soldiers patrolled the streets of Quebec. Nearly five hundred people were arrested without warrant but only sixty-two ended up being charged with any offense. Although the majority of Canadians supported the implementation of the Act, a vocal minority staged protests around the country decrying the use of the military in what was seen as essentially a criminal matter. Vancouver mayor Tom Campbell issued a statement saying that he could use the provisions of the Act to clean out the hippies in Vancouver. He quickly backtracked after a storm of protest, including from the federal government, which pointed out that this was not the intent or proper use of the Act.

For all the turbulence of the times, there was a great optimism among the young. We felt we could change the world, change it into a better place with more freedom and greater understanding. While some things were clearly for the better, such as the art, the music, the sexual revolution, women's liberation, and the confrontation with racism, it's difficult some forty years later to say that the "revolution" was successful. Some things are better. Some are worse. Life is like that.

In 1968 I opened a small studio-cum-darkroom in a shopfront on Yew Street, half a block off Fourth Avenue, and began freelancing photos to the newspapers and looking for customers. The first photos I published were in the *The Province*. I should remember how it came to be, but I don't. I just know that one of the first photos was of jazz great Lionel Hampton at Isy's Supper Club on West Georgia Street. A few weeks later I shot Little Richard there. After that, I began to do some of the big concerts that came into town.

It was pretty hectic as I wasn't allowed to use the newspaper facilities: after a shoot I'd race to my darkroom, hoping I had something useable, develop the film, make a print (or perhaps two), and then hightail it to the newspaper offices in the newly built Pacific Press building on Granville Street, near the south end of the Granville Bridge. Time was tight. Often shows didn't begin until after 9:00 or 9:30 and the deadline for photos was 11:00. It didn't leave me much time to get a shot and come up with a print. Sometimes I drove down the street waving the print out the window, trying to dry it as I sped along the quiet streets in my old VW Karmann Ghia. It was tight but fun. And you always had to have a shot — that's the unwavering rule of newspaper photography. After all, there was a hole in the paper where your photo would go with the review and if you didn't have a useable photo, well, you had a very short career in newspapers. Editors are funny that way: they expect you to come up with the goods, on time, every time. I may have handed in some still damp prints but I never missed a deadline.

For a number of years I fed photos to Vancouver's "underground" newspaper, the *Georgia Straight*, which in its early days managed to outrage just about everybody at some time or another, and was the most persecuted newspaper in Canada's history. I don't remember ever getting paid for anything I gave to the *Straight*, but if I did it was very little. I didn't really care. This was about photography, not money.

In May, 1969, the *Straight* published a two-page spread of my Aldergrove Pop Festival pictures. A couple of days later I heard a large motorcycle draw up at my shop front. A biker with a beard, tattoos and denim came through the door. He was as big as a truck, and looked mean as a cut snake.

"Are you Vlad, the photographer?" he bellowed at me.

I wasn't sure whether to admit to it or not but the shop front was plastered with photos. This wasn't looking good. I couldn't figure out what he was after. He asked whether I had taken the photos of the Aldergrove Festival and again, it was hard to deny as my name was all over them. A big smile broke through the beard; he grabbed my hand and shook it vigorously.

"Man, they were great shots. Can we get some of our colours?"

Of course! I had a photo published of his motorcycle gang crawling all over the stage during an act, wearing their colours, the large patch on the back of their denim jackets that identified their gang. For the next month or so I had gang members dropping in at the shop, sitting around on the floor smoking (I didn't have chairs), their big bikes parked out front. They turned out to not be as tough as they thought they were, but they certainly added an element of colour to my place, an element that wasn't good for clients. Fortunately, they eventually got bored with me and disappeared. I never even saw any of them on the streets around Fourth Avenue after that.

For the audience a concert is an aural experience, but for the photographer it's a visual event. Photography is all about light; the word itself means "writing with light." If there's not enough of it there to make an image on film you carry your own light, or you go home and put up your feet. Without adequate light, you have nothing. The question is, what's adequate? It appeared that the night-clubs and the early concerts didn't seem overly concerned about lighting. A black stage, a spot or two and that was it. Even worse, sometimes they used a blue or red spot. Nothing you can do then as you can't use a flash during a performance. Might as well sit down and listen to the music. But you can't do that either; you have to get a shot. How far can the film and the developing be pushed to come up with a useable print?

I was always a black and white photographer and for concerts I used only Kodak Tri-X film. It's rated at 400 ASA, which is not nearly enough for most entertainment situations, so I pushed it to 800, 1200 and even 1600, four times its rating. This is pushing the film to its very limits. The result is a very "thin" negative with not much detail in the blacks and often over-exposed faces. The skill lies in creating a print from a negative that you shouldn't be able to print — but I didn't know that it couldn't be done. I learned pretty quickly how to breathe life into these near dead negatives, and even if the shot wasn't exactly award-winning, it was printable in a newspaper. Pushing film like this creates grain but sometimes the grain adds to the appeal of the photo, giving it an interesting texture. I spent hours and hours experimenting with film, developers and print-making, tweaking processes to come up with a useable and interesting print.

Although the lighting at that time couldn't compete with modern concerts with their flash and dash, security was far easier. With a camera around your neck you often got access in front of the stage. More than once a roadie even beckoned me up on stage to shoot from the wings, which would be impossible today without a long drawn-out negotiation with the promoter and security guards and the artist's manager, and passes of various colours hanging around your neck. Security was much more relaxed. It was another fifteen or so years before John Lennon was murdered and rock stars felt they were targets.

Having worked under tight deadlines with poor lighting, shooting in the daytime was a breeze. I covered all kinds of daytime events — demonstrations, the "be-ins" in Stanley Park, pop festivals. In 1969 I covered the Aldergrove Pop Festival, the Paradise Valley Pop Festival and a big festival in nearby Seattle. It was the year of festivals. From August 15 to 19 the most famous festival of all took place at Woodstock. The year ended with the Rolling Stones headlining the infamous Altamont Speedway Free Festival in December. An audience member, Meredith Hunter, pulled out a gun and was stabbed by one of the Hells Angels gang members that were hired (for $500 worth of beer) as security guards. Three others died in accidents. It signalled the end of the peace and love "hippie era."

Much has been written lately about rock photography. While taking photos at concerts has its own problems, such as lighting, crowds, and access to a good spot to shoot from, in other respects it is similar to any kind of shoot. You always try to get a shot that says something about the subject, the event and, inevitably and unconsciously, about the photographer. The 1969 photo I took of Eric Clapton when he was with Blind Faith has an almost religious quality to it, embodying the famous graffiti "Clapton is God," which began appearing all over London in 1965 when he played with John Mayall and the Bluesbreakers. In another shot, Leo Lyons, bass player for Ten Years After, throws his bass into the air, hair flying, a smile on his lips. It shows something not only about Leo and his style, but about the exuberance and the joy of rock and roll. It's one of my favourite pictures. I have two photos of Janis Joplin in this collection. One shows her hard-drinking, hard-living life, on and off stage, as she drinks from a bottle of tequila, lemon slice in hand. But the other photo, a close-up, shows another side of Joplin: the soulful blues singer, the gentle, vulnerable Janis that made her one of the greatest female blues singers of her generation.

I loved taking street pictures of the life around me. I never did much nature photography and I hated setting up shots, fiddling with lights and backdrops, posing people. Studio work was not for me. I liked to work with what was there in front of me. Just leave it alone and become invisible, and work out the problems as you go along. For me, capturing the moment meant letting the moment reveal itself and being ready when it came. I practiced this on the streets of Vancouver, learned how to pre-focus and estimate exposure so that when it came time to take a photo, I'd need as little adjustment as possible. There are many photographs being taken all the time but only a few capture this moment. Speed is essential, as things change instantly and if you're not ready, the shot's gone.

There is a certain ambiguity to many street photos. Who are these people, what are they doing? The photo "Two men and a lady, 1969" invites the viewer in to wonder about the moment: why does the woman look so worried? What's on her mind? The three stand on the corner, waiting for the light to change, each in his or her own world — the loneliness of the city.

My first newspaper job where I was an employee and actually received a steady salary was at the *Lions Gate*

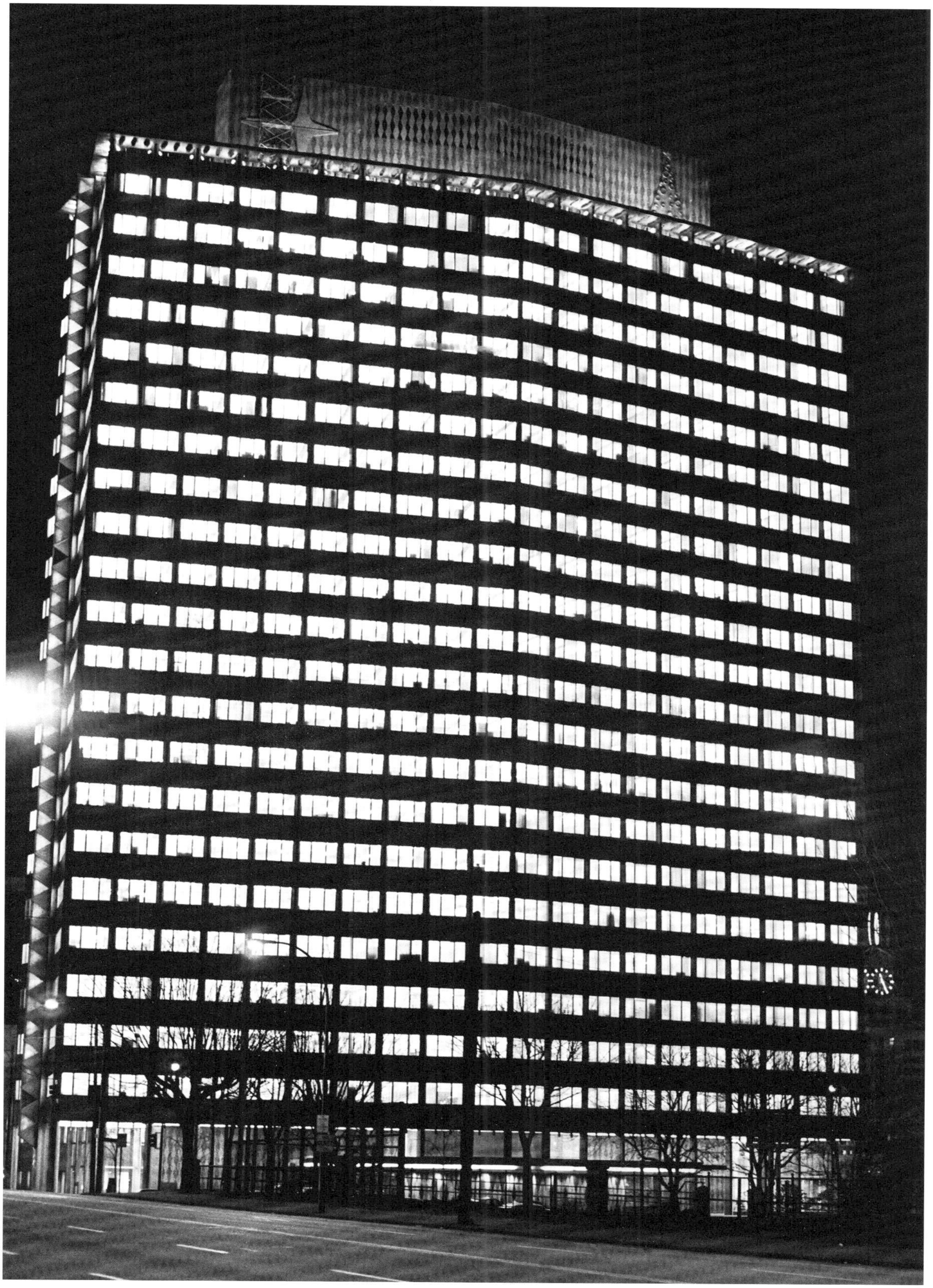

British Columbia Hydro Building, winter 1970.

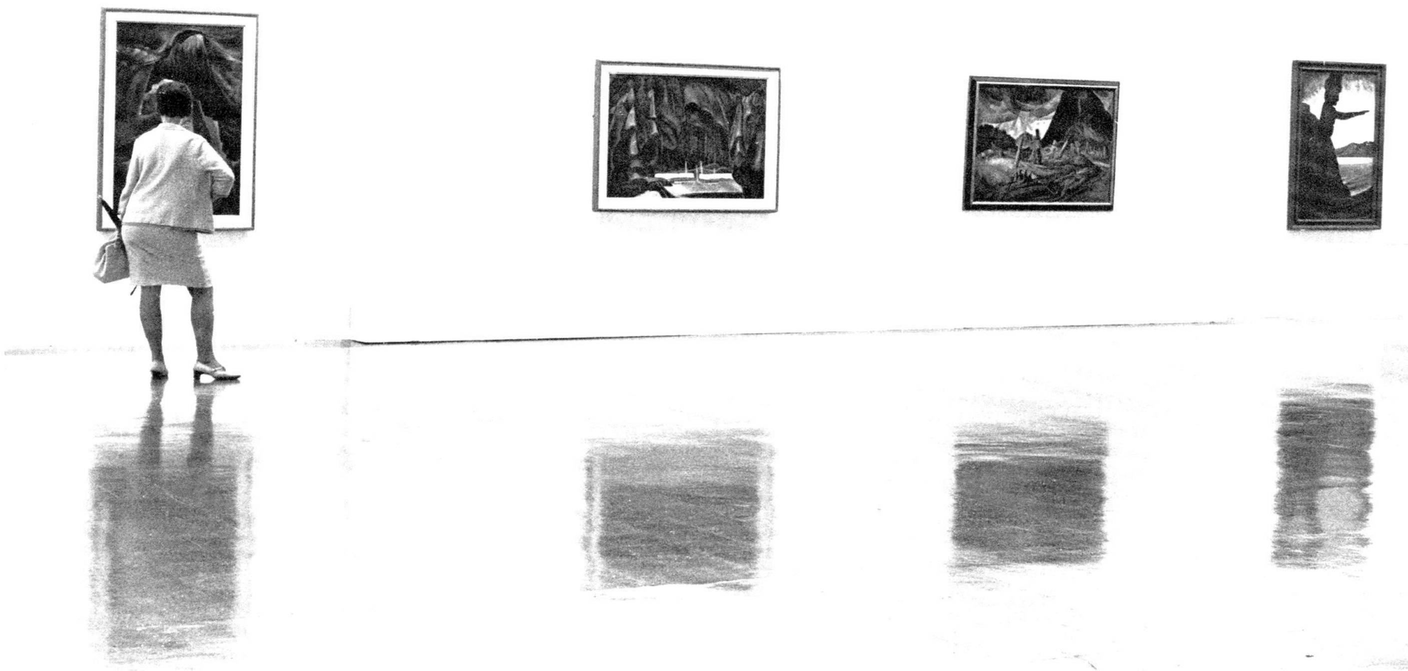

An exhibition of Emily Carr paintings at the Vancouver Art Gallery, in its West Georgia Street location, 1969.

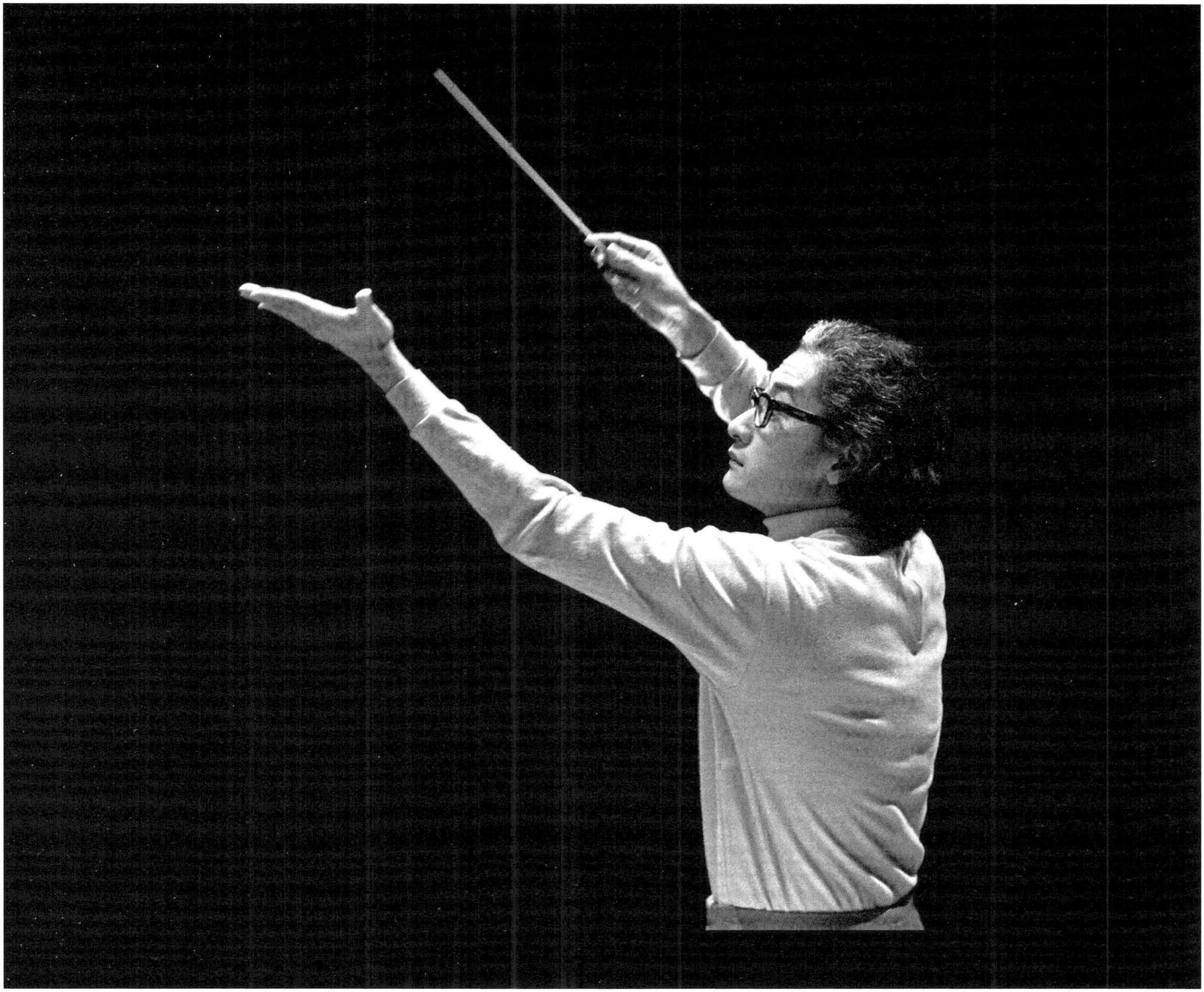

Kazuyoshi Akiyama, the dynamic new conductor of the Vancouver Symphony Orchestra, 1971.

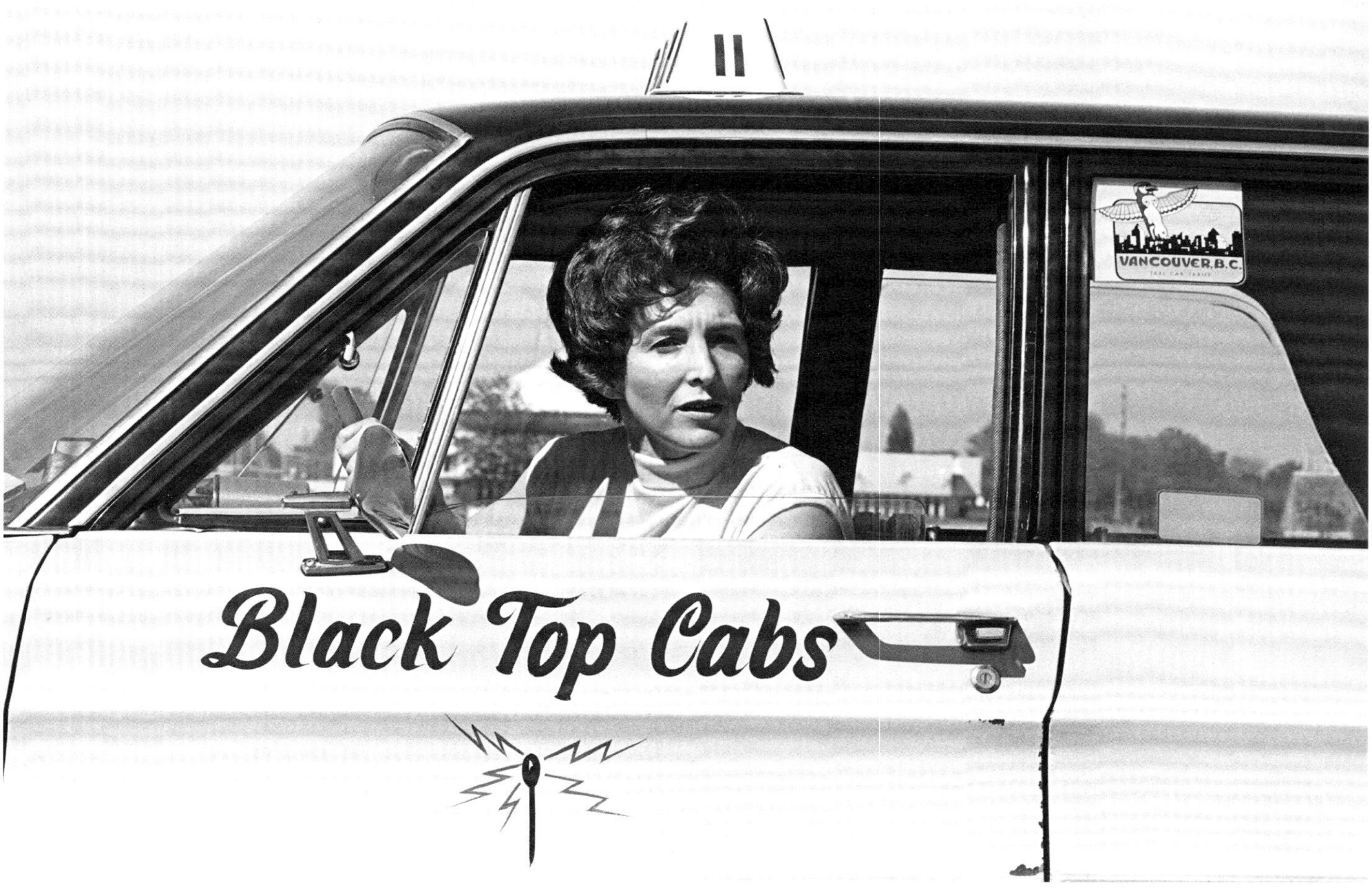

Driving cab was a somewhat controversial occupation for a woman when I shot this photo for an article in 1969.

Granville Street, October 1969.

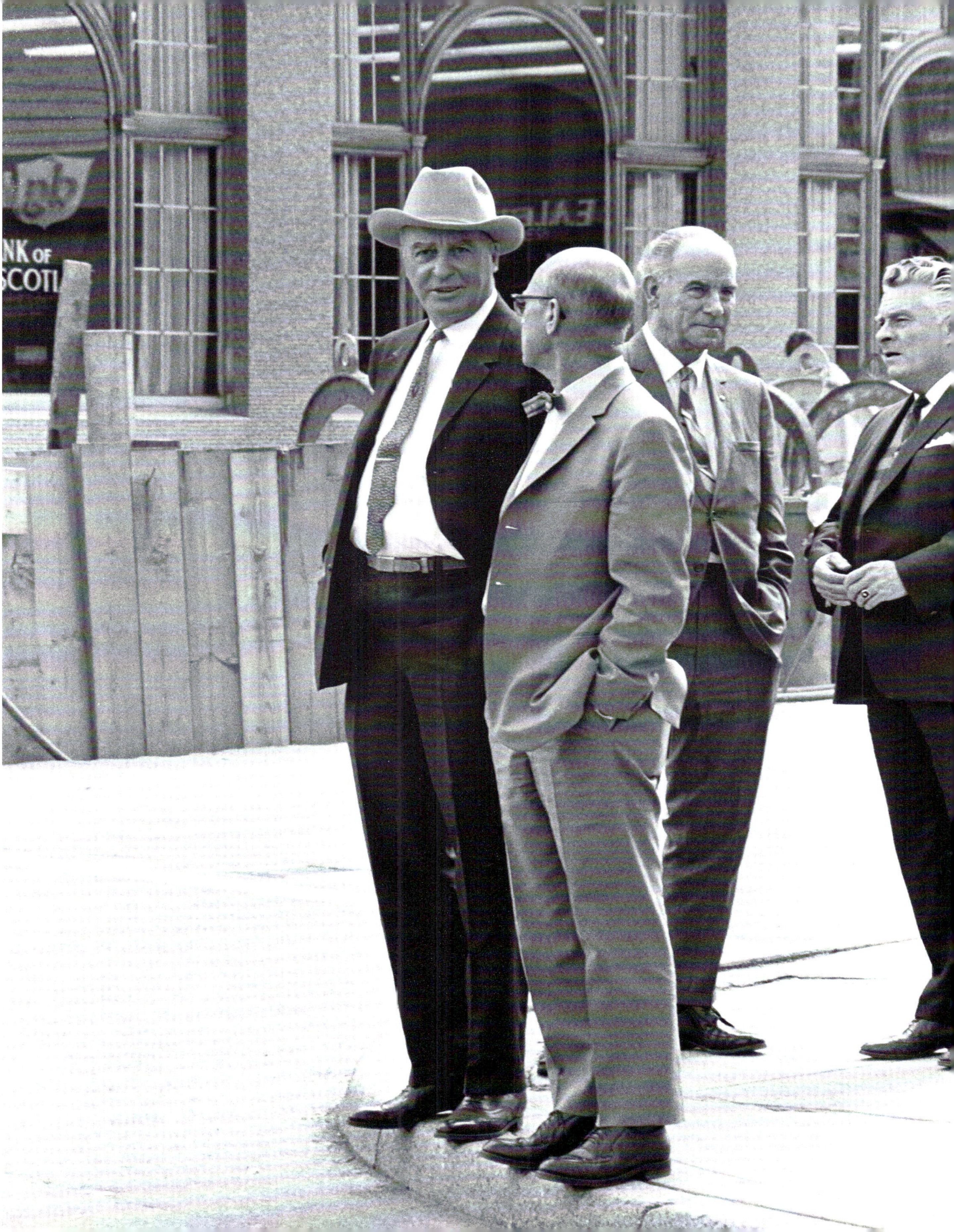

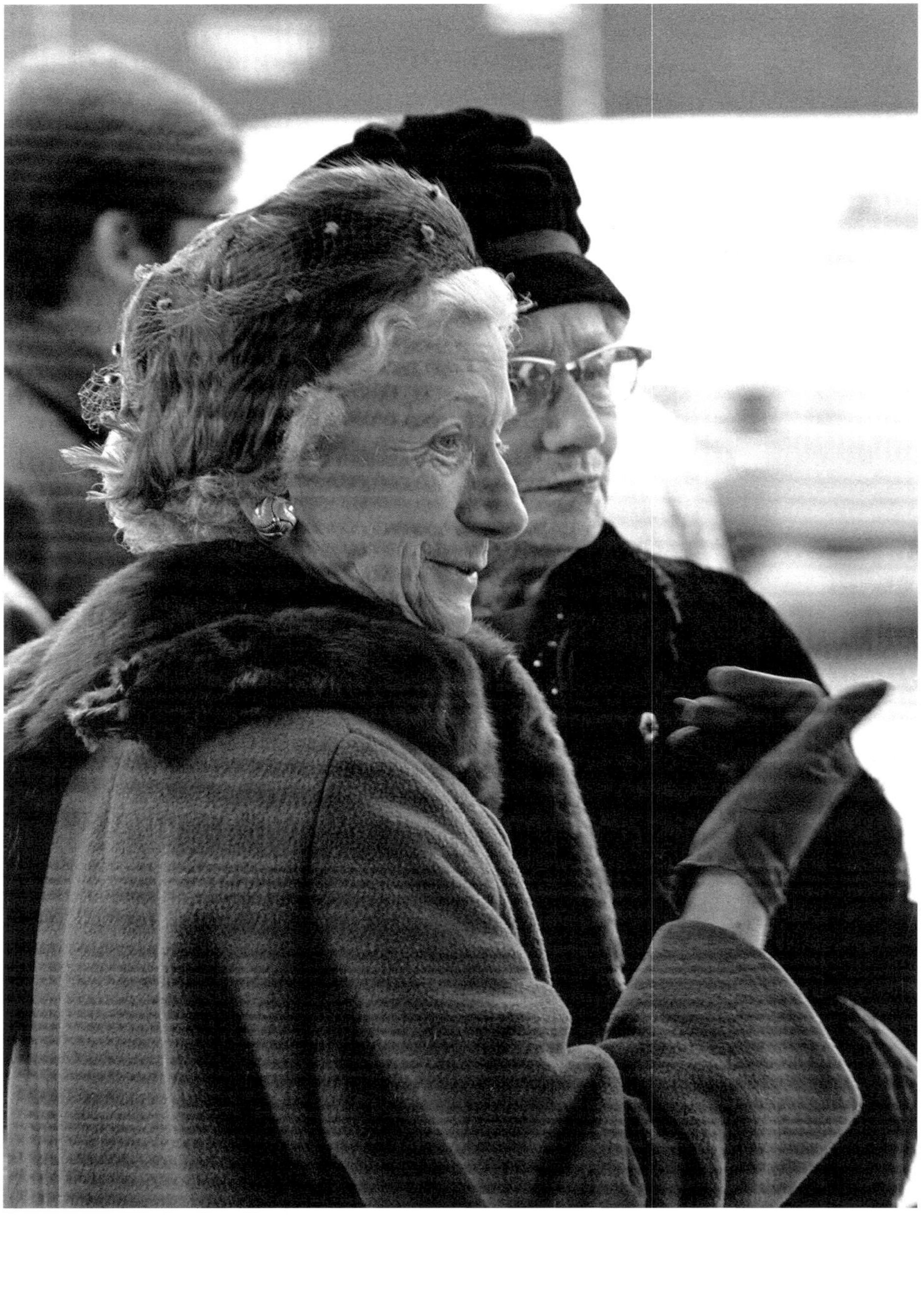

 Watching the Hare Krishnas singing and dancing, 1970.

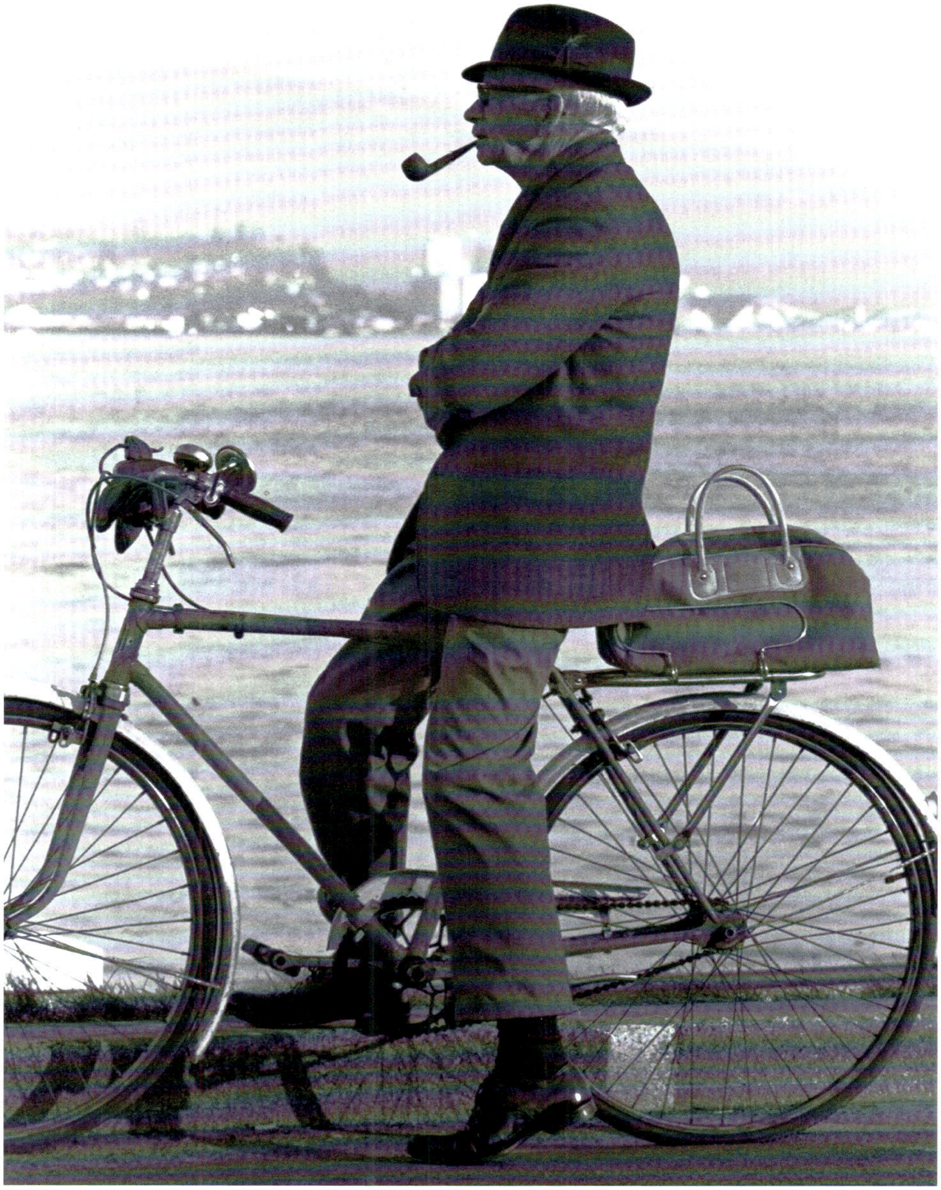

Pioneer cyclist on Stanley Park seawall, 1968.

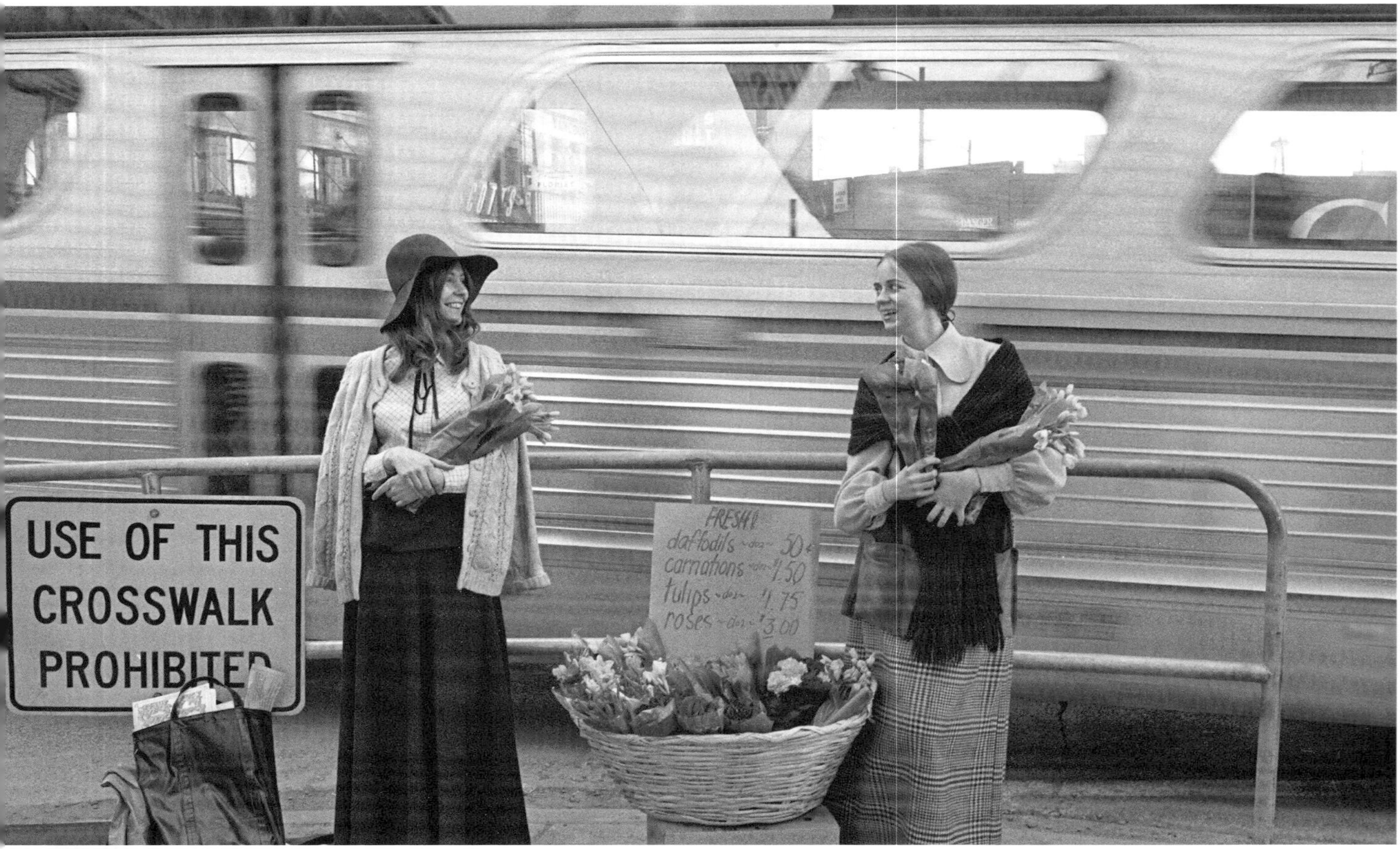

Flower girls at the corner of Georgia and Granville Streets, 1970.

Two men and a lady, Burrard Street, 1969.

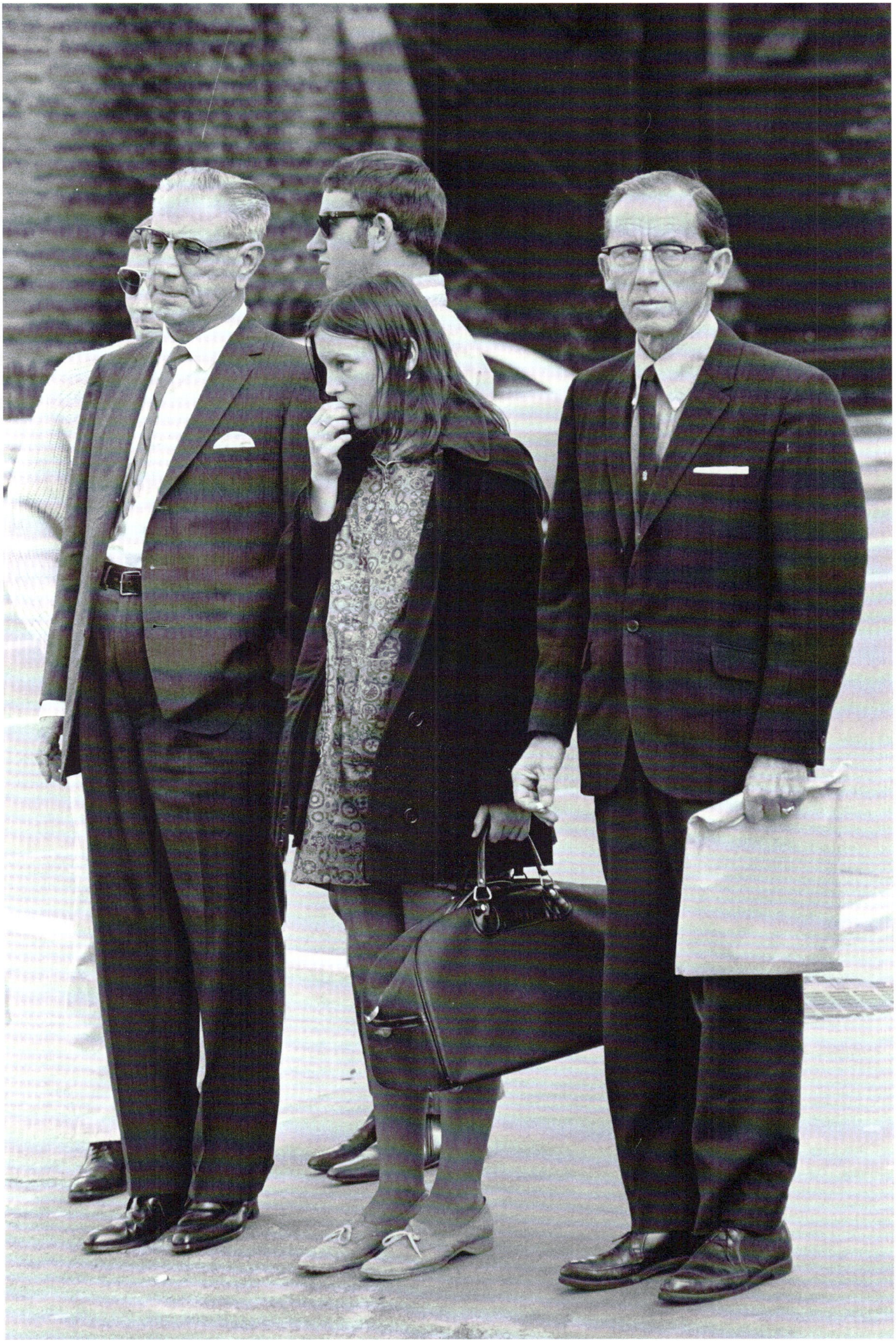

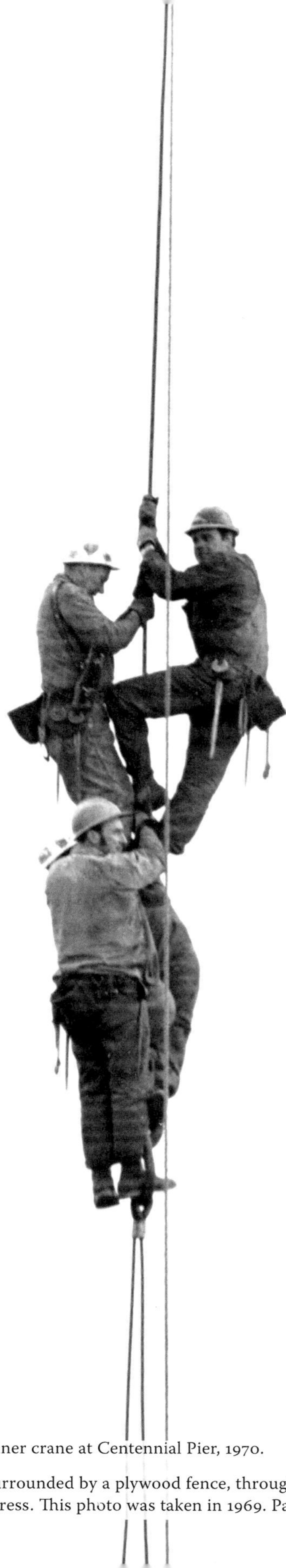

Riggers building a new container crane at Centennial Pier, 1970.

The Pacific Centre site was surrounded by a plywood fence, through which holes were cut so passers-by could view construction progress. This photo was taken in 1969. Pacific Centre opened in 1971.

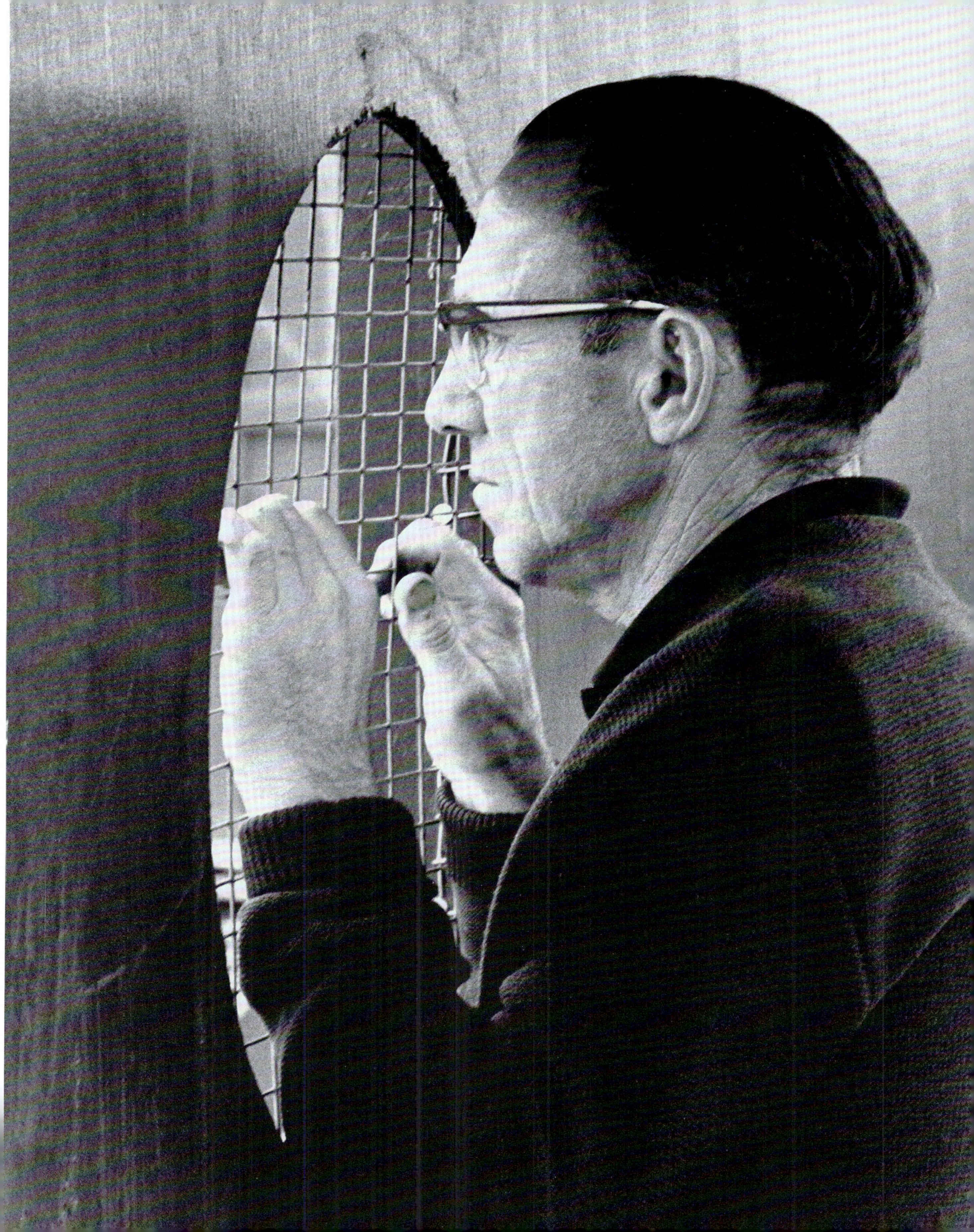

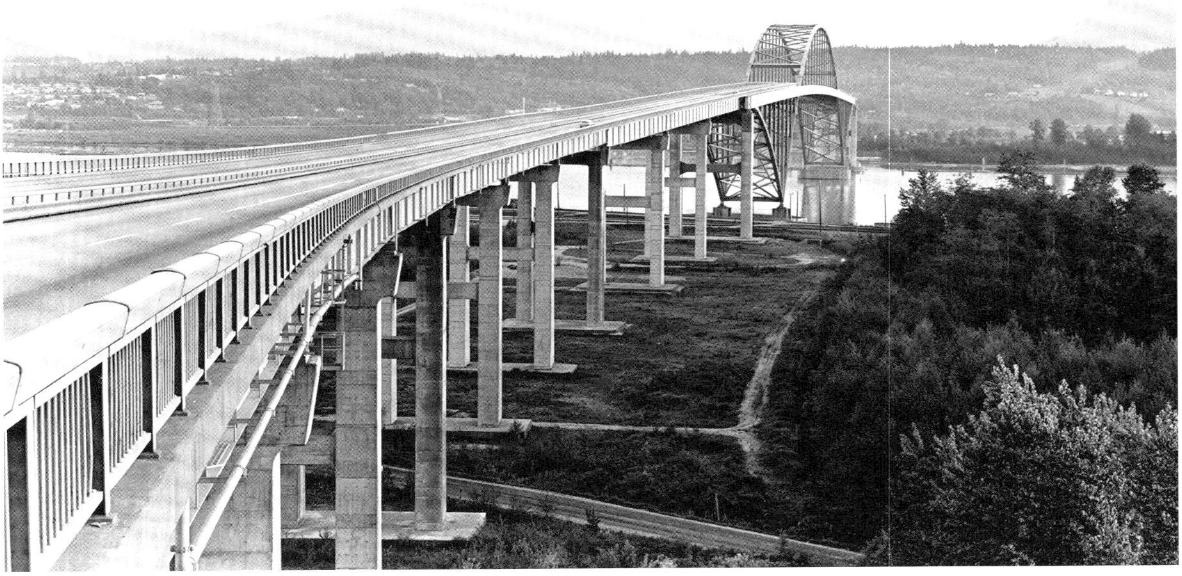

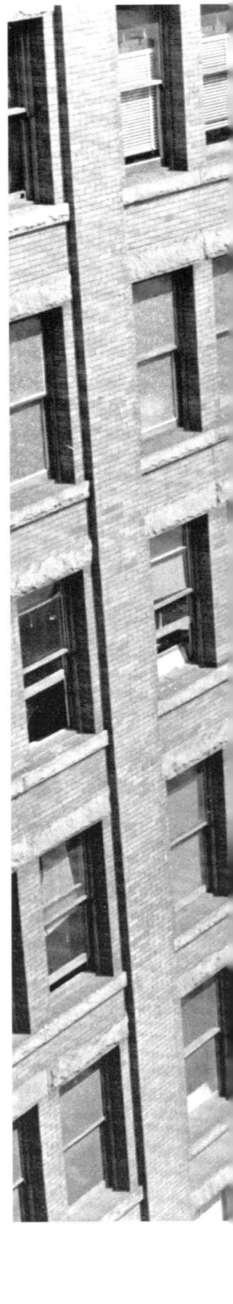

Port Mann Bridge, 1970. It had opened in 1964, connecting Vancouver to suburbs in the Fraser Valley.

Gastown, 1970.

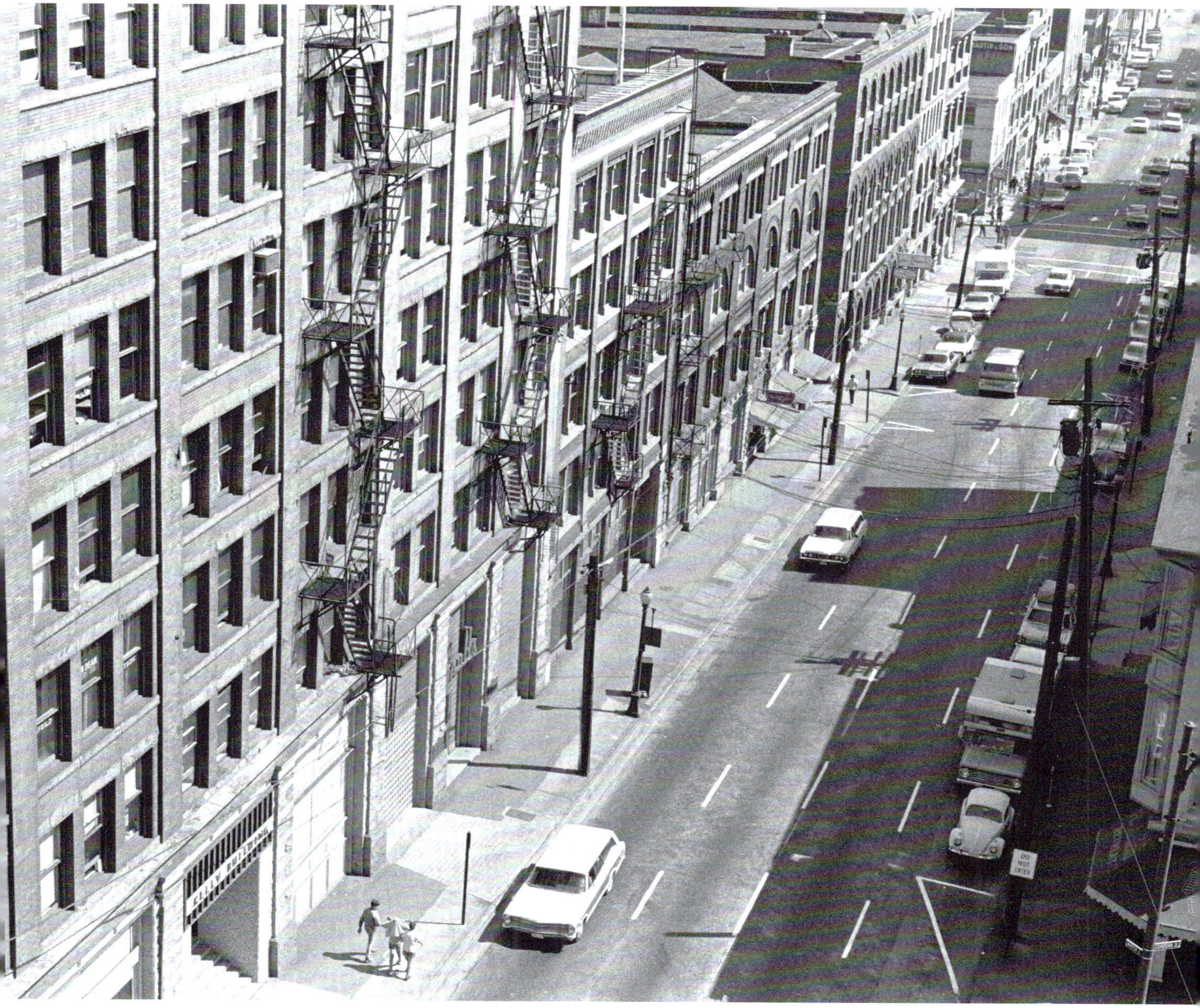
DO
NOT
ENTER

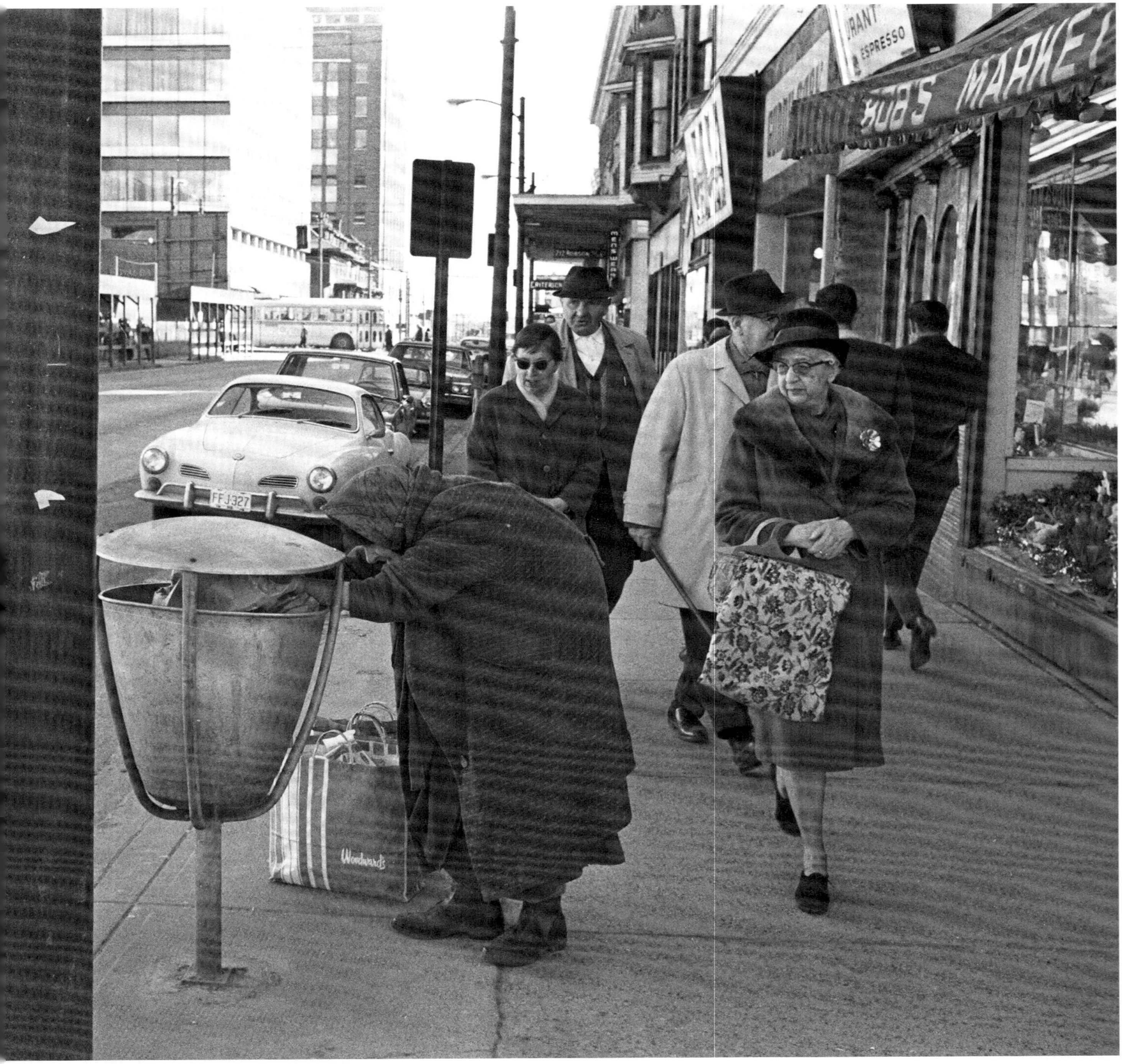

Not everyone was doing well. Robson Street at Howe, 1970.

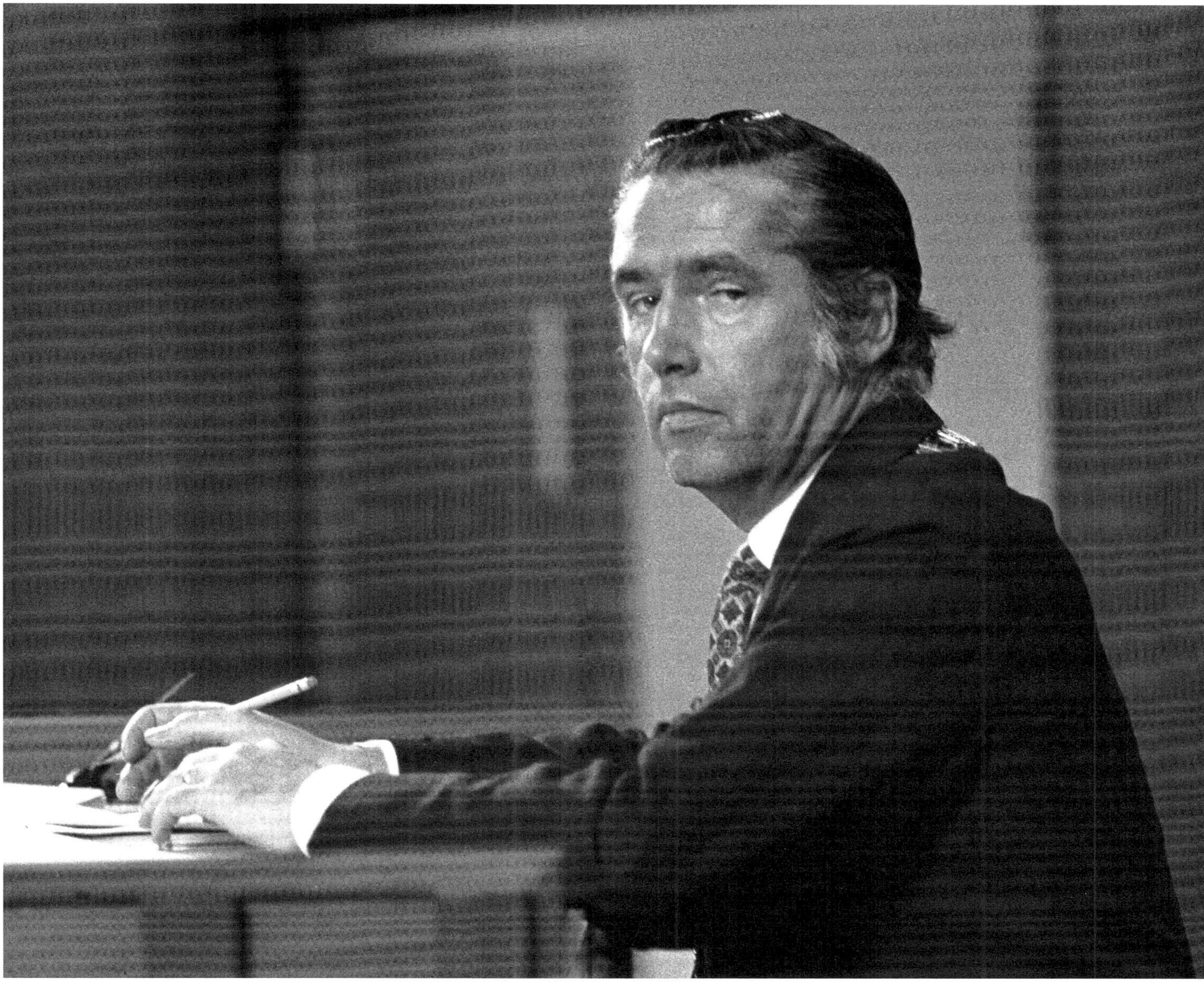

Vancouver Mayor Tom "Terrific" Campbell, a land developer, presides over a contentious council meeting, 1970.

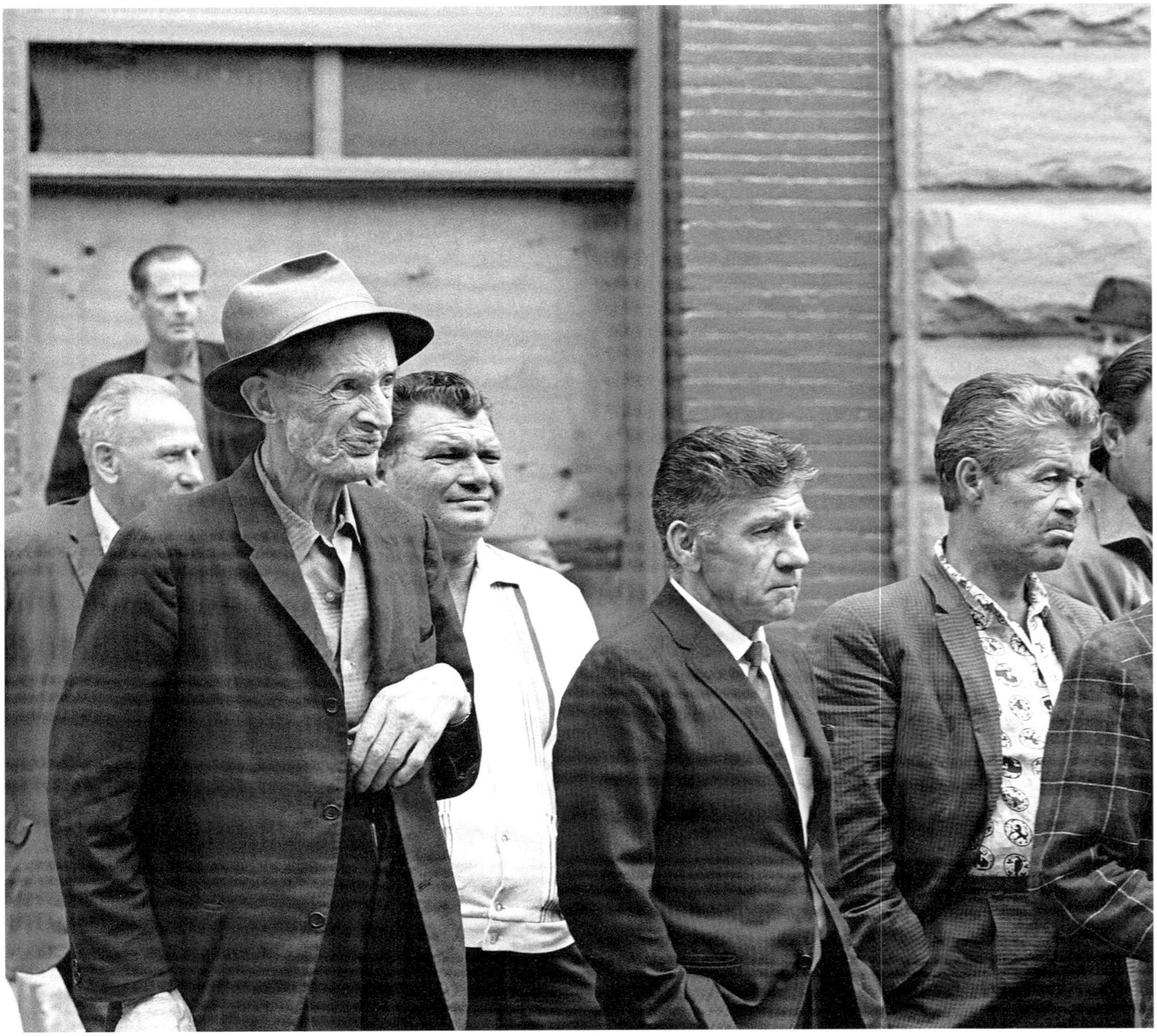

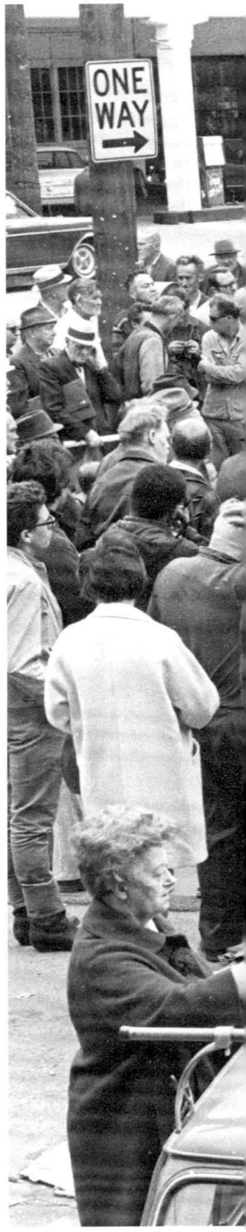

Participants at an August, 1970 outdoor meeting at the foot of Carrall Street, organized by the Downtown Tenants Association, responding to plans to displace Downtown Eastside residents via redevelopment. Long-time city alderman Harry Rankin is the speaker.

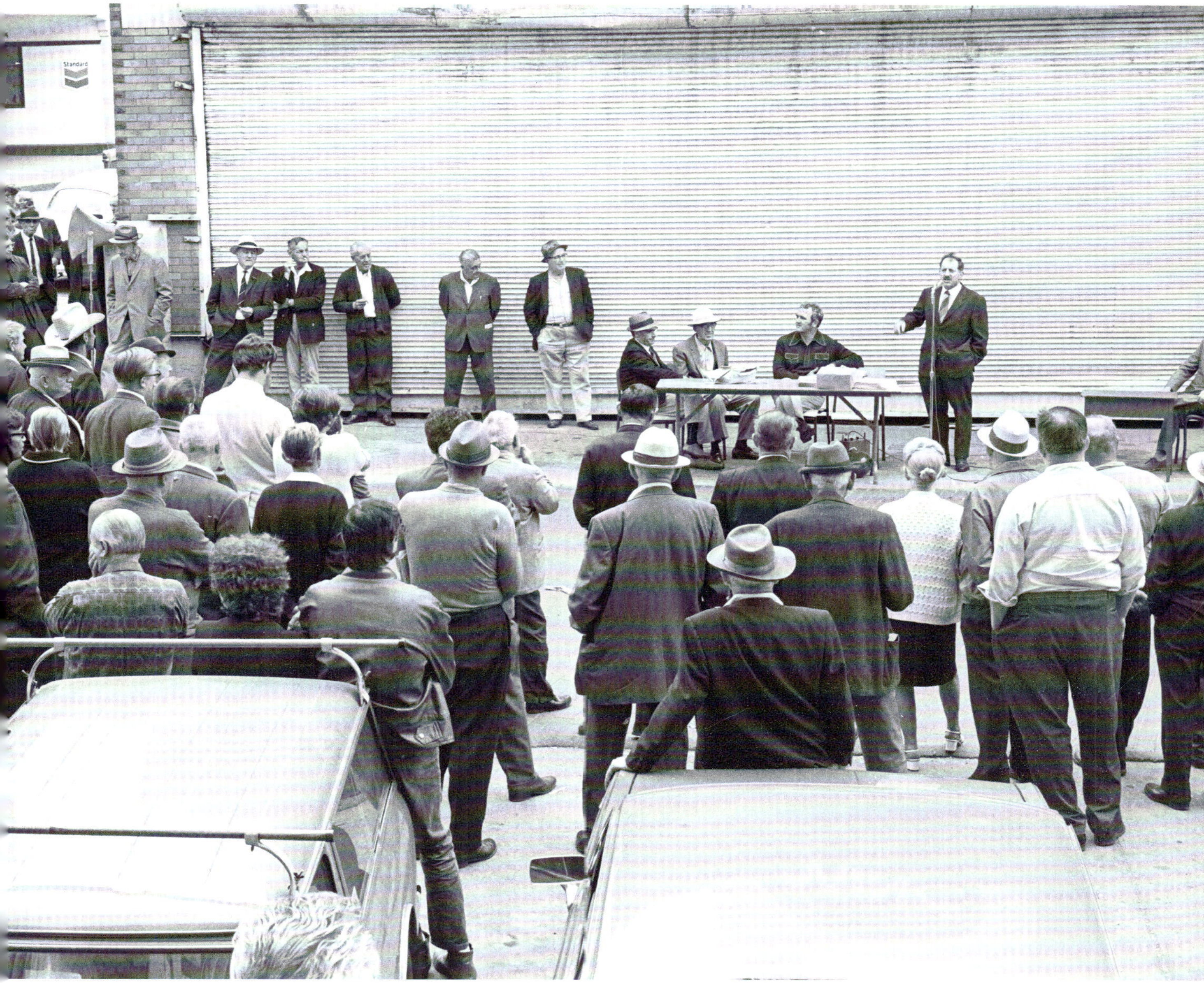
Standard

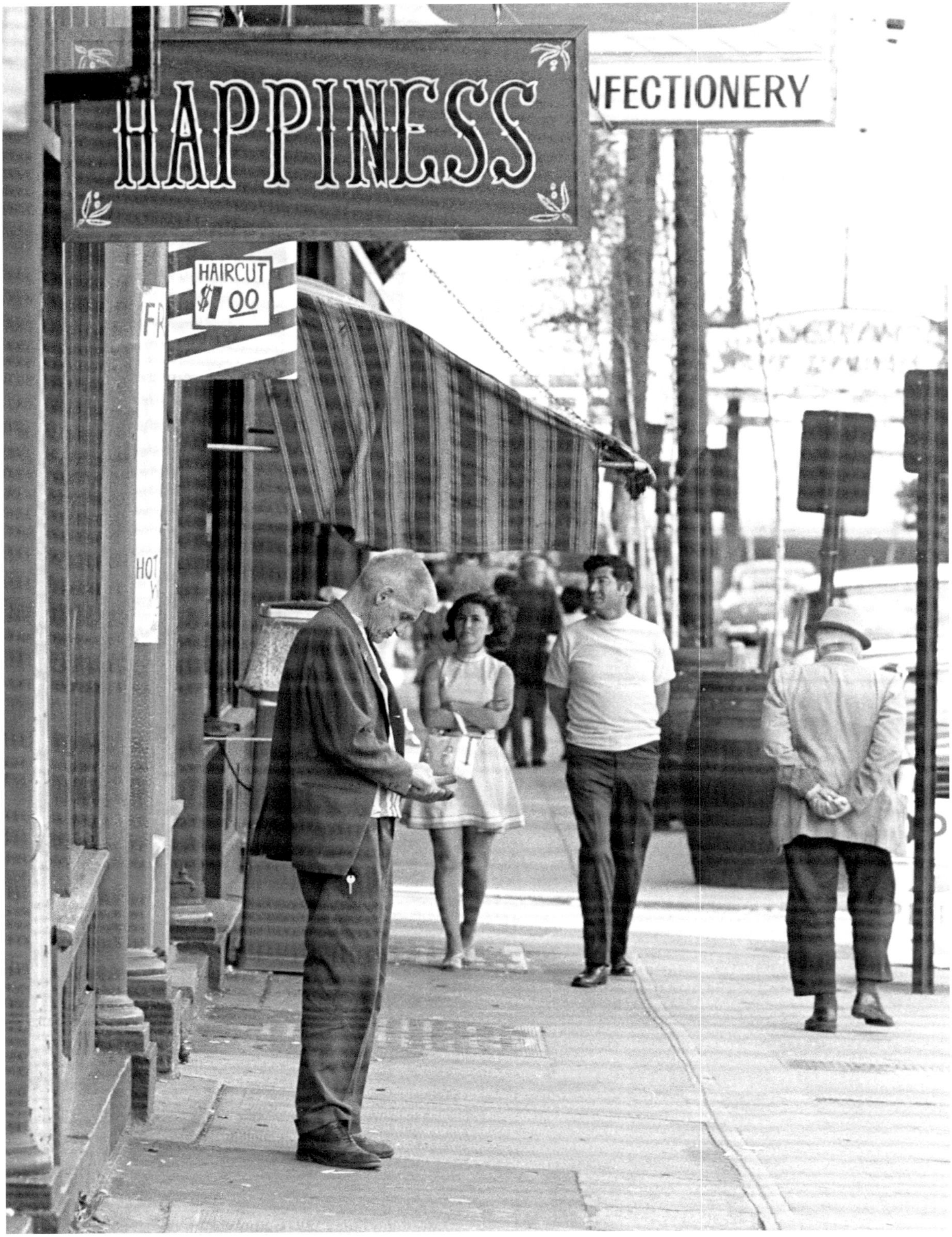

East Hastings Street, Fall 1970. Happiness was a consignment store for local craftspeople run by Roger Brewton, who helped found the Vancouver Free University.

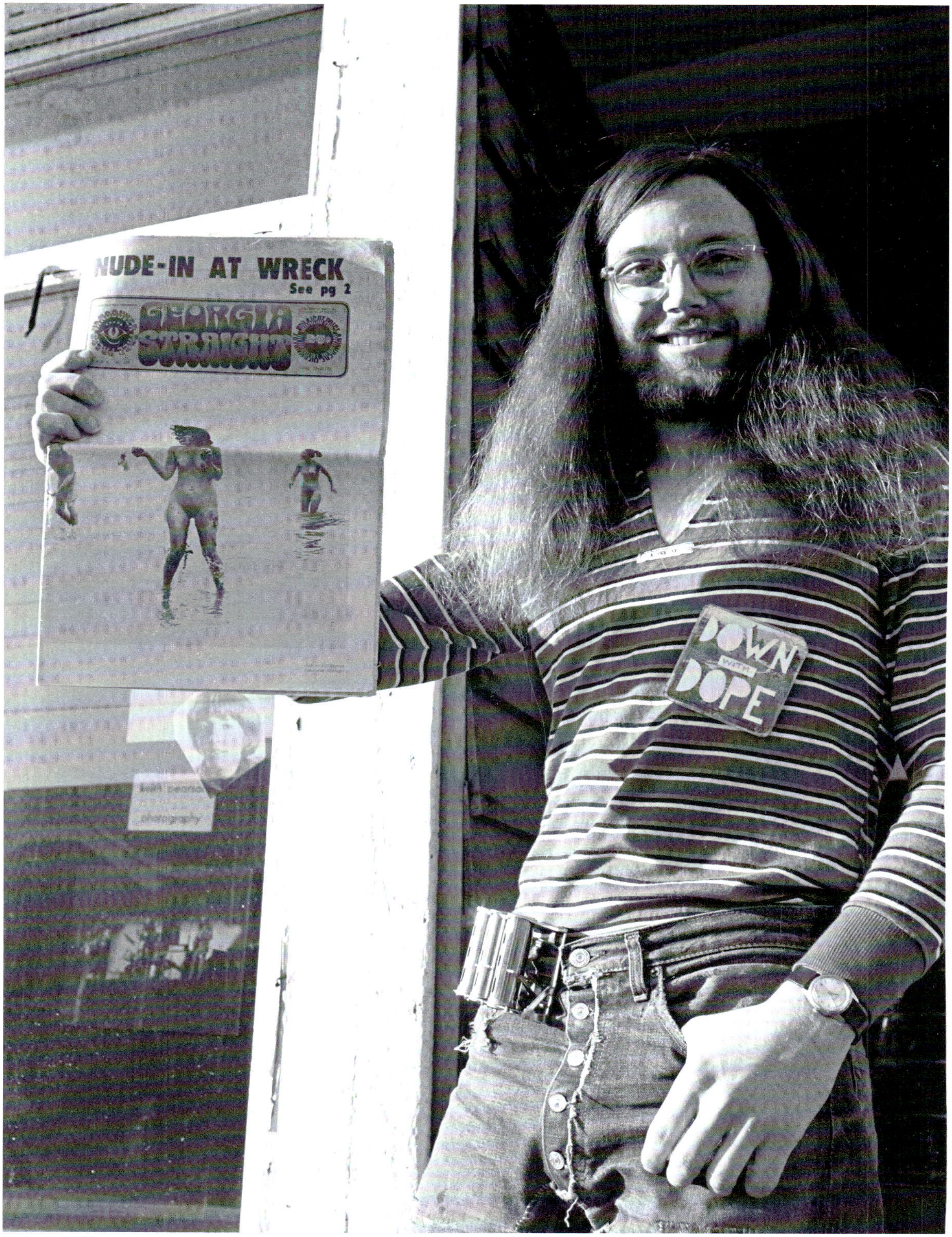

Korky Day, Wreck Beach pioneer and *Georgia Straight* salesman, August 1970.
The *Straight* features a story on a "nude-in" that helped establish Wreck as a nude beach.

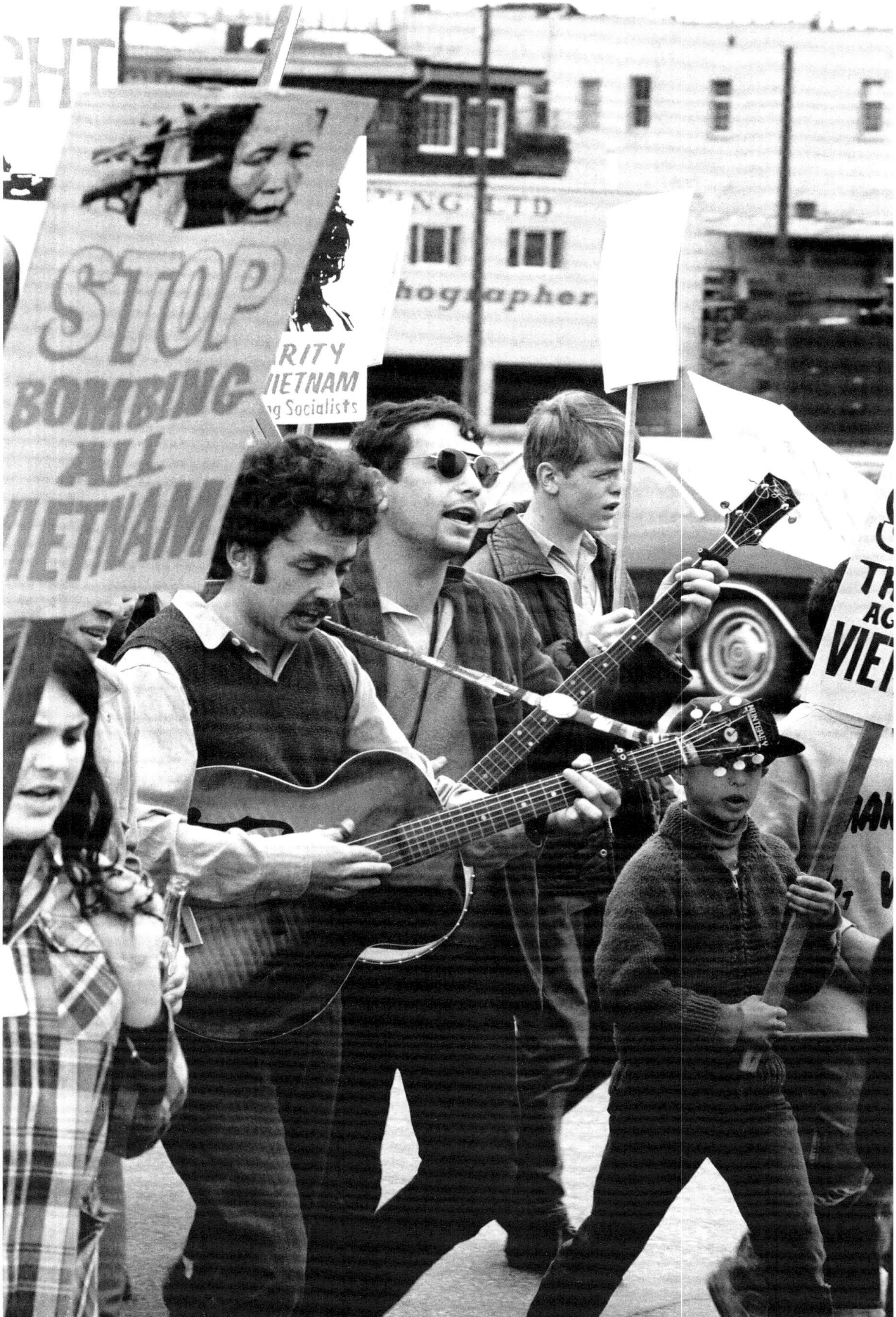
STOP
BOMBING
ALL
Socialists

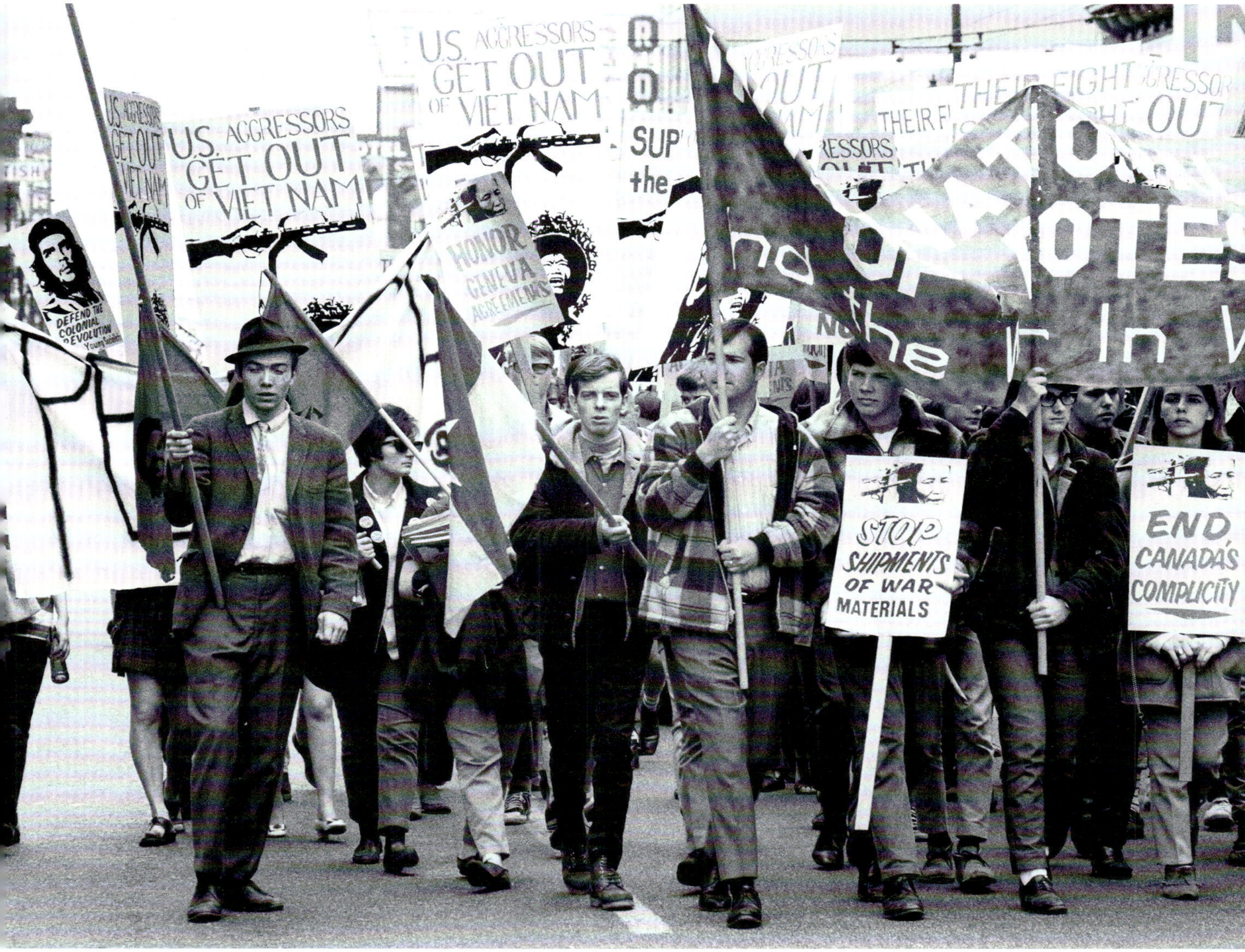

International Day of Protest organized by the Canadian Student Association to End the War, October 21, 1968, drew anti-Vietnam War protesters.

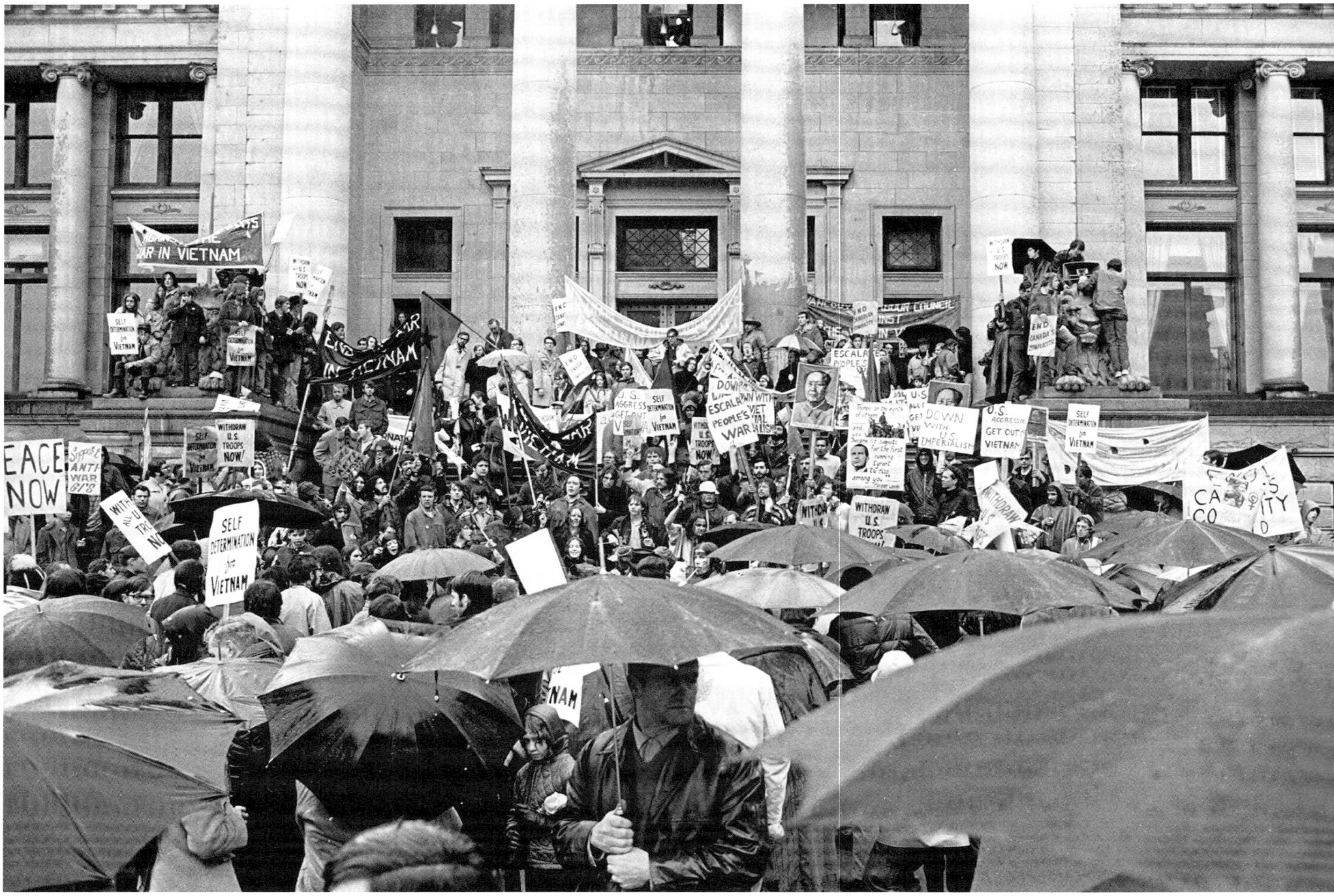

An anti-Vietnam War demonstration held in Vancouver on November 15, 1969 drew about 4,000 marchers on the same day that the Moratorium March in Washington, DC brought out half a million demonstrators.

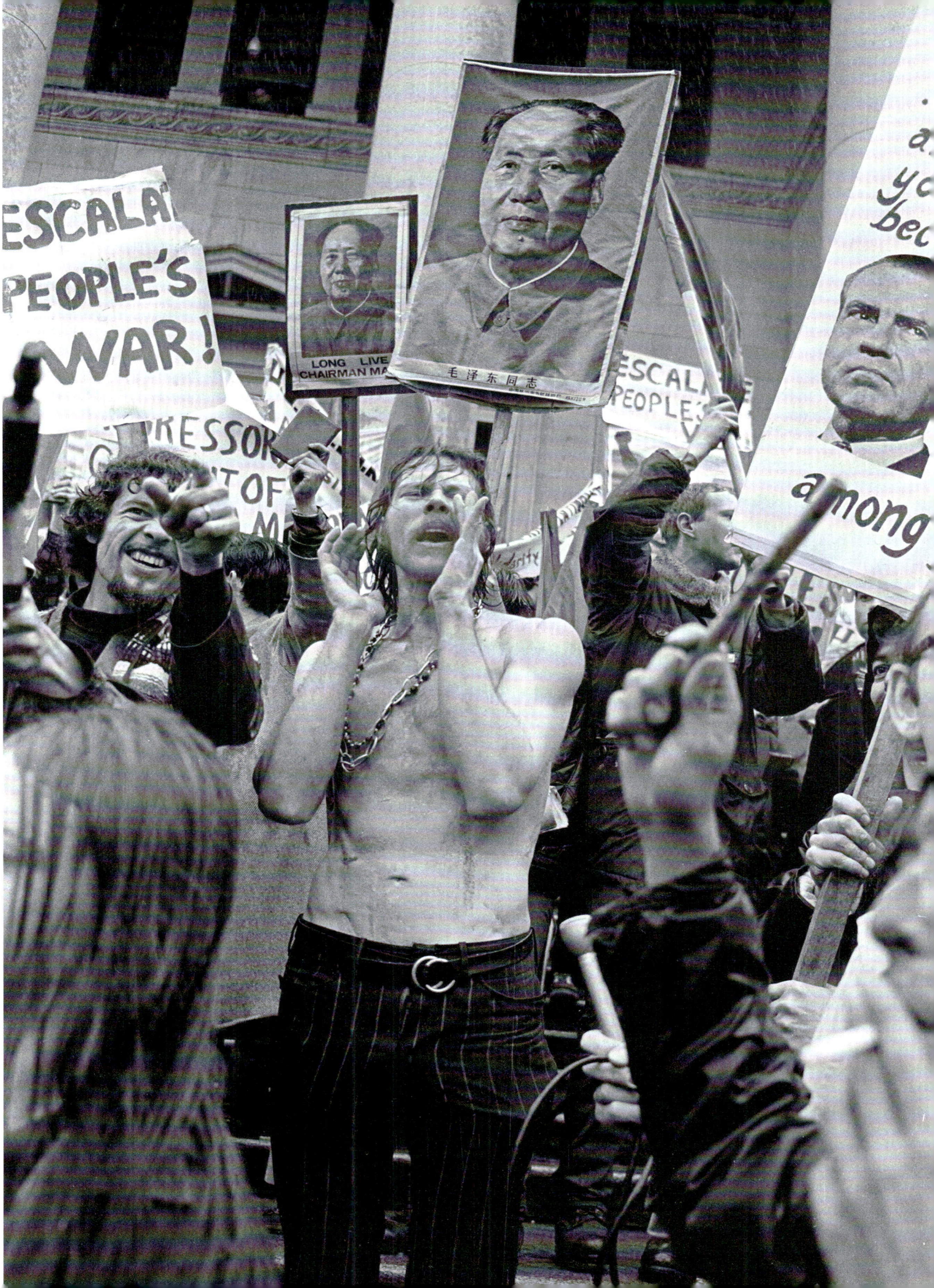
ESCALAT
PEOPLE'S
WAR!
LONG LIVE
CHAIRMAN MA
毛泽东同志
ESCALA
PEOPLE'S
among

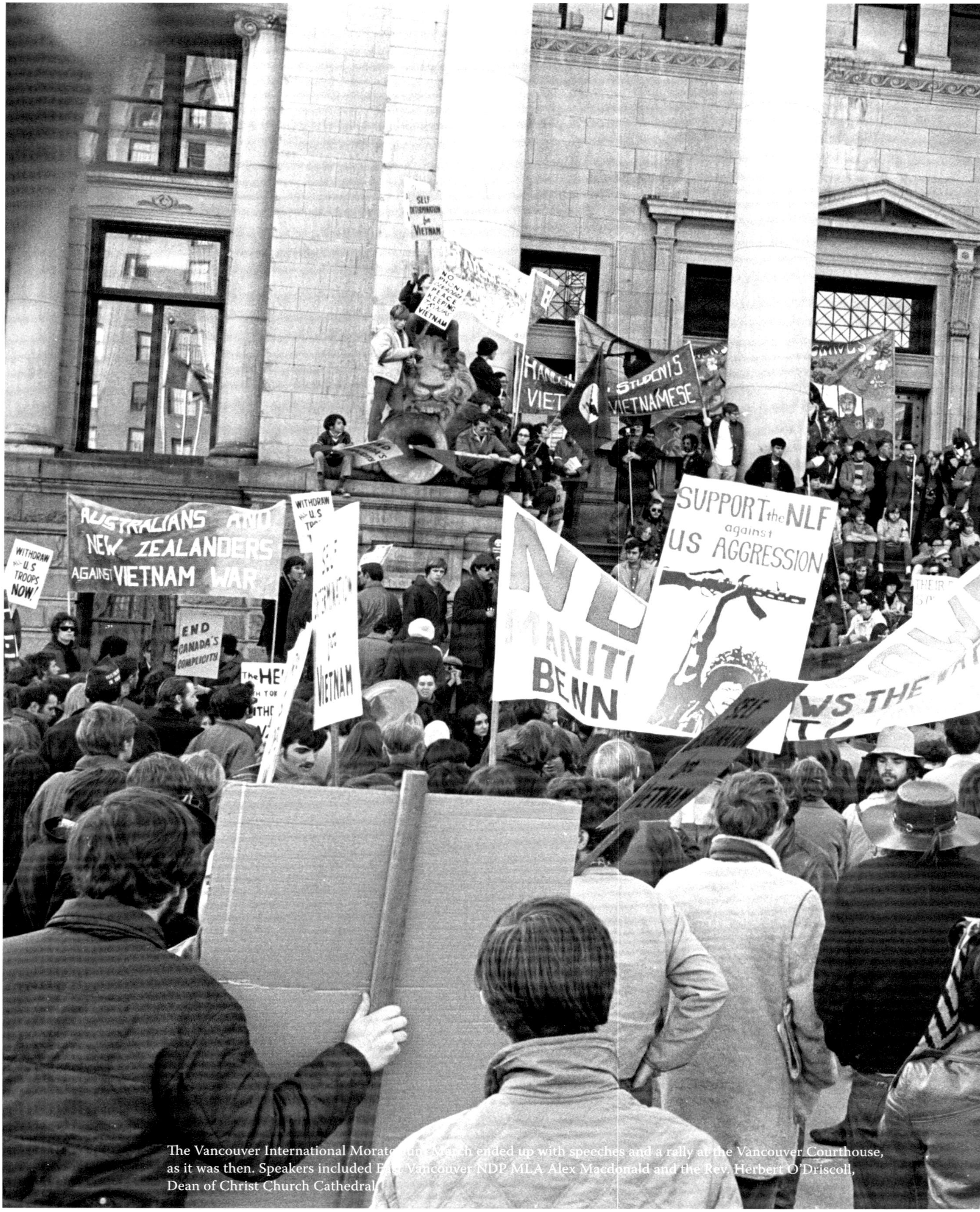

The Vancouver International Moratorium March ended up with speeches and a rally at the Vancouver Courthouse, as it was then. Speakers included East Vancouver NDP MLA Alex Macdonald and the Rev. Herbert O'Driscoll, Dean of Christ Church Cathedral.

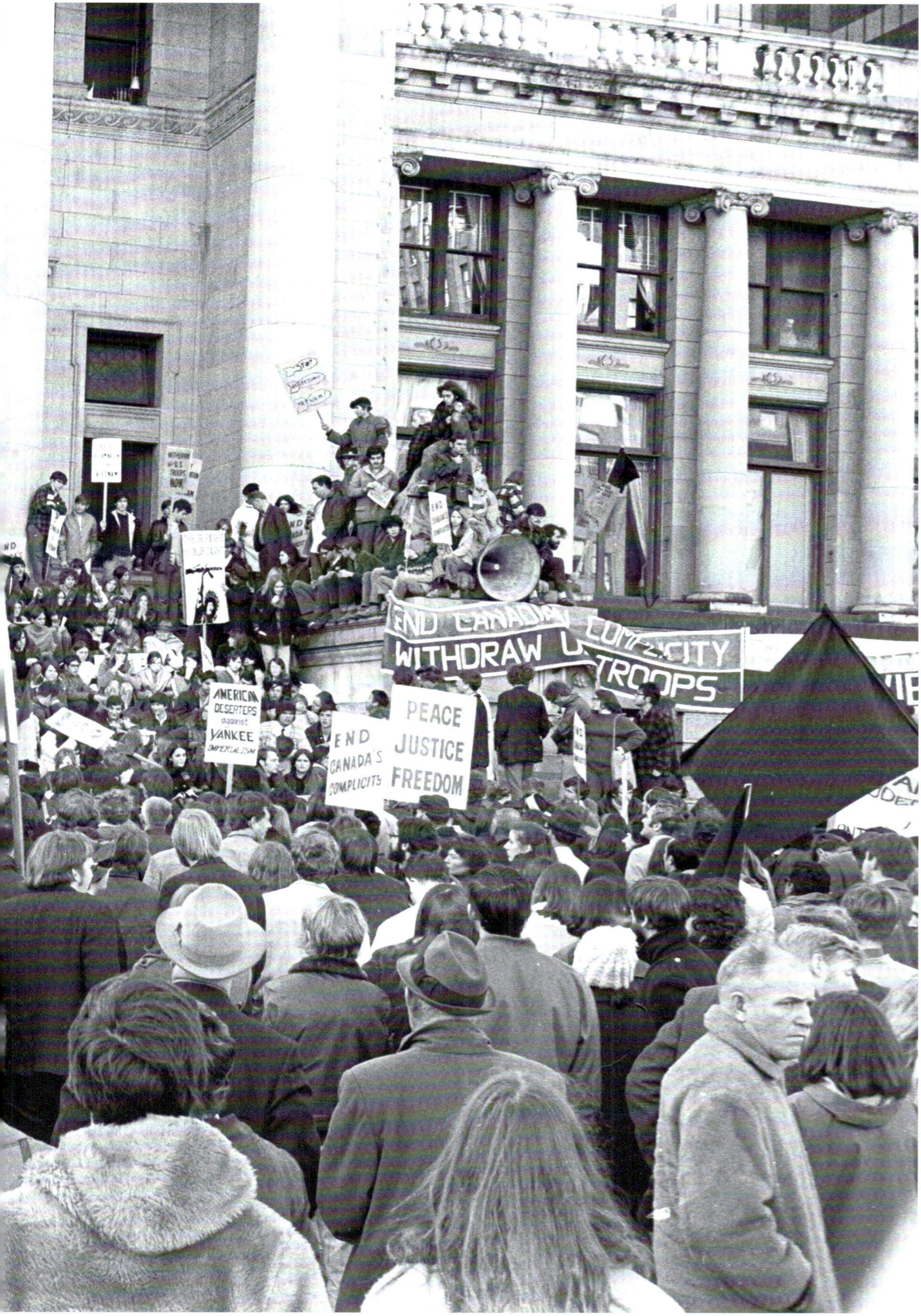
WITHDRAW
TROOPS
AMERICAN DESERTERS against YANKEE IMPERIALISM
END CANADA'S COMPLICITY
PEACE JUSTICE FREEDOM

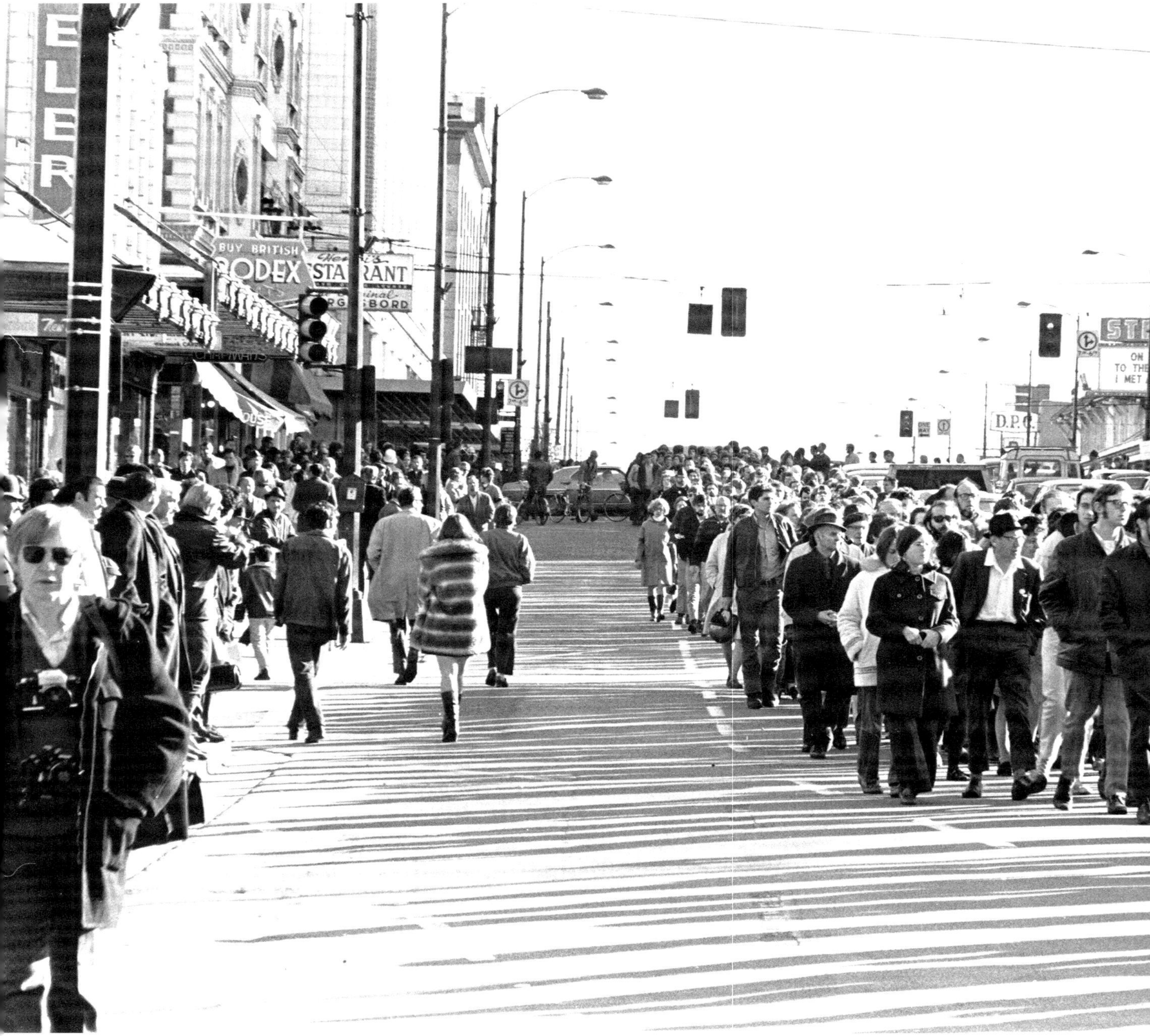

International Moratorium Day march, November 15, 1969.

Young demonstrator watches the demonstration from atop a stone lion at the courthouse.

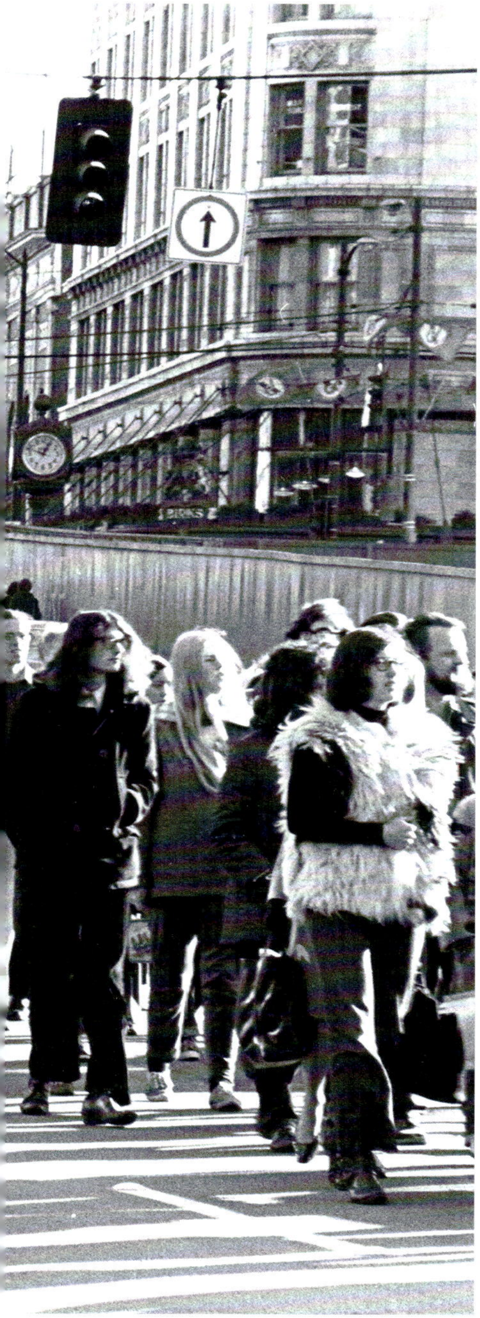

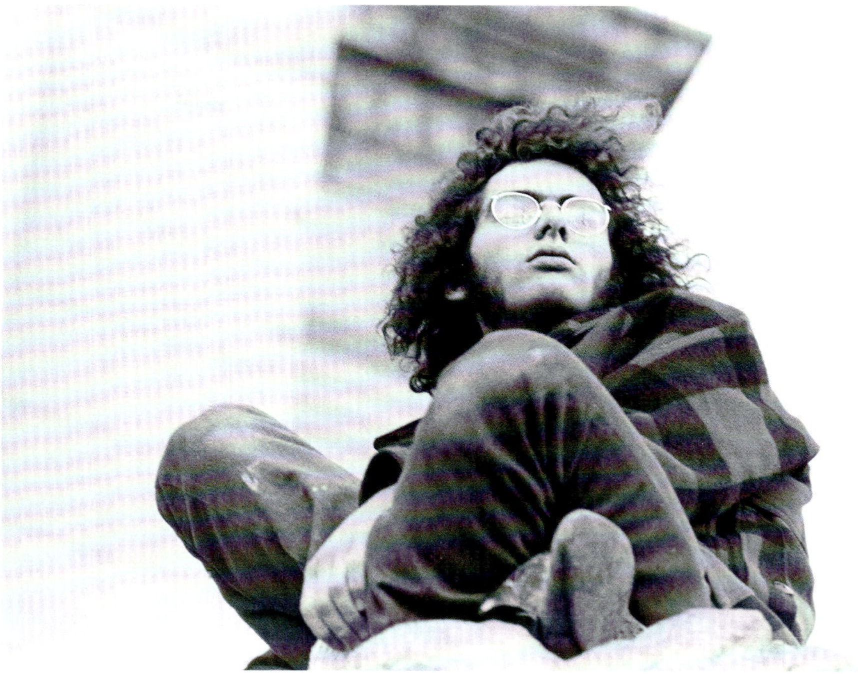

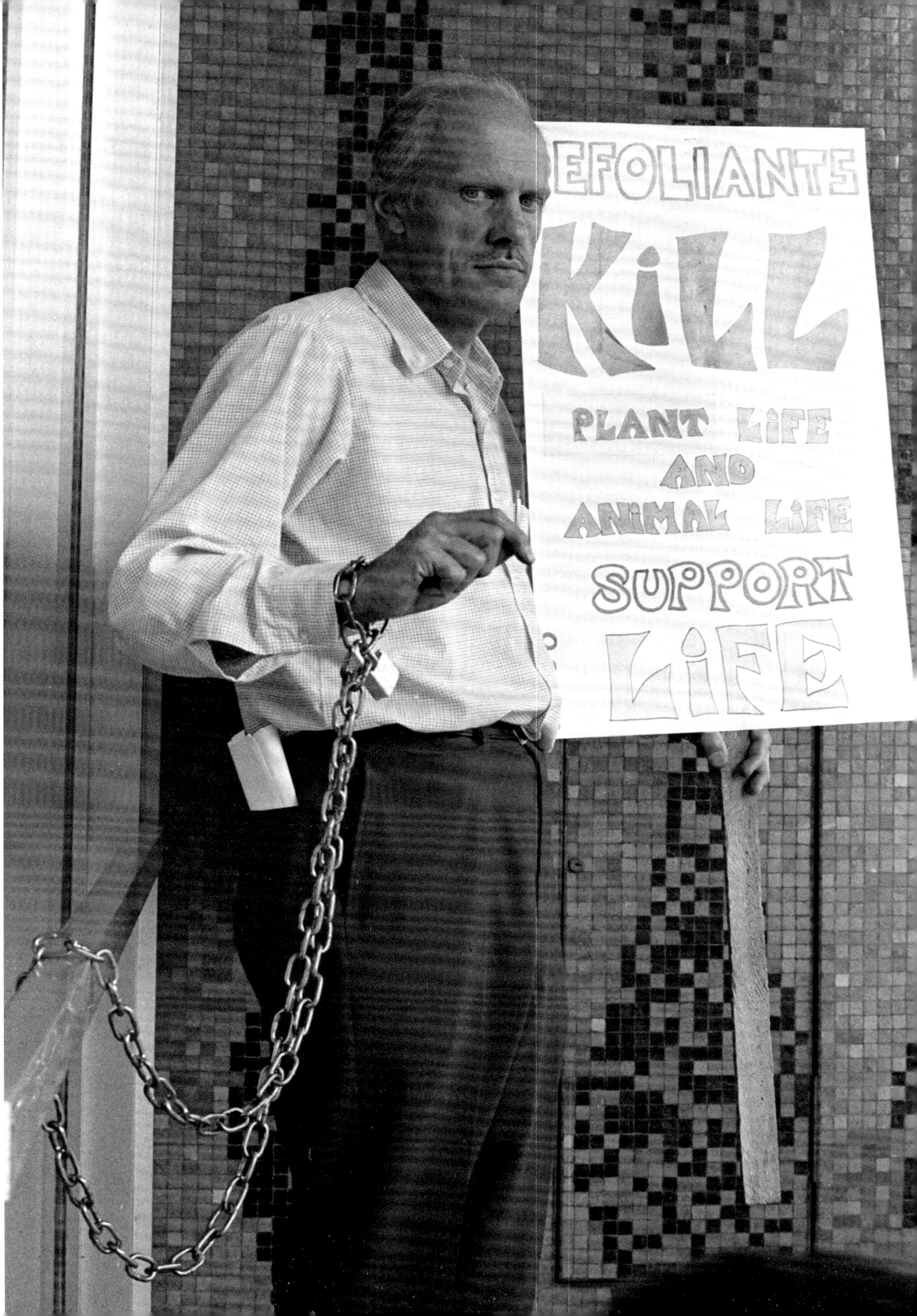
EFOLIANTS
KILL
PLANT LIFE
AND
ANIMAL LIFE
SUPPORT
LIFE

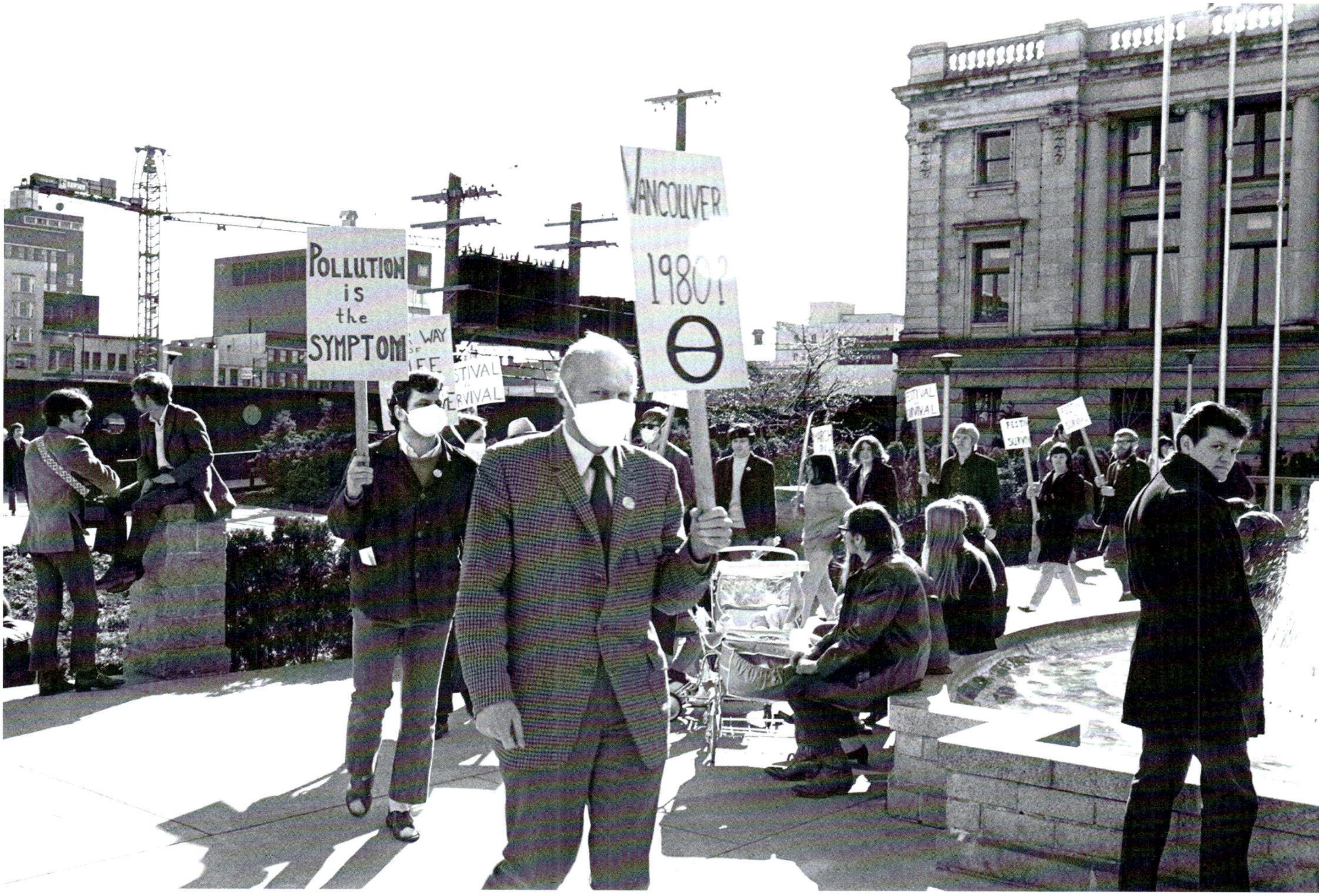

The Society Promoting Environmental Conservation (SPEC) was founded in 1969 to raise awareness of environmental issues. At a demonstration on July 17, 1970 at the BC Hydro building, Delta activist Bill Brewer chains himself to the doors as part of a protest against pesticide spraying by the publicly owned utility.

A late winter anti-pollution protest held at the Vancouver Courthouse, February, 1970.

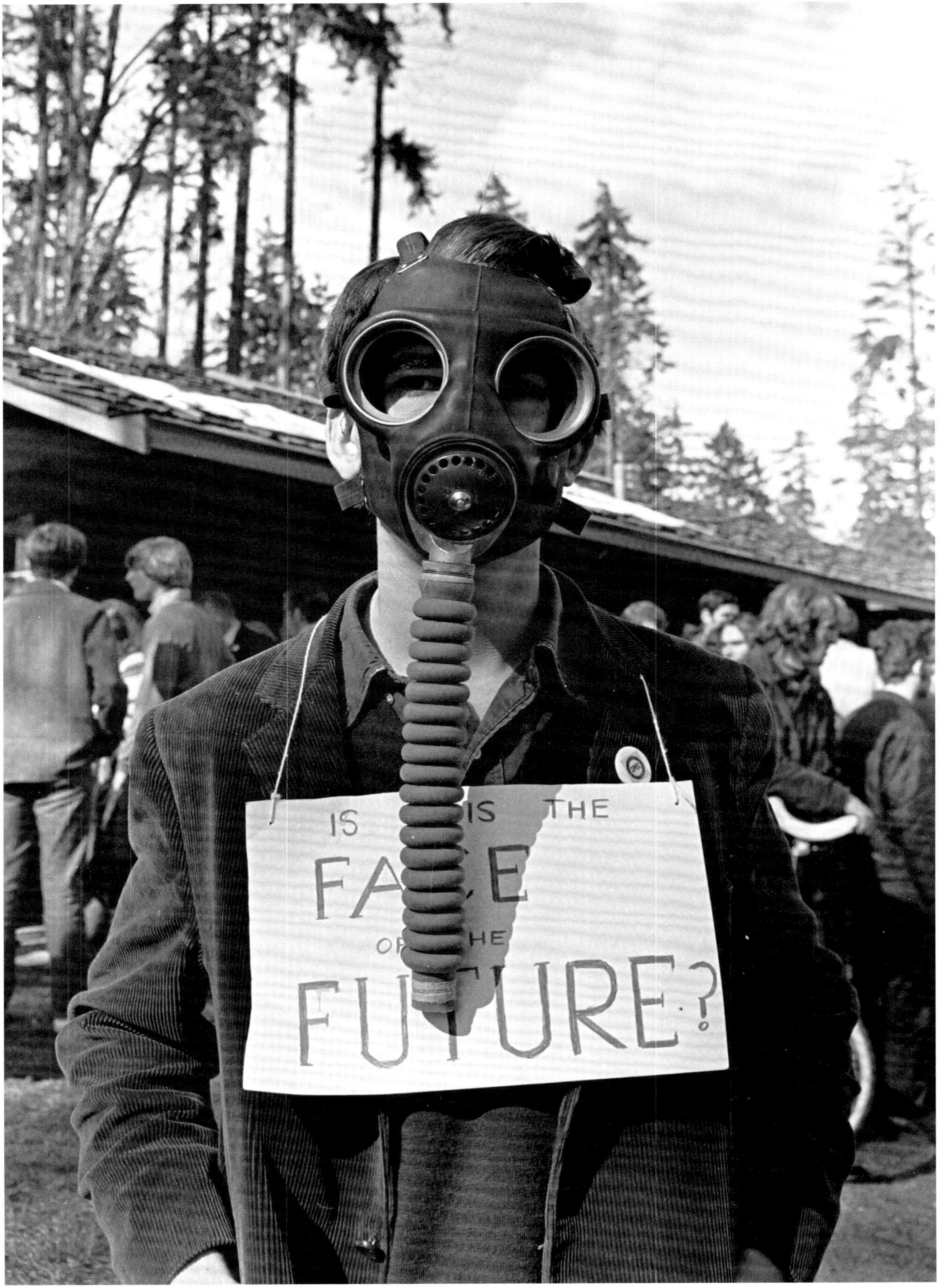
IS THE
FUTURE?

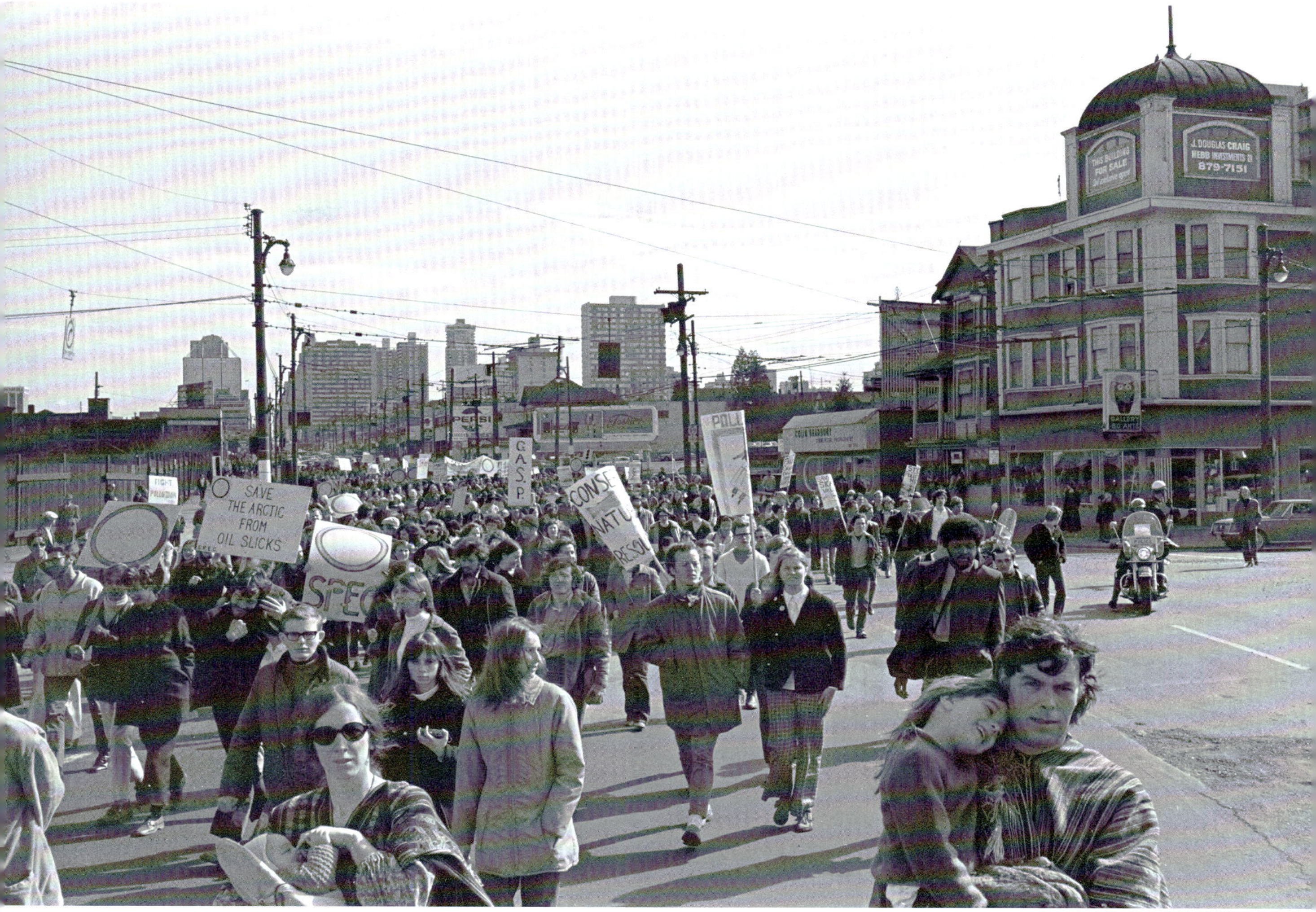

Another demonstration inspired by environmental concerns, the Festival for Survival on March 20, 1970, saw protesters march from downtown to Stanley Park.

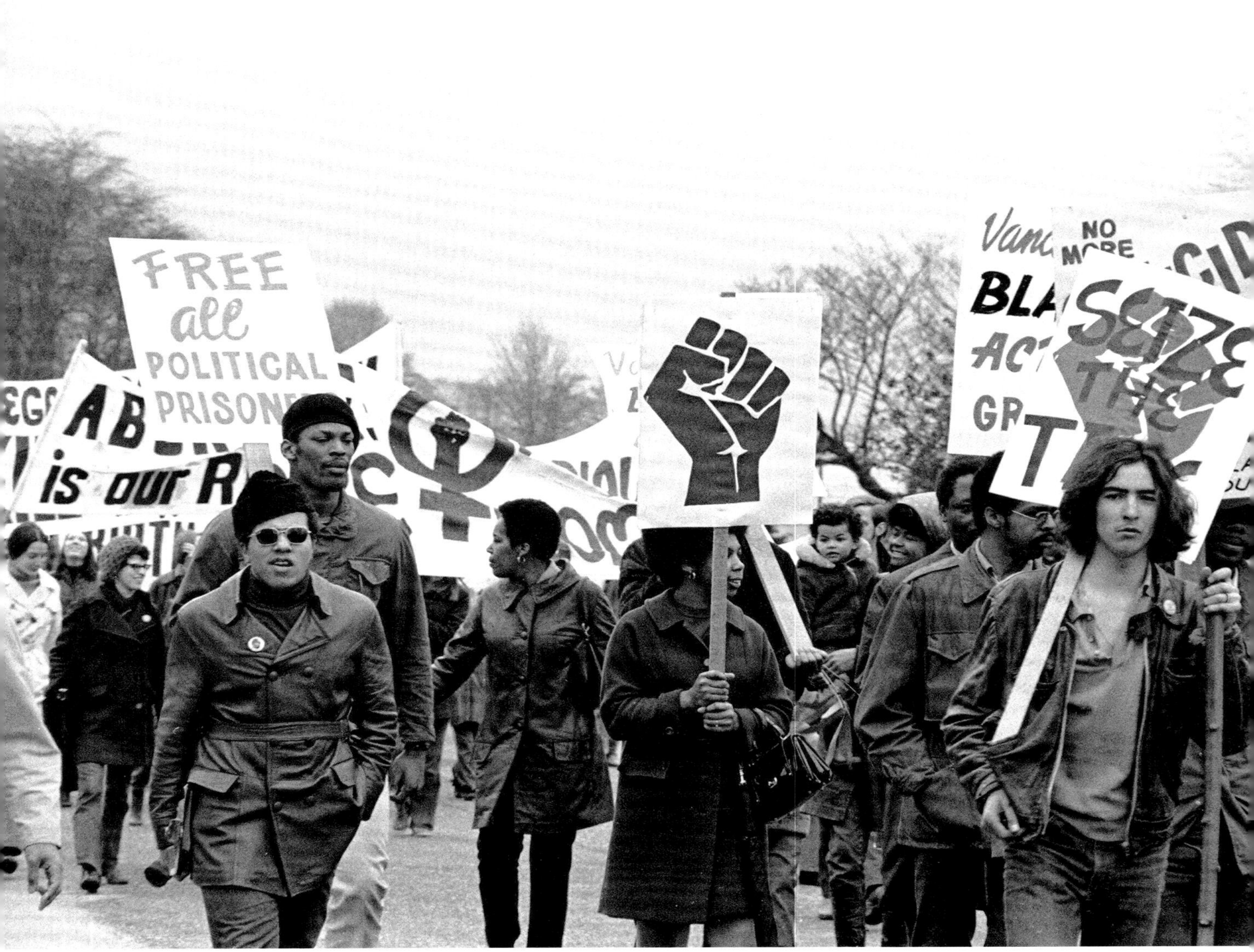

A testier demonstration took place on March 14, 1970, when between 350 and 500 people, part of a March Against Frustration, "liberated" the Burrard Bridge, frustrating citizens who were trying to drive across the bridge.

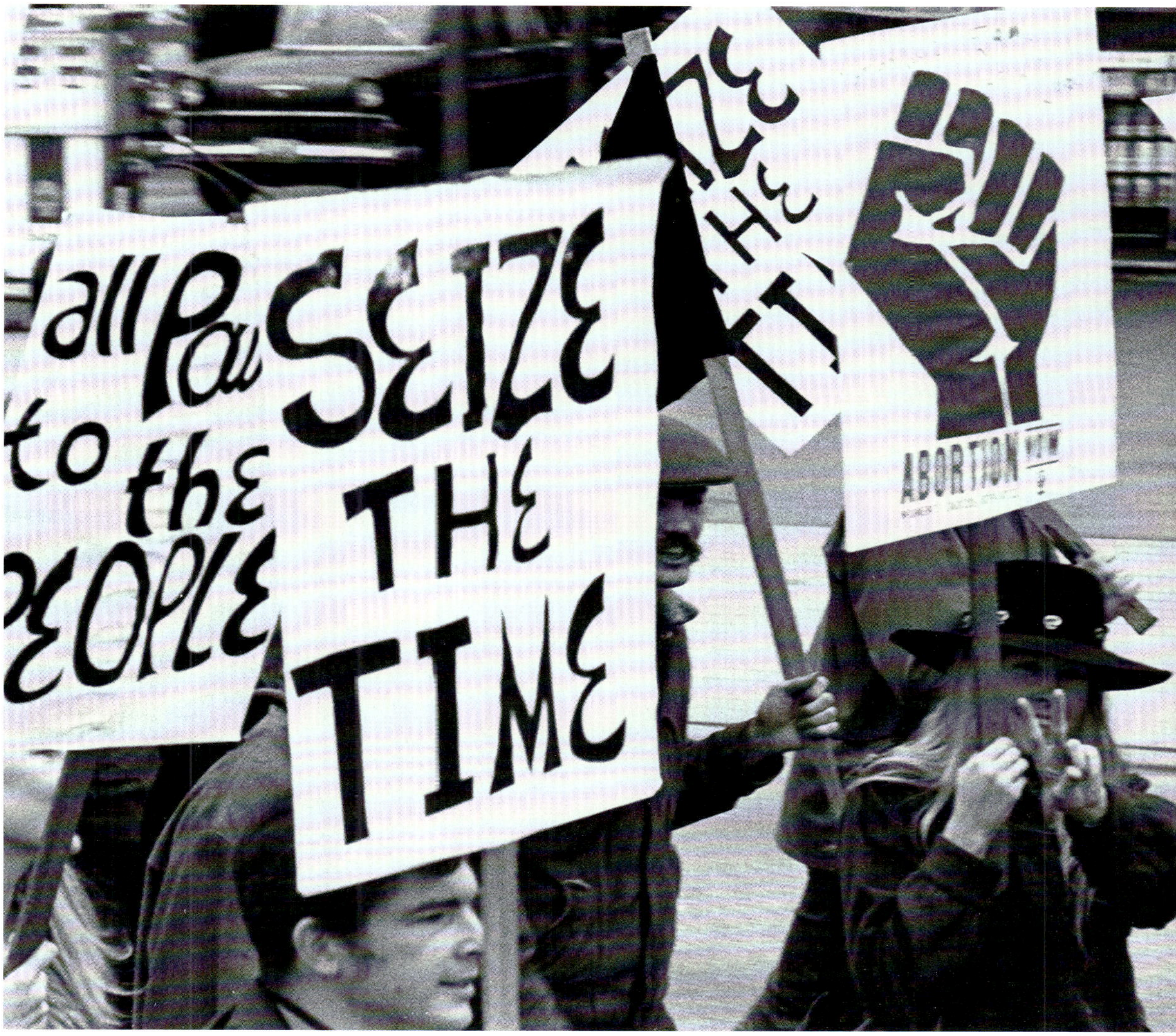
SEIZE THE TIME
ABORTION

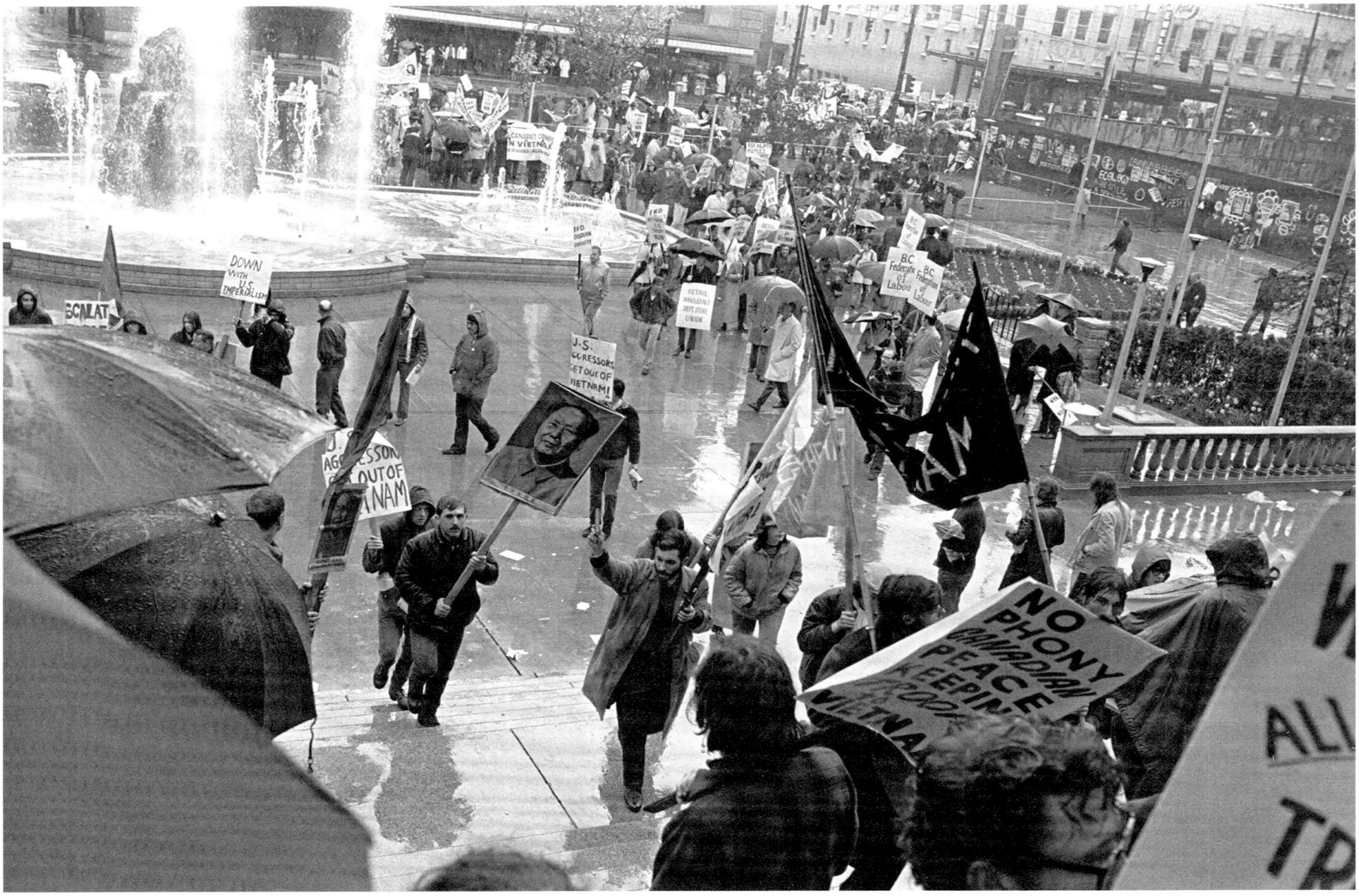

March Against the War in Vietnam, April 18, 1970. Between 300 and 400 protesters marched from Thornton Park on Main Street to the courthouse on Georgia Street. Some Yippies (members of the Youth International Party), who had performed an "exorcism" at the Vancouver Police Department headquarters on Main Street, joined the march, handing out flutes and sparklers.

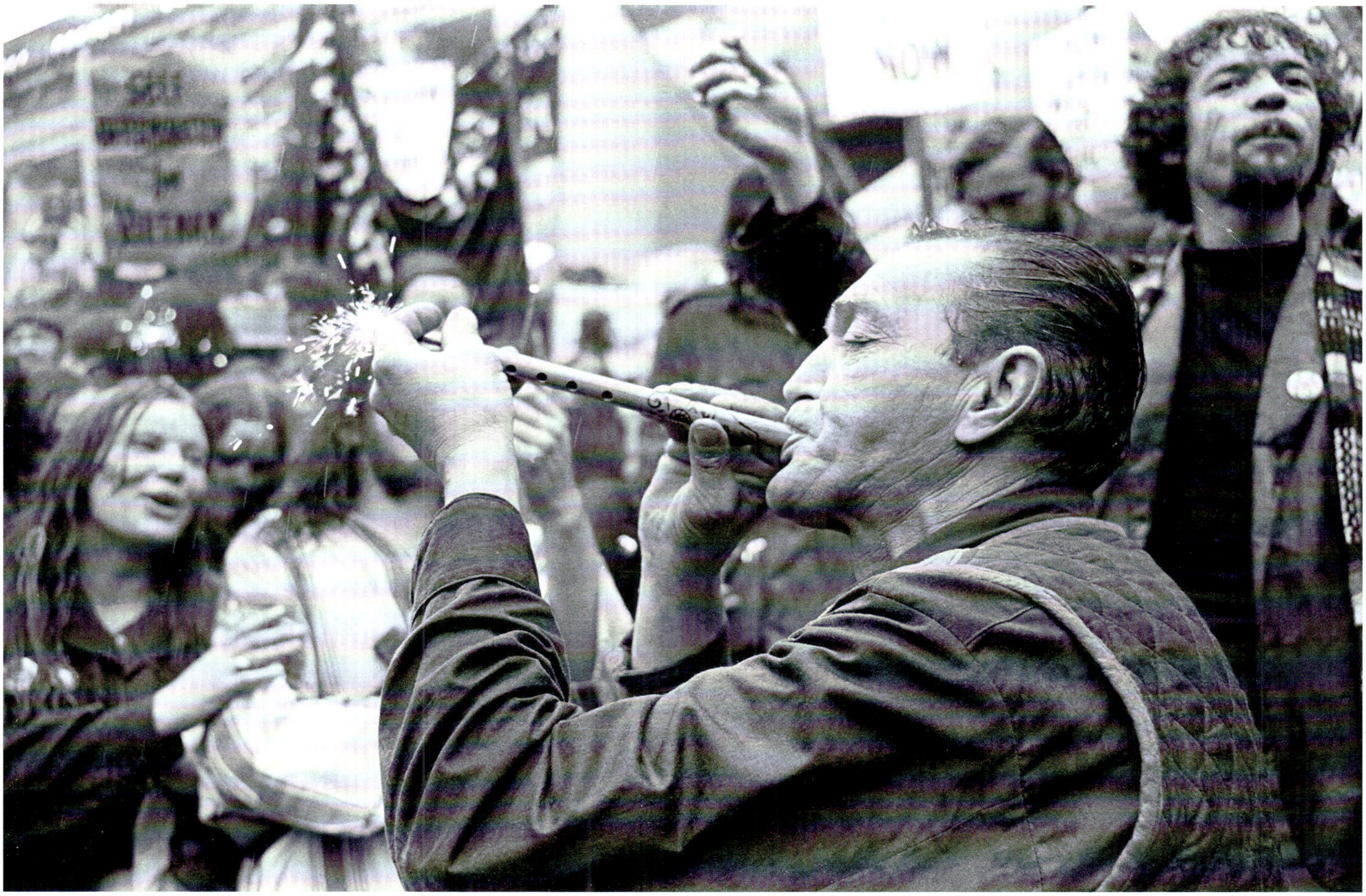

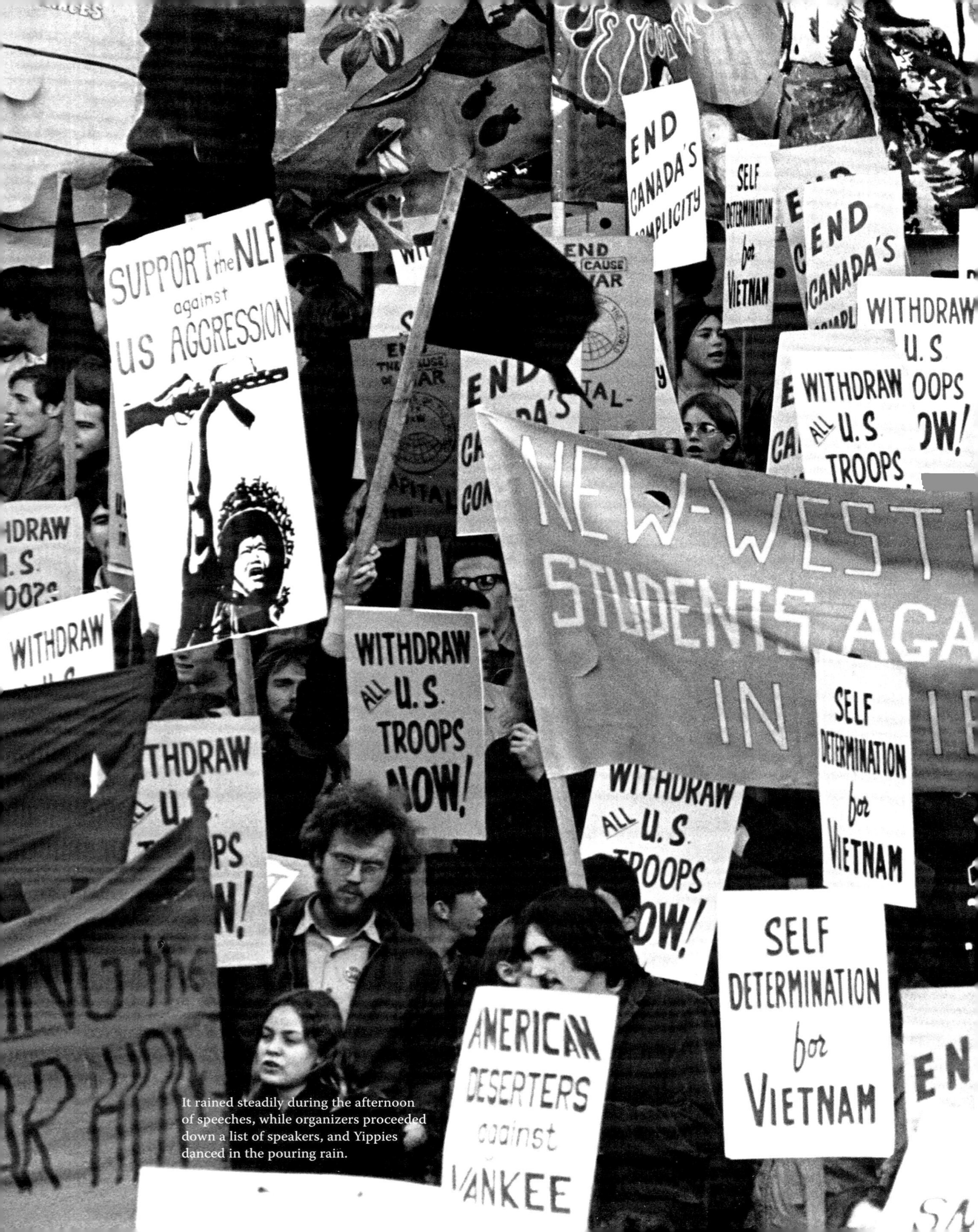

It rained steadily during the afternoon of speeches, while organizers proceeded down a list of speakers, and Yippies danced in the pouring rain.

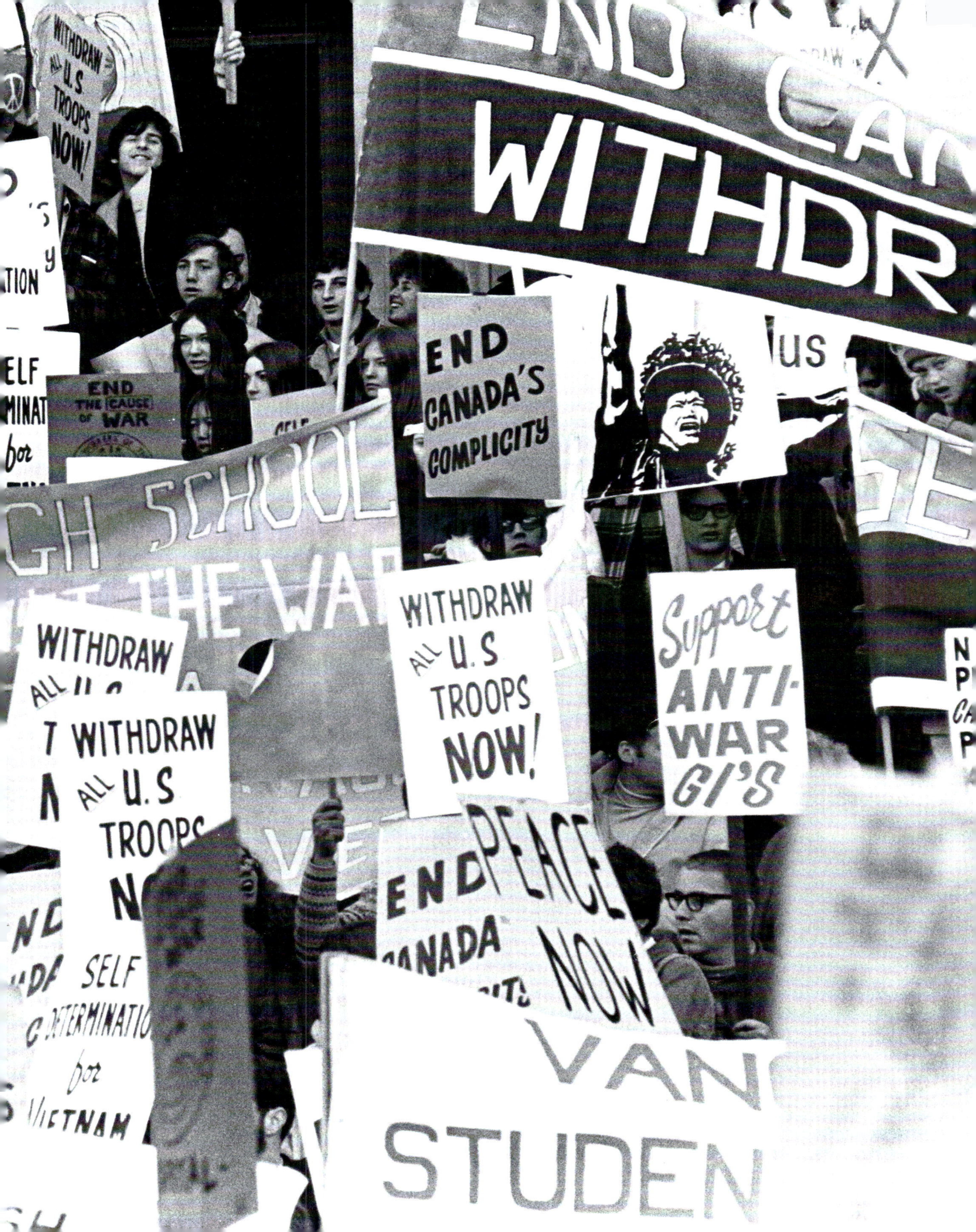
WITHDRAW ALL U.S. TROOPS NOW!
WITHDR
END THE CAUSE OF WAR
END CANADA'S COMPLICITY
GH SCHOOL
THE WAR
WITHDRAW ALL U.S TROOPS NOW!
Support ANTI-WAR GI'S
WITHDRAW ALL U.S TROOPS
PEACE NOW
SELF DETERMINATION for VIETNAM
VAN
STUDEN

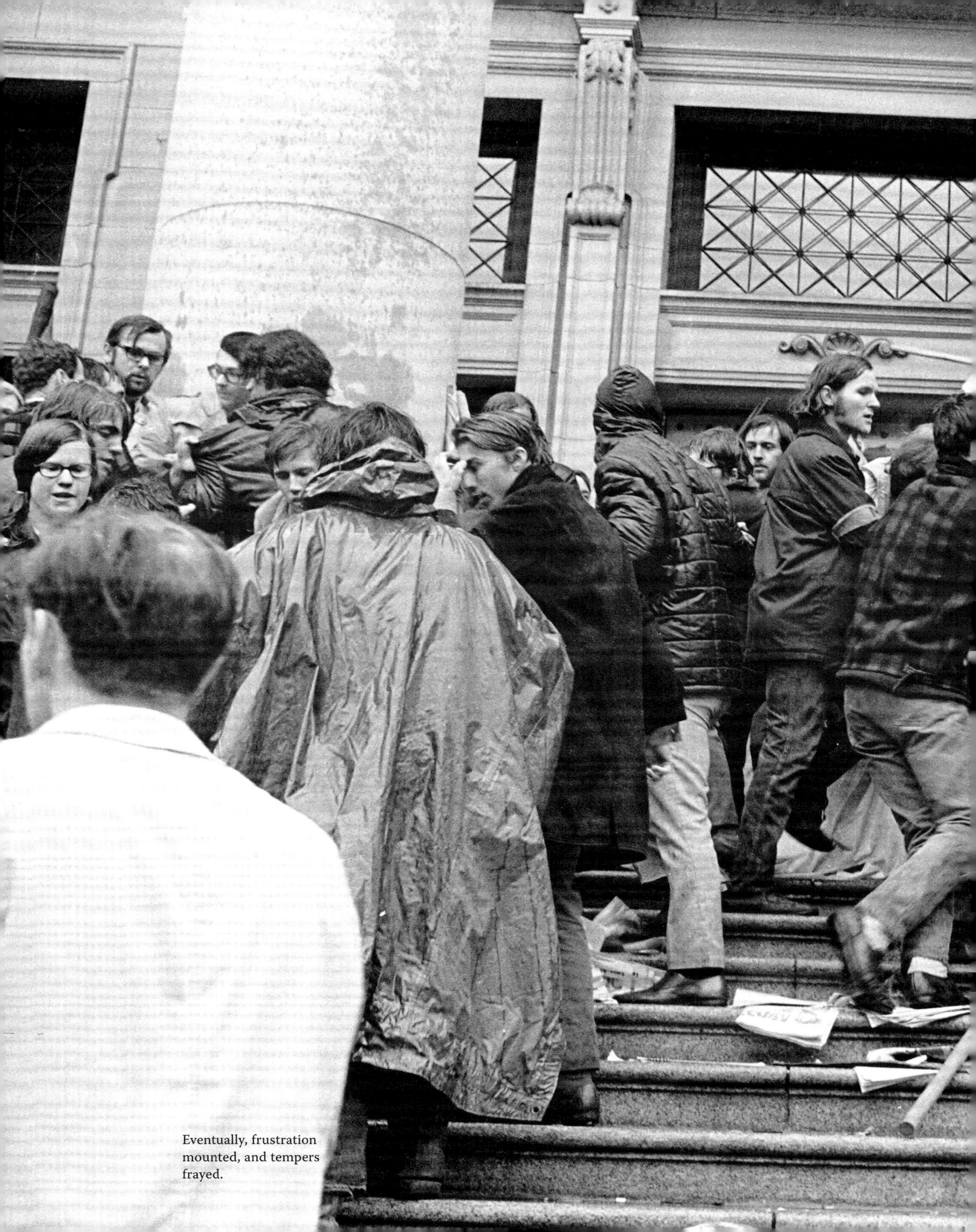

Eventually, frustration mounted, and tempers frayed.

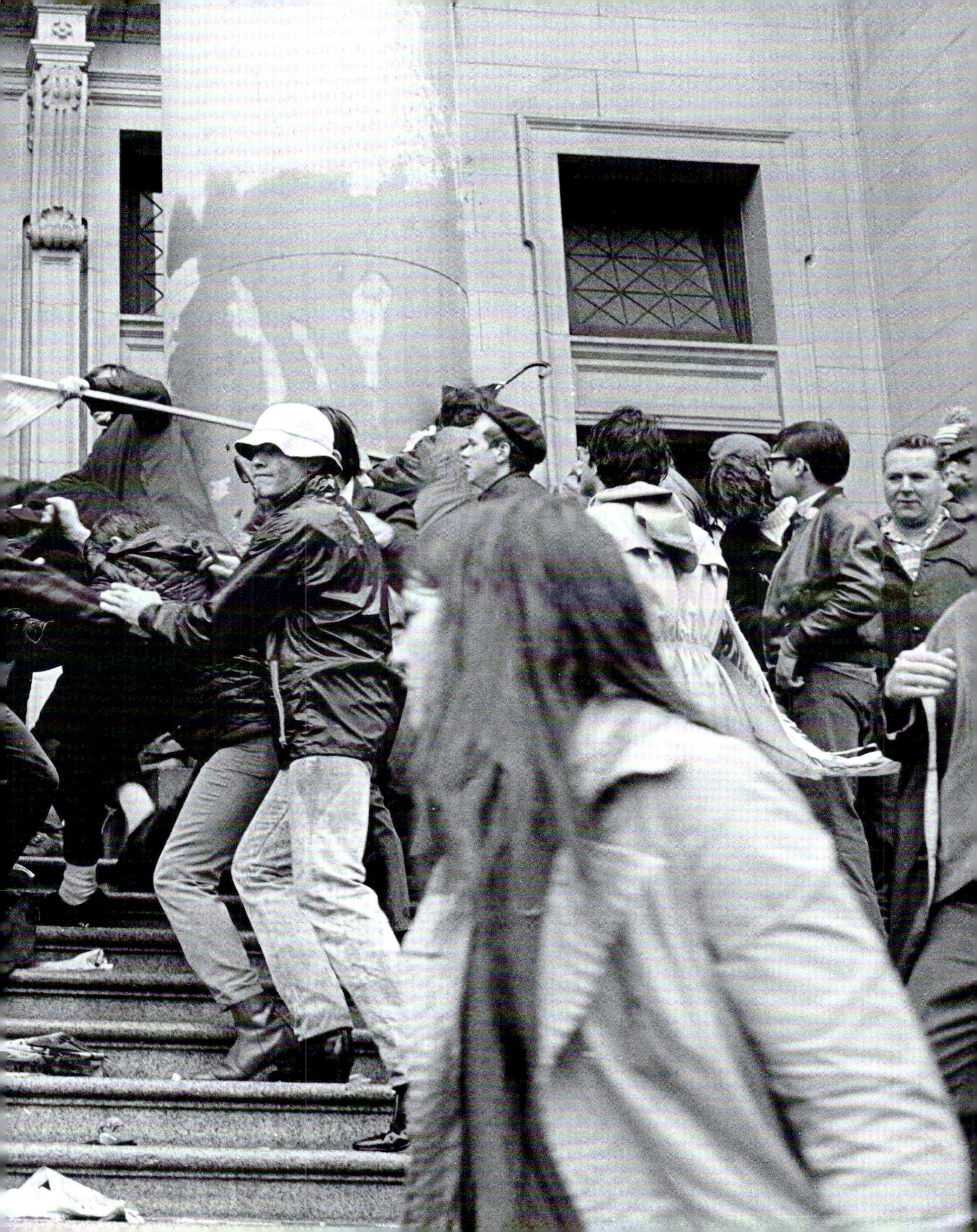

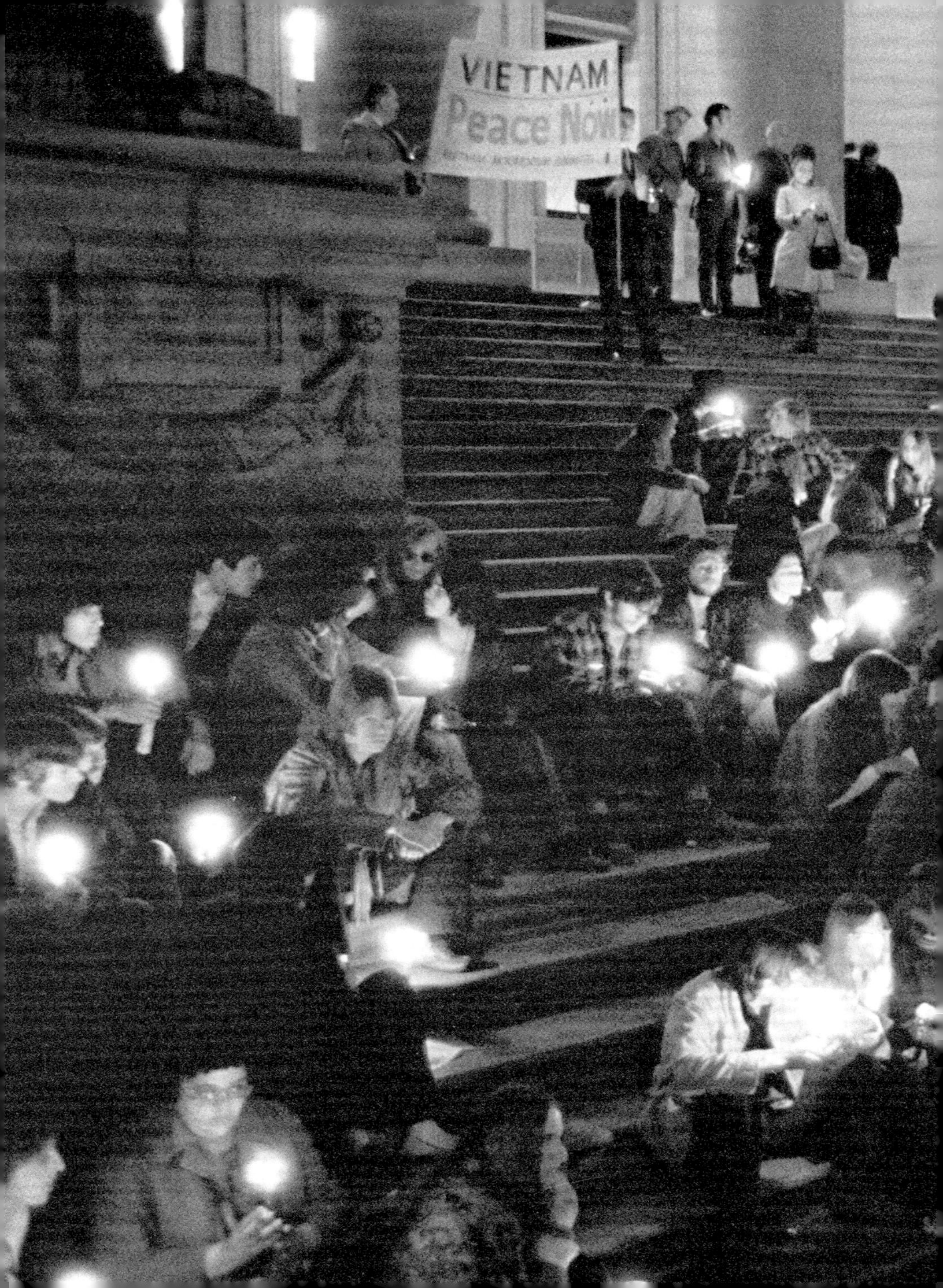
VIETNAM
Peace Now

The next night, after the sodden afternoon demonstration, many protesters returned for a night-time candlelight vigil on the same courthouse steps.

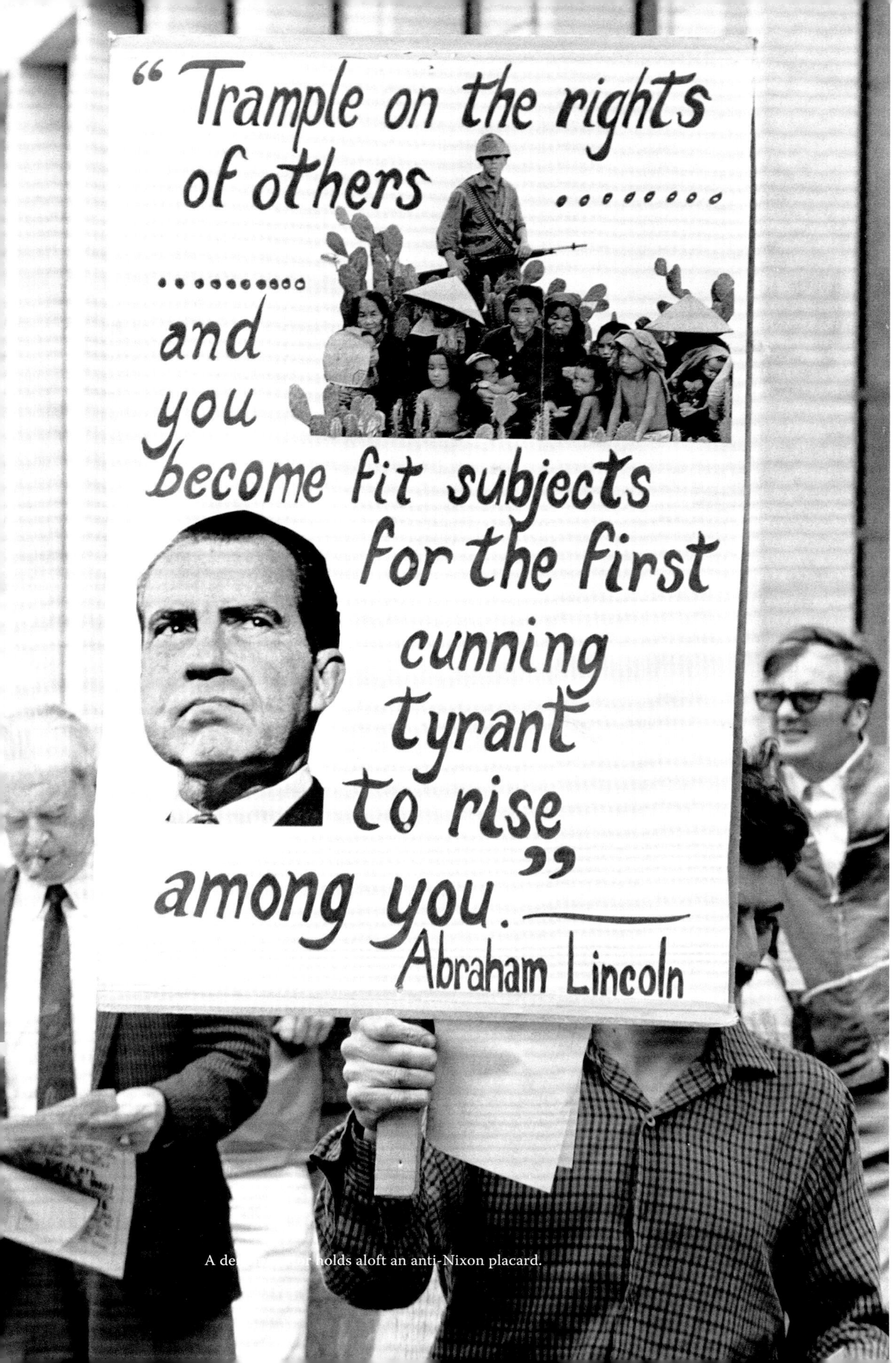

A de[illegible]r holds aloft an anti-Nixon placard.

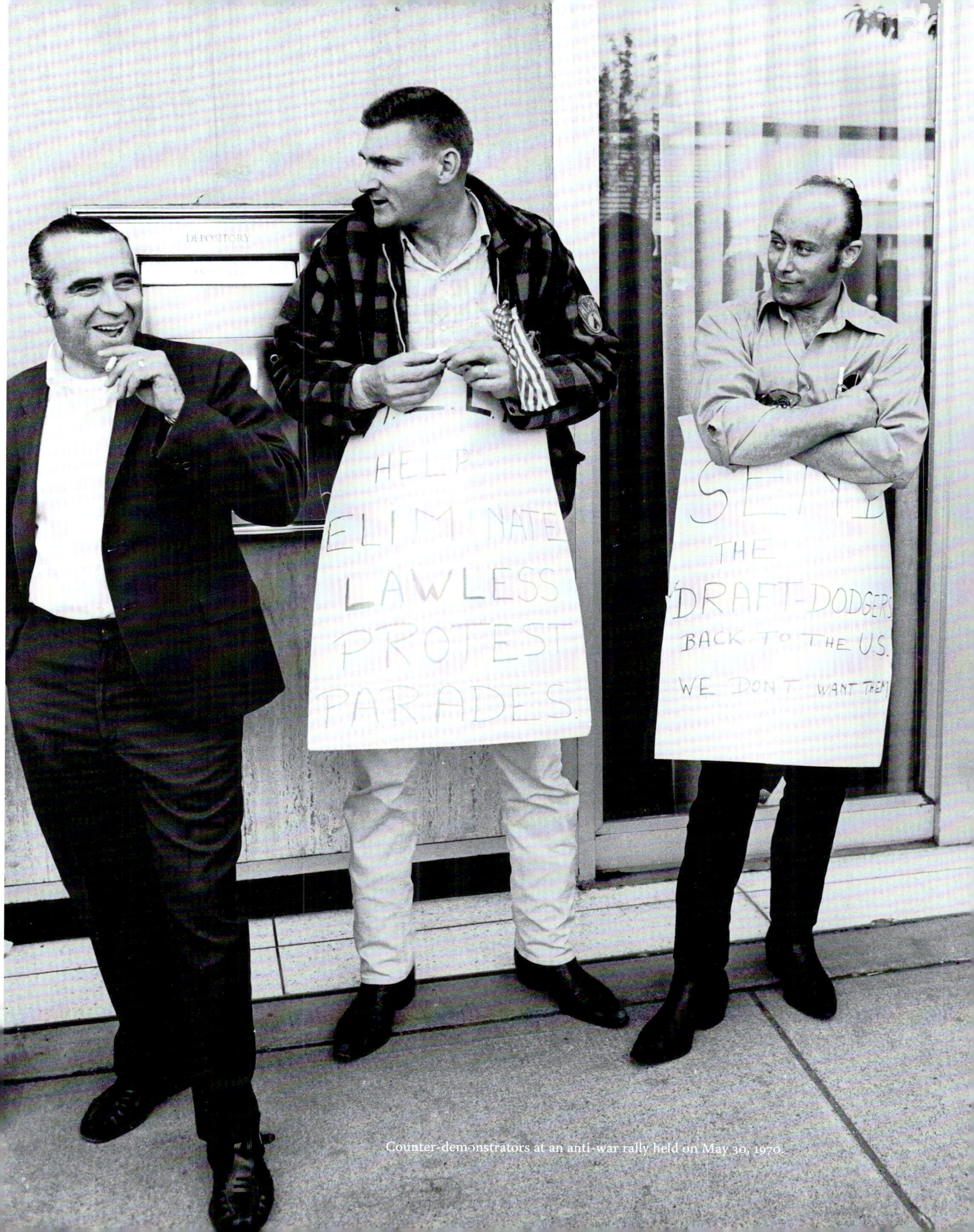

Counter-demonstrators at an anti-war rally held on May 30, 1970.

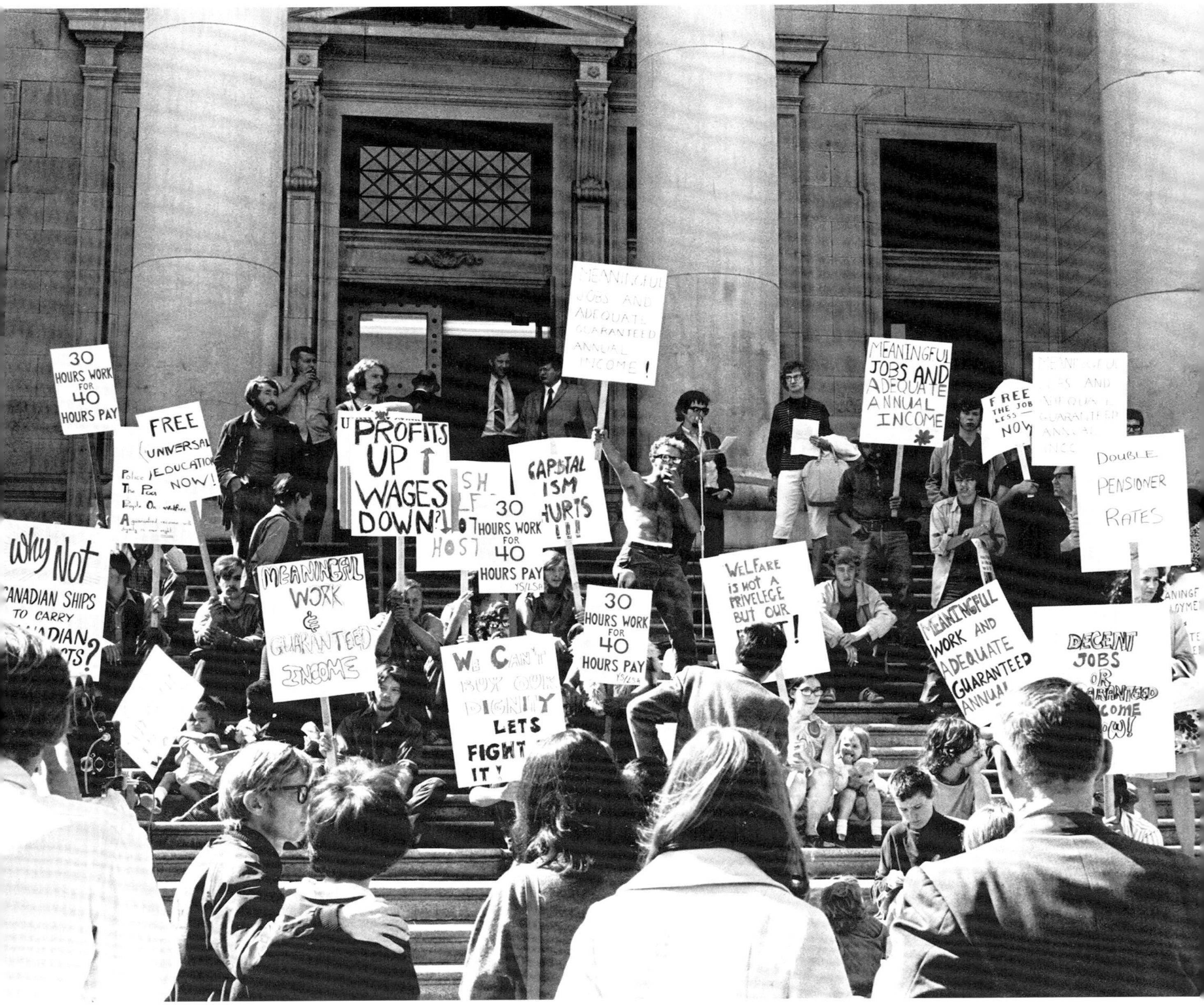

A rally on the courthouse steps, on August 1970, targeted economic issues and growing concerns about joblessness.

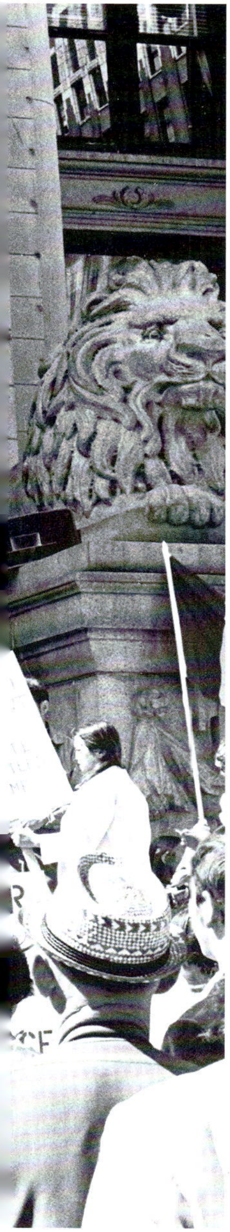

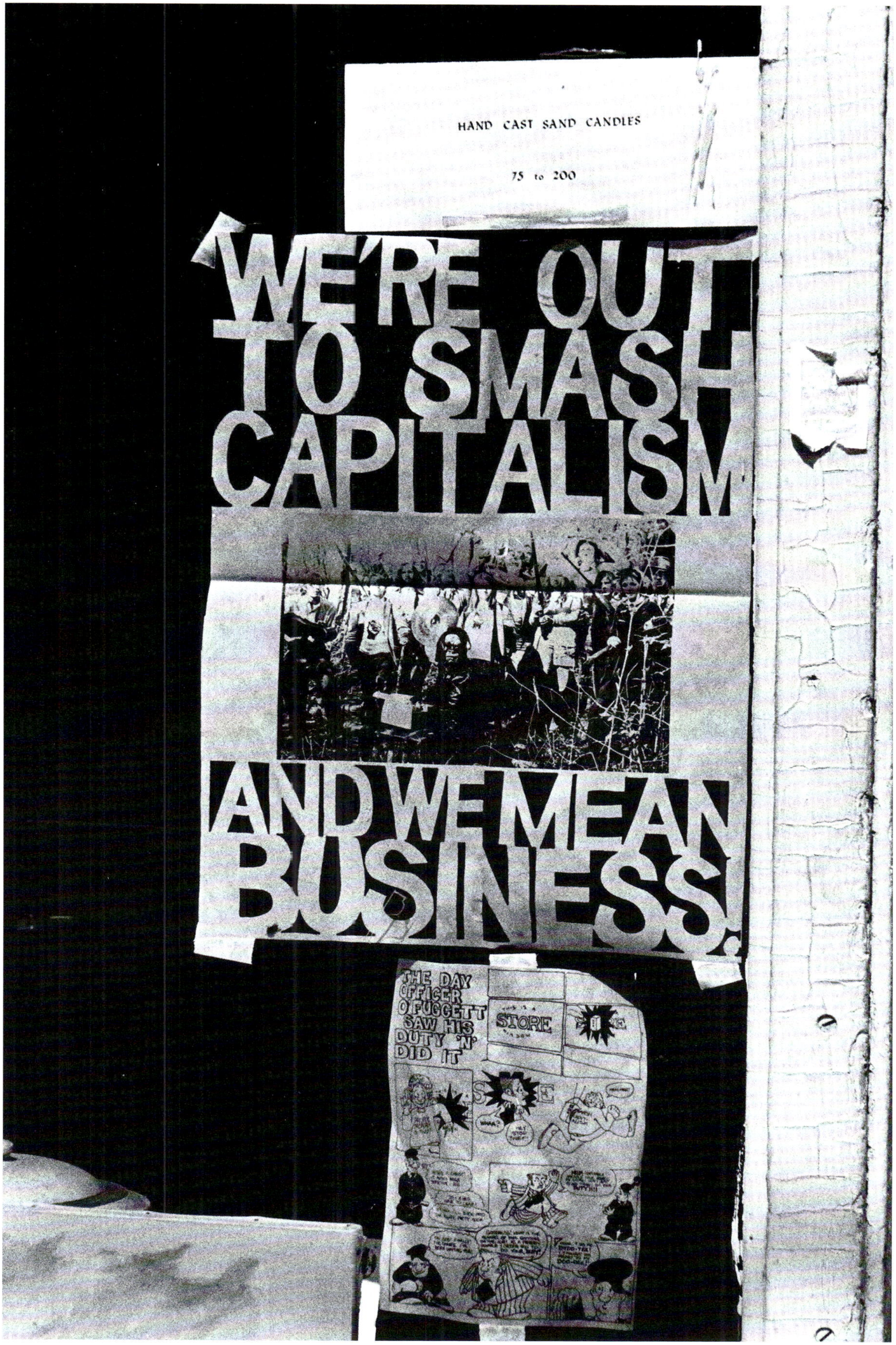
HAND CAST SAND CANDLES
75 to 200
WE'RE OUT TO SMASH CAPITALISM
AND WE MEAN BUSINESS!
THE DAY OFFICER O'FUGGETT SAW HIS DUTY 'N' DID IT
STORE

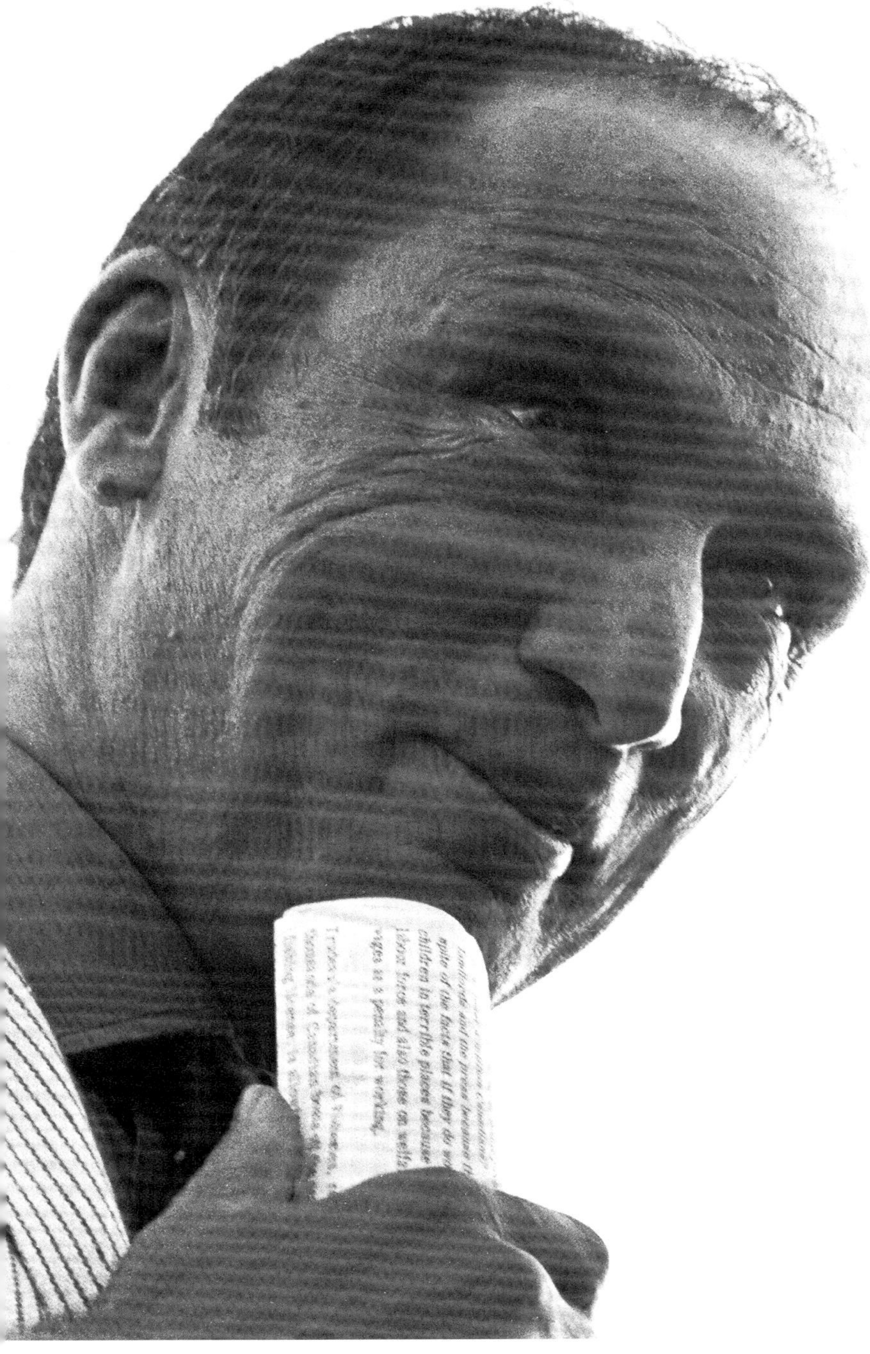

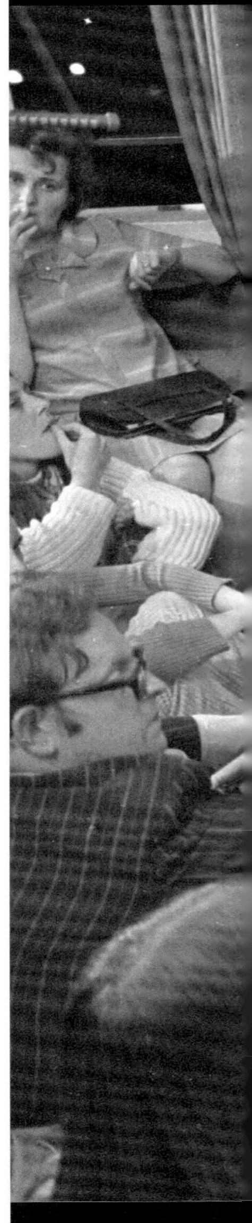

Prime Minister Pierre Elliott Trudeau tries to wield his charm while skirting protesters on his way into a $50 a plate Liberal Party fundraiser held at Seaforth Armoury, August 8, 1969.

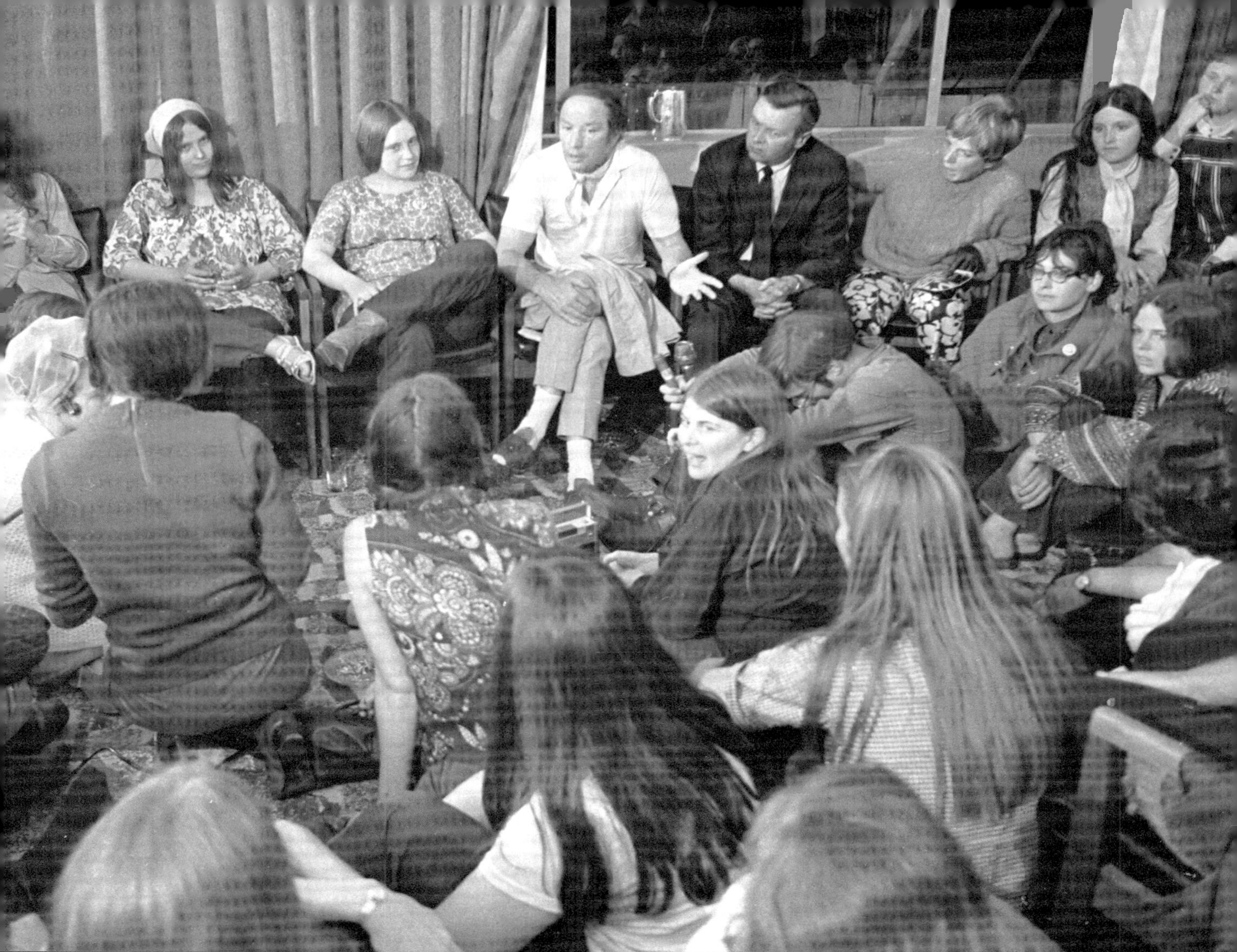

On June 14, 1970, leaders of Vancouver's feminist community demanded and got an audience with Trudeau at the Bayshore Inn. A Catholic who had been opposed to abortion, Trudeau admitted to the meeting that he was reconsidering his views

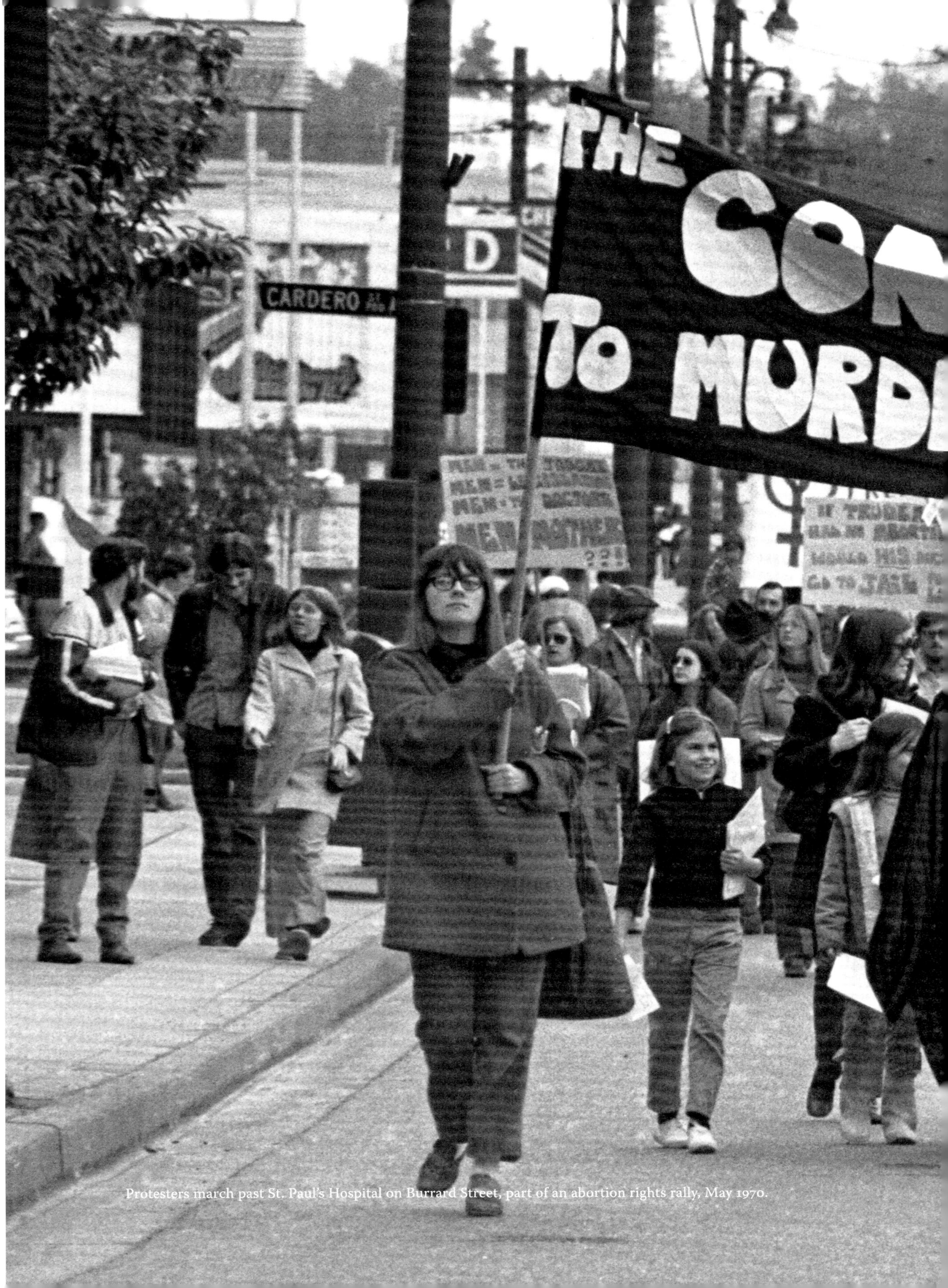

Protesters march past St. Paul's Hospital on Burrard Street, part of an abortion rights rally, May 1970.

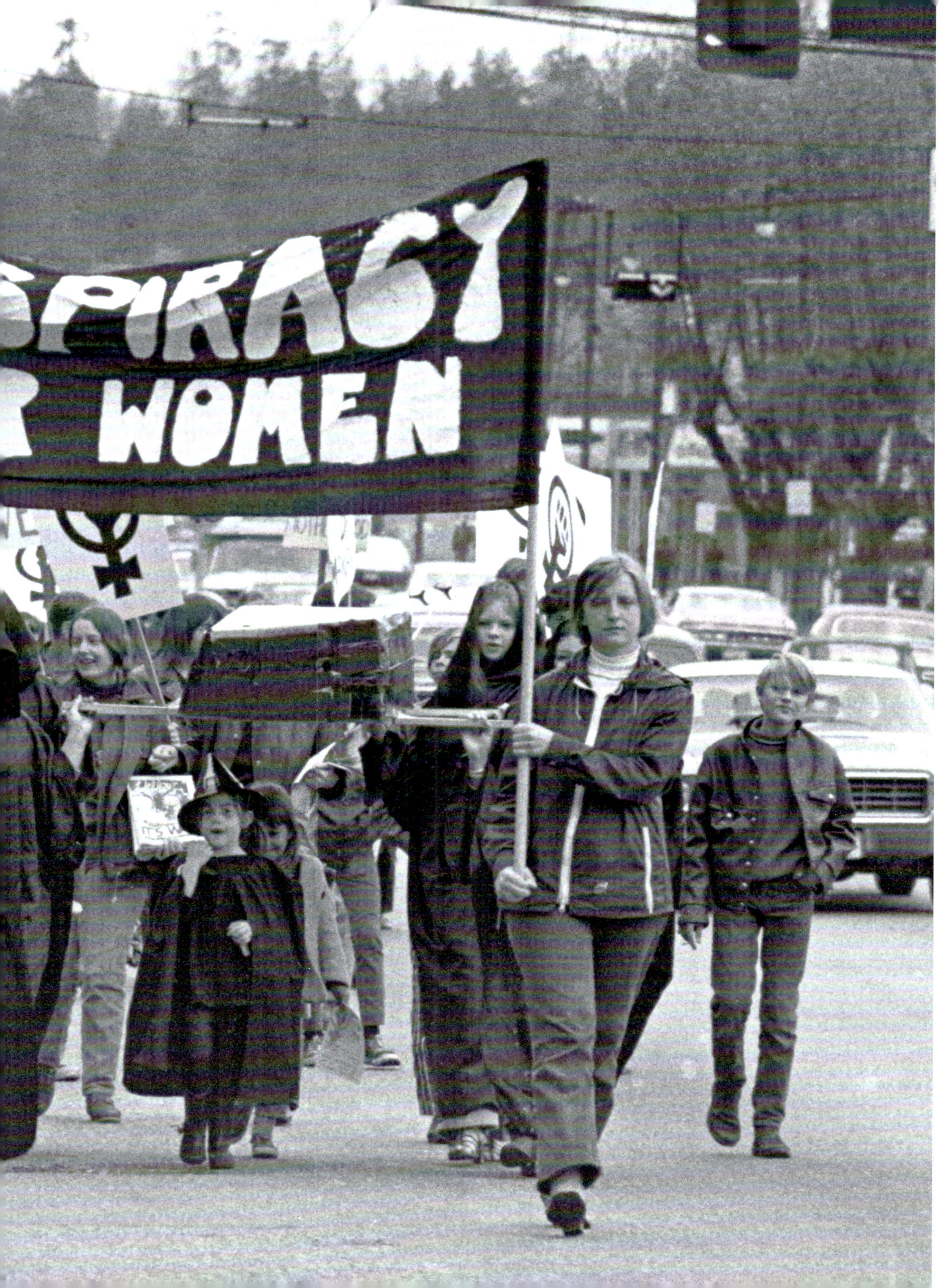
SPIRACY
WOMEN

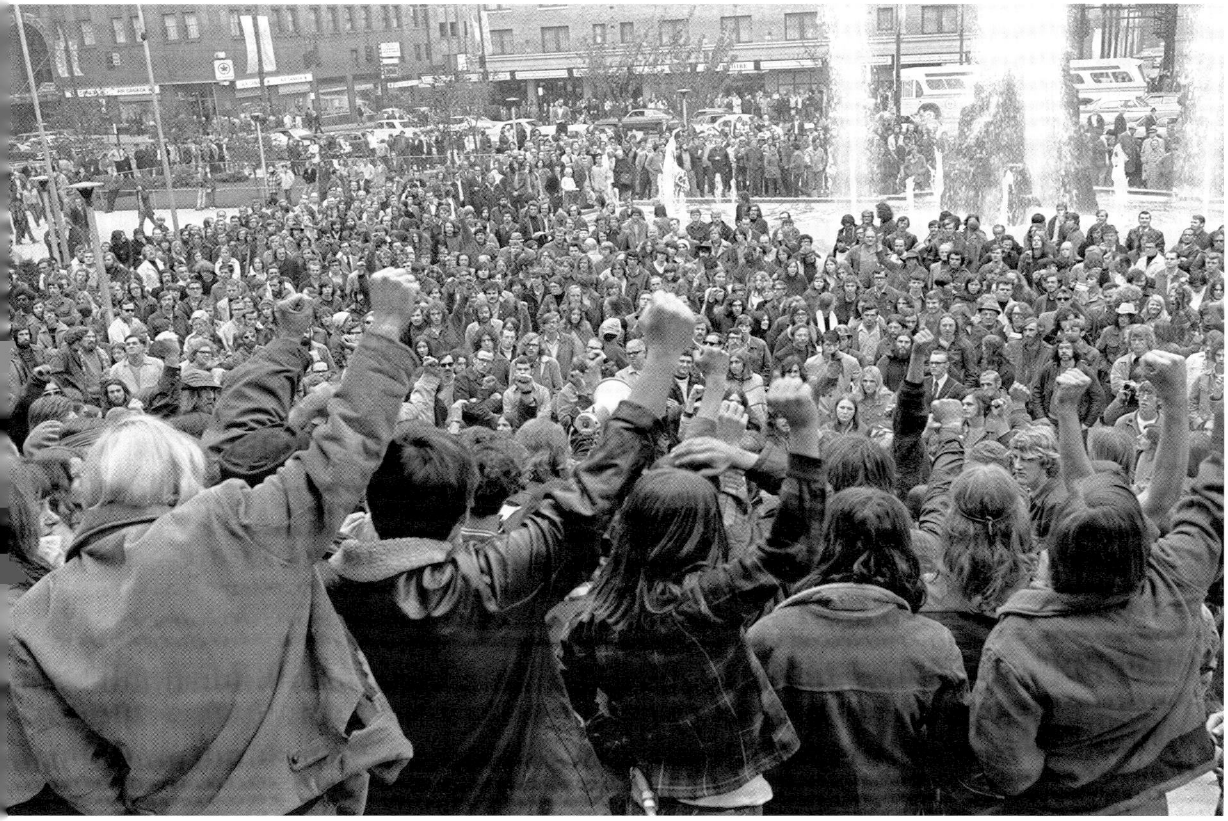

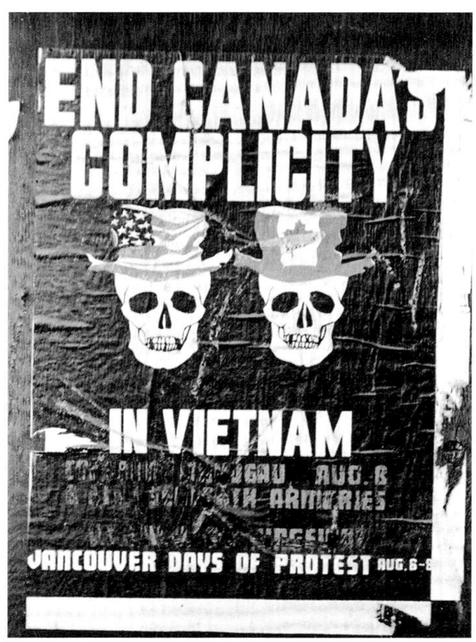

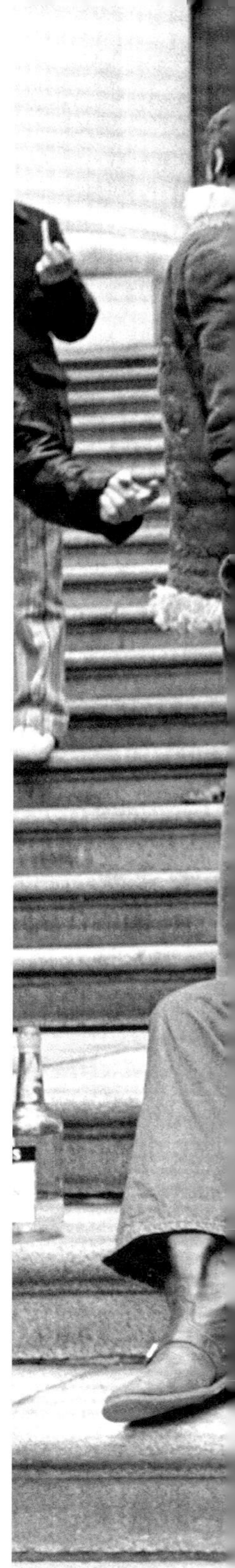

Trudeau's invocation of the War Measures Act to counter the panic set off by the kidnapping of Pierre Laporte and James Cross by the Front de libération du Québec sparked massive protest demonstrations across the country. In Vancouver, a demonstration on October 17, 1970, organized by the Vancouver Liberation Front to protest the eviction of tenants from the Jericho Hostel, escalated into a much larger rally at the courthouse.

An anti-Vietnam War poster created for the Vancouver Days of Protest, August 6 to 8, 1970.

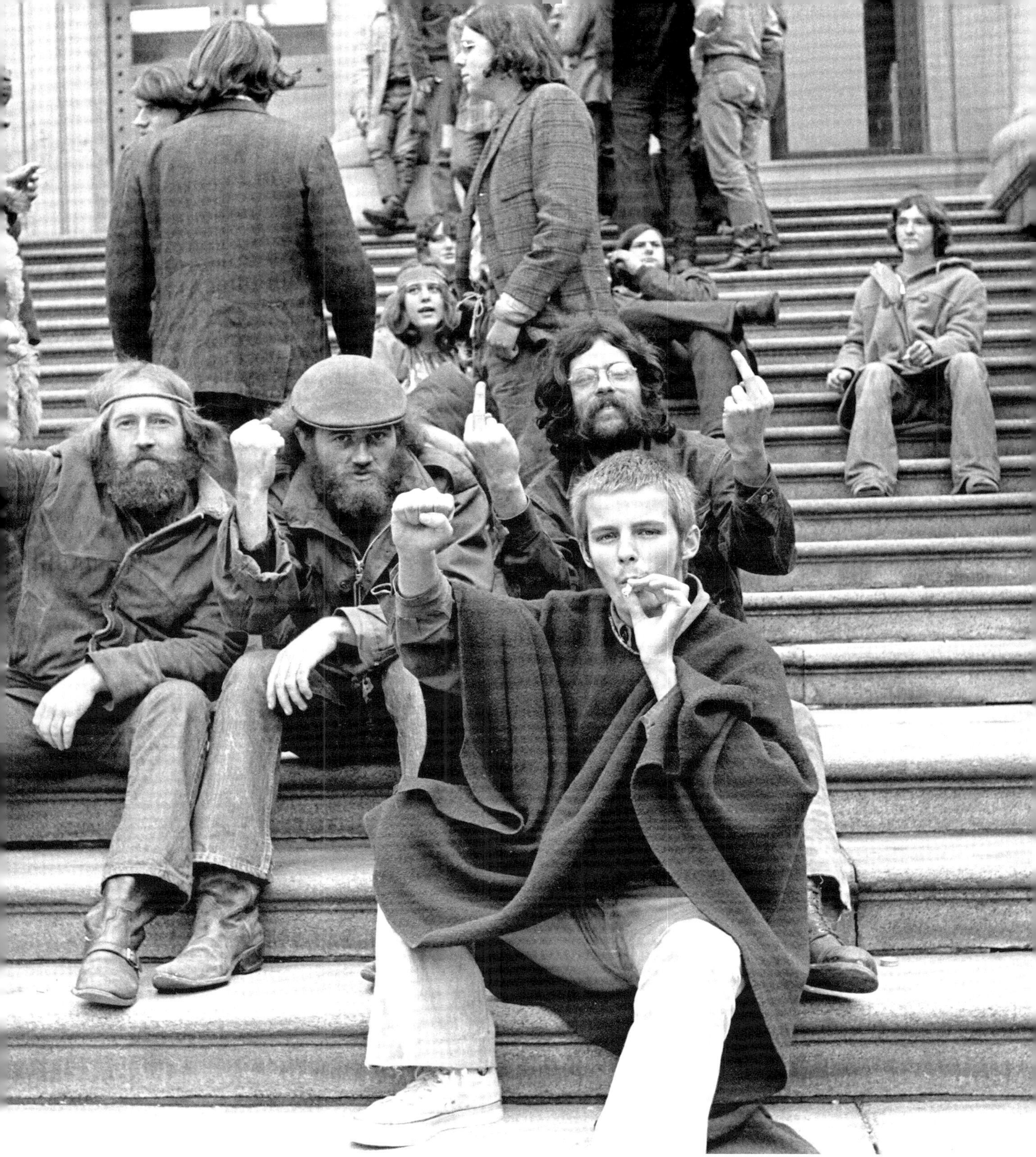

On December 20, 1970, Cesar Chavez, leader of the United Farm Workers Organizing Committee, came to Vancouver to speak at a rally seeking Canadian backing for a boycott of California grapes in support of the American farm workers who were on strike for better pay and conditions.

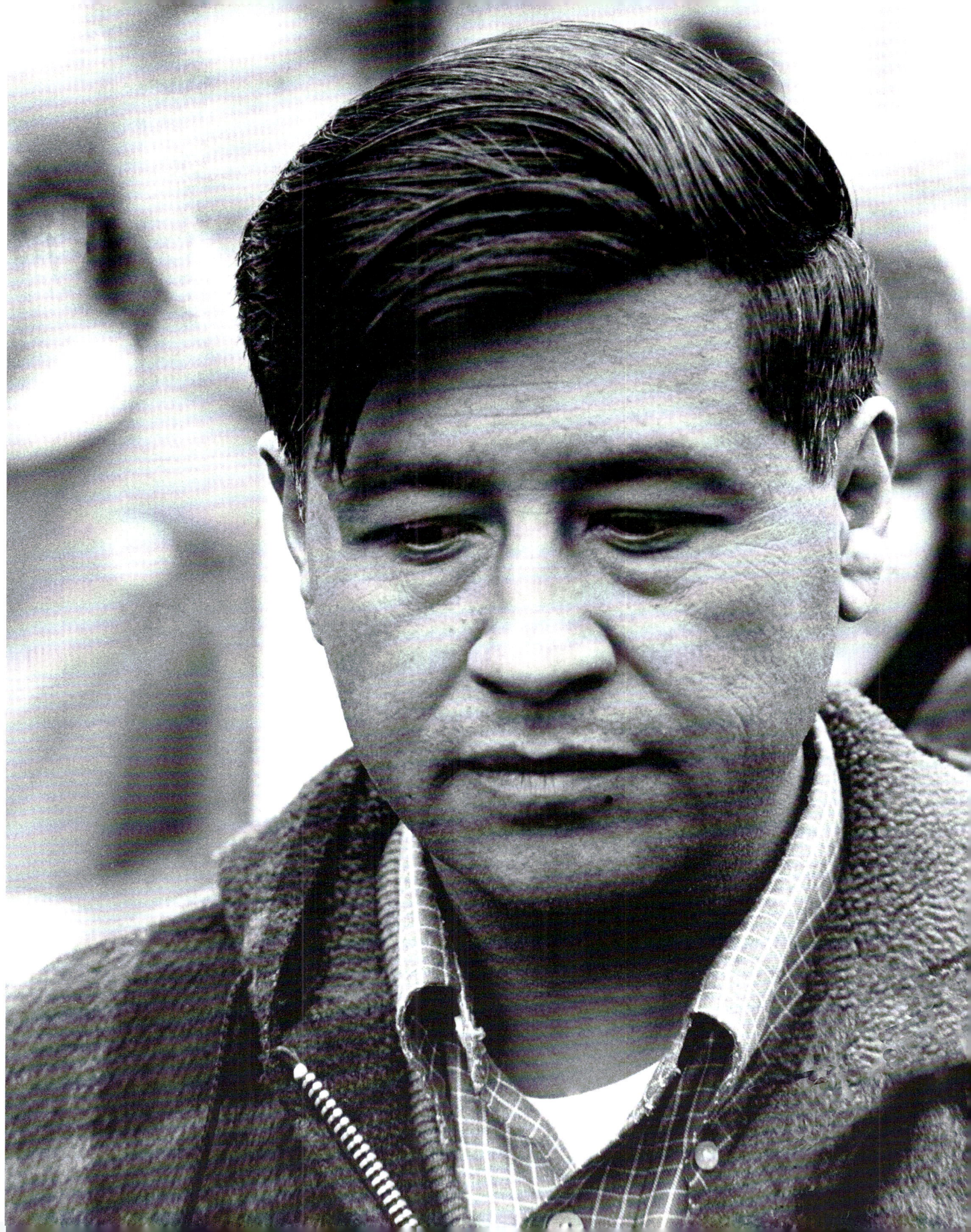

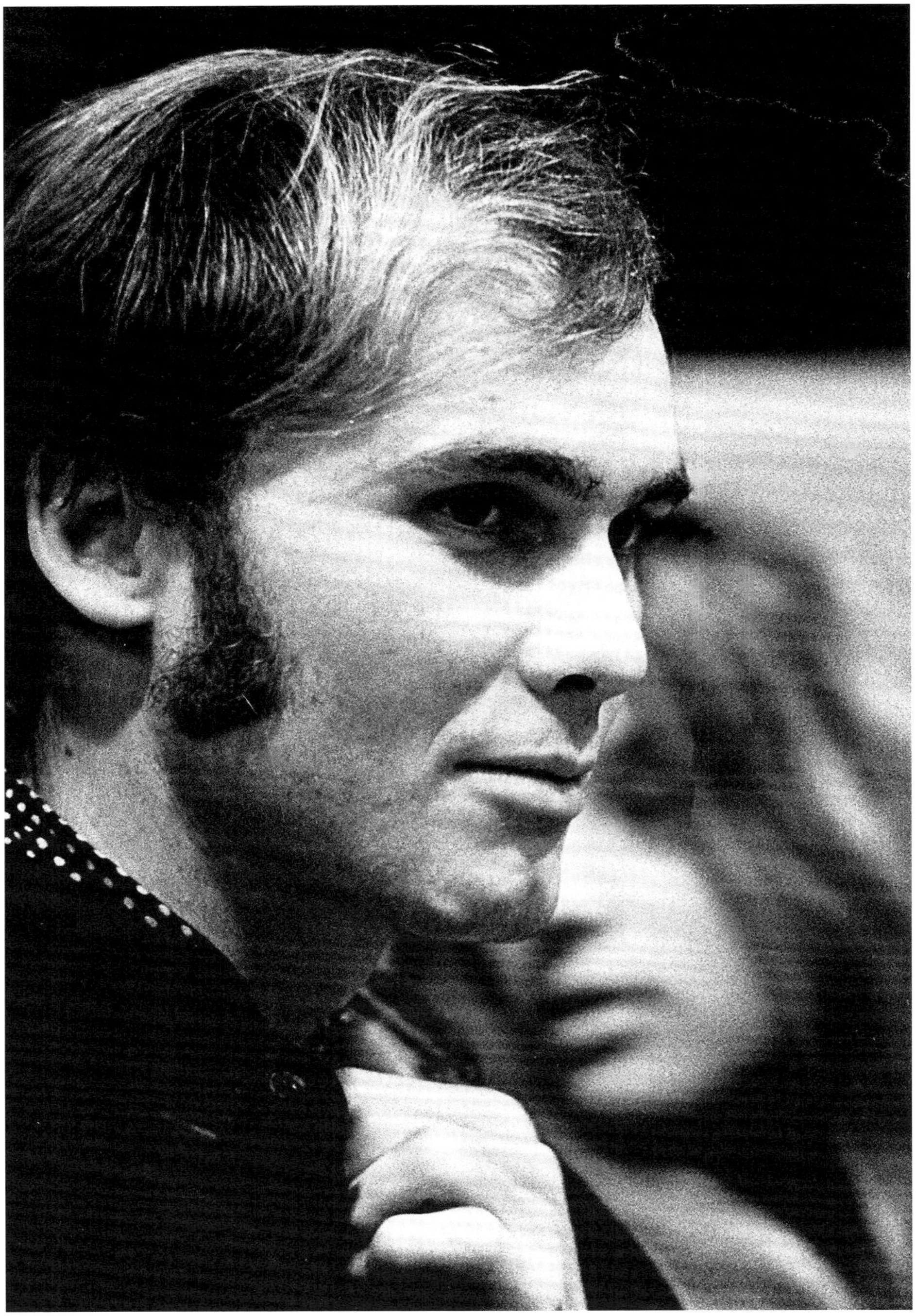

Gary, Aldergrove Rock Festival, May 17 & 18, 1969.

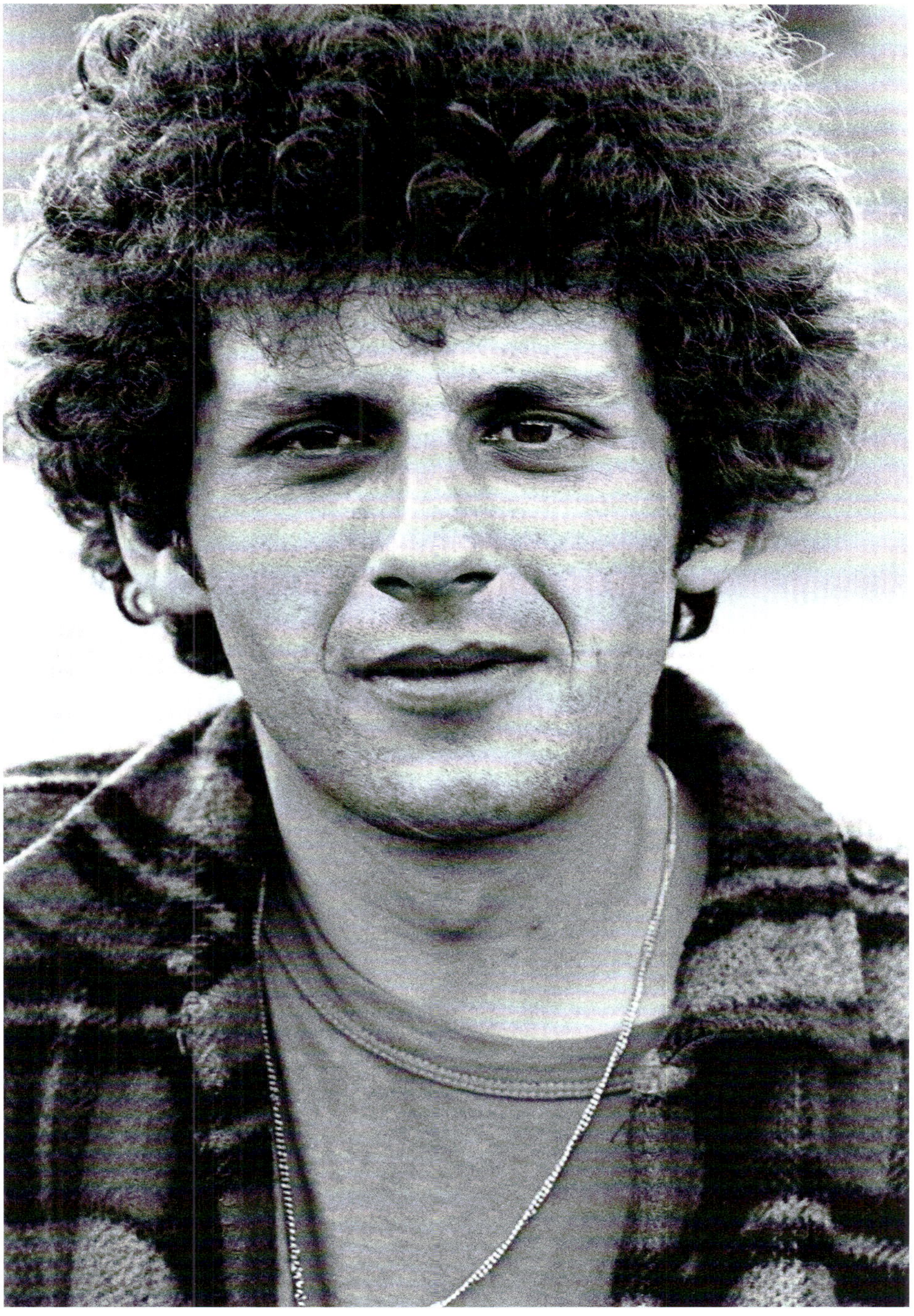

Dal, Aldergrove Rock Festival, May 17 & 18, 1969.

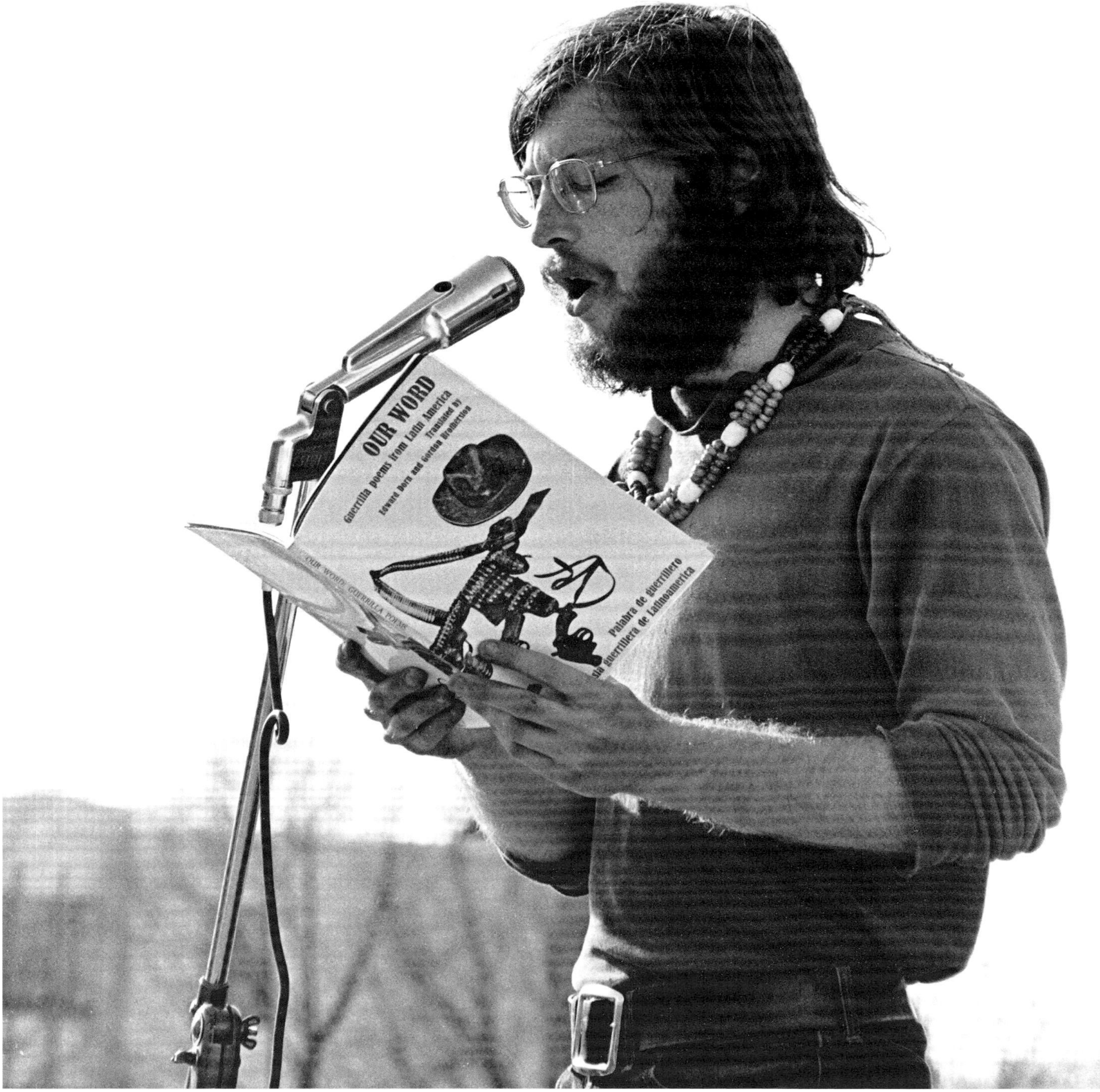

UBC Open House, March 6 & 7, 1970. Concurrent with the university's boosterish celebration, the Industrial Workers of the World sponsored a counter-Festival of the Oppressed, featuring speakers, bands, street theatre, and poetry readings.

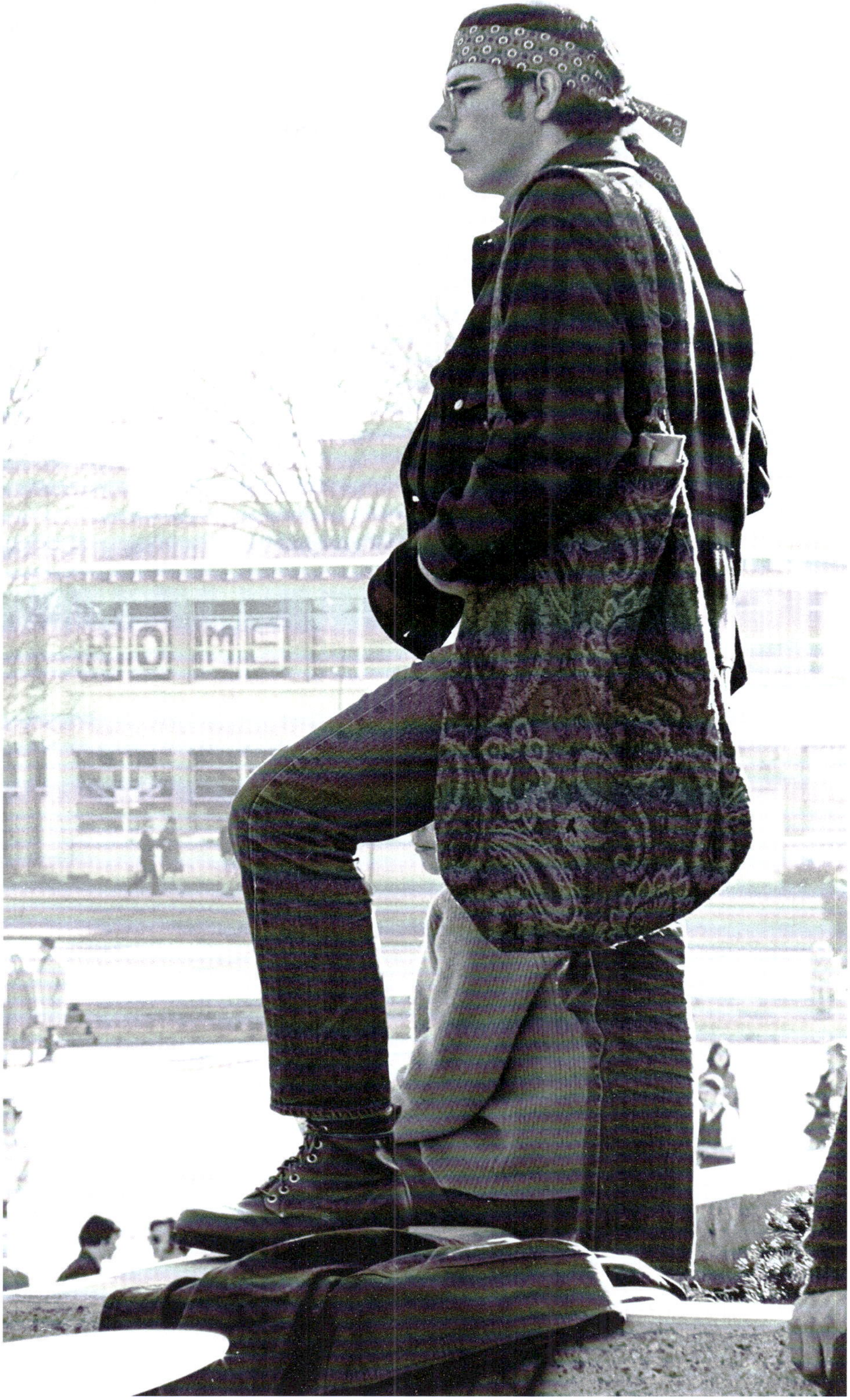
HOME

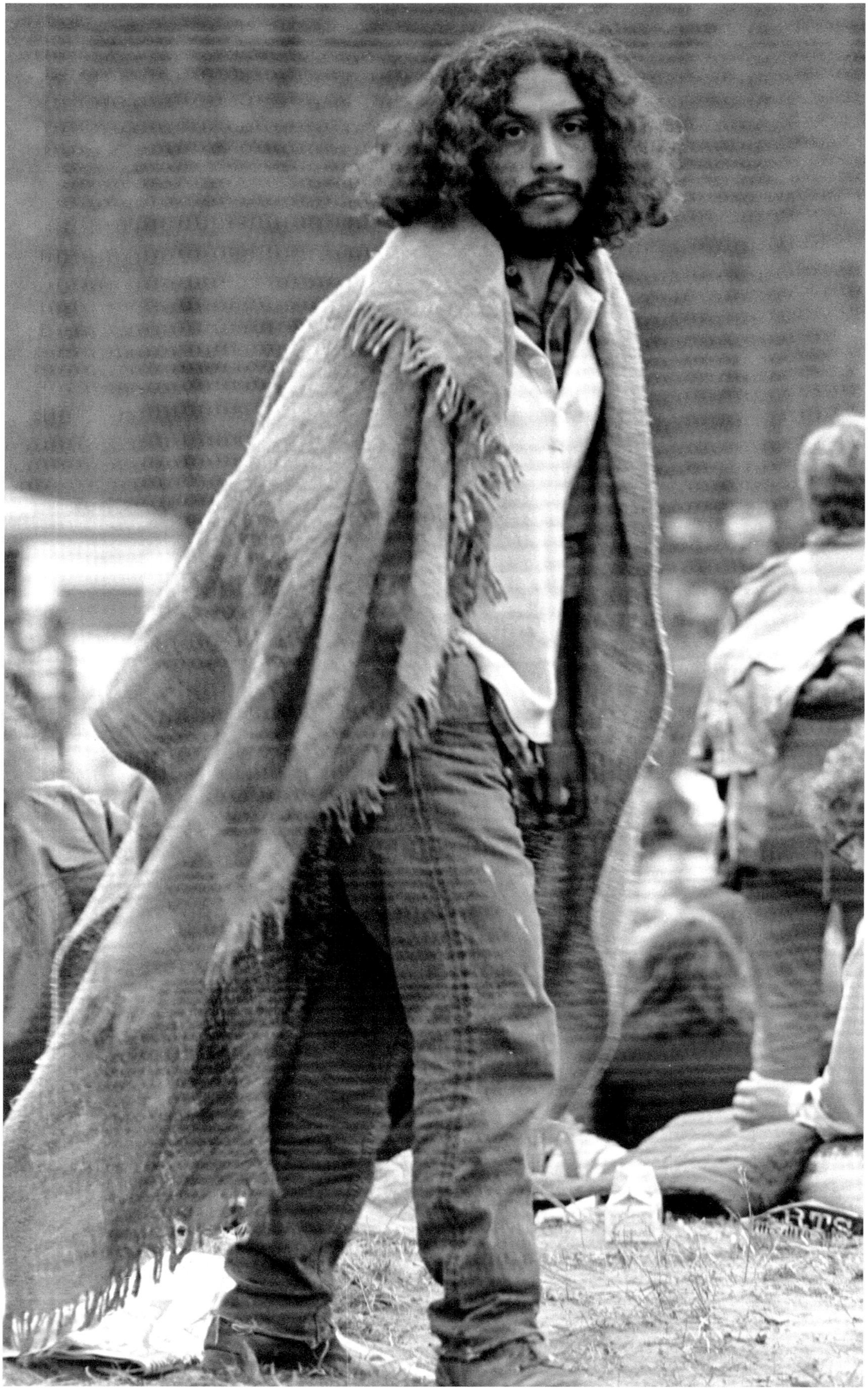

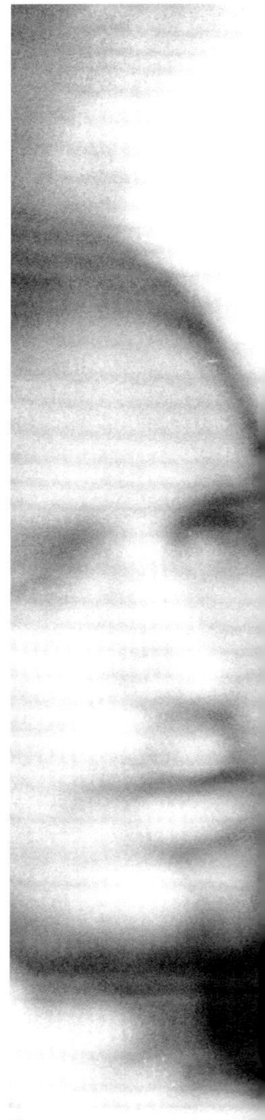

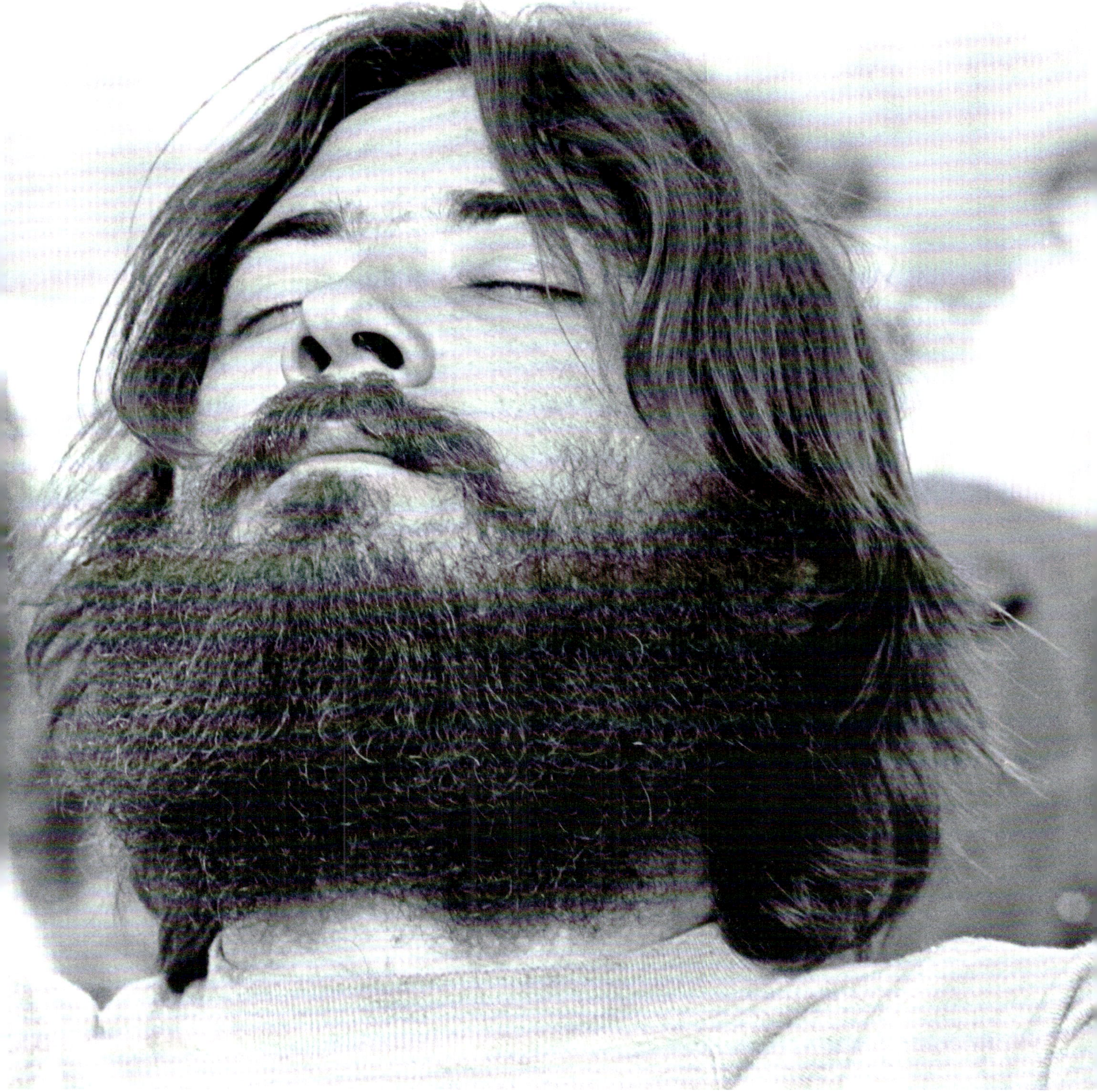

Fourth annual Easter Be-In, Prospect Point, Stanley Park, March 29, 1970. The first three had been political protests in nature. The 1970 Easter Be-In, and a handful of subsequent be-ins, were organized as commercial ventures, and featured big-name rock acts such as Country Joe and the Fish.

Groovin at Strawberry Mountain Fair, near Mission, May 16 – 17, 1970, which featured Country Joe & the Fish, Small Faces, Redbone, and Seals & Crofts.

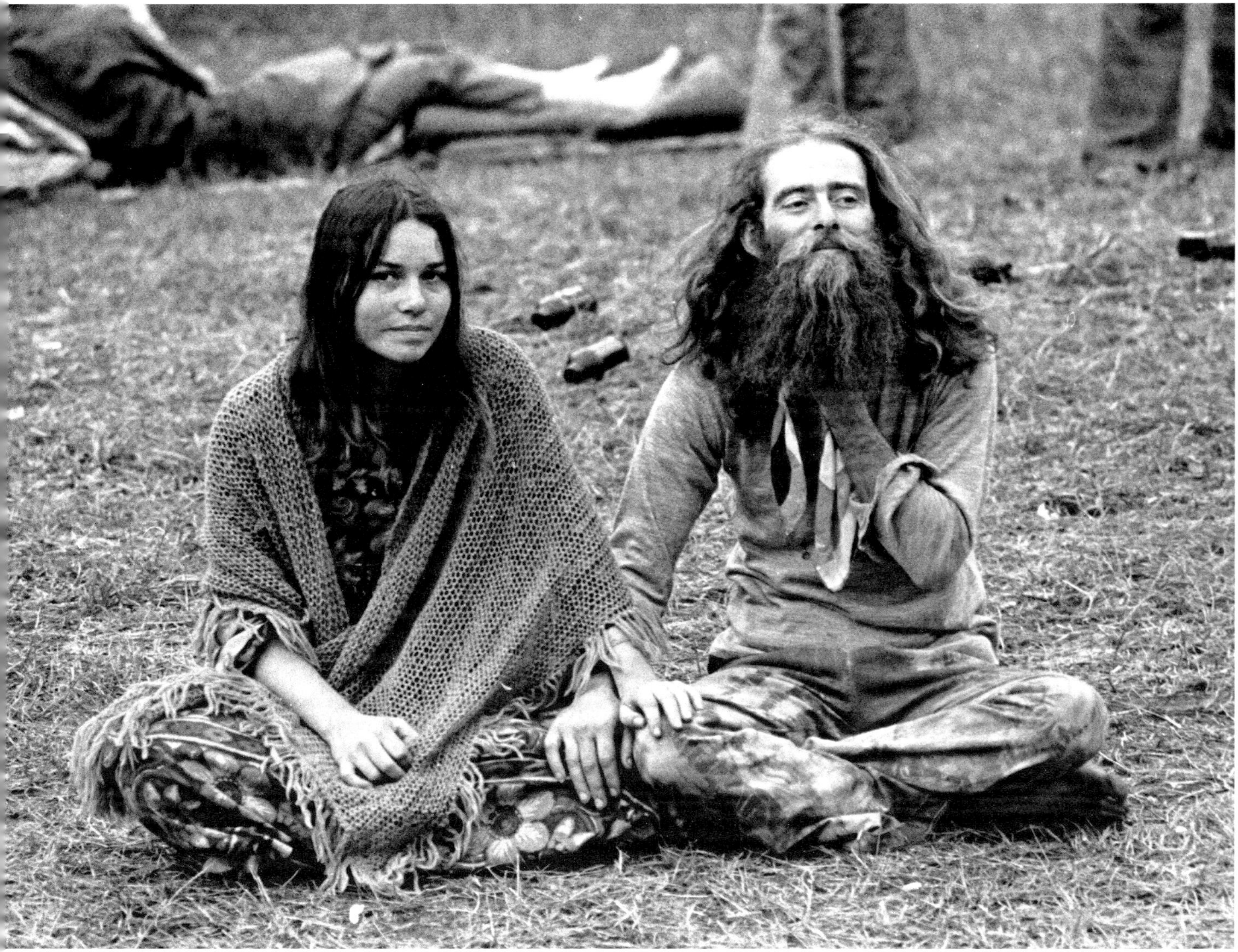

Strawberry Mountain Fair, near Mission, May 16 & 17, 1970.

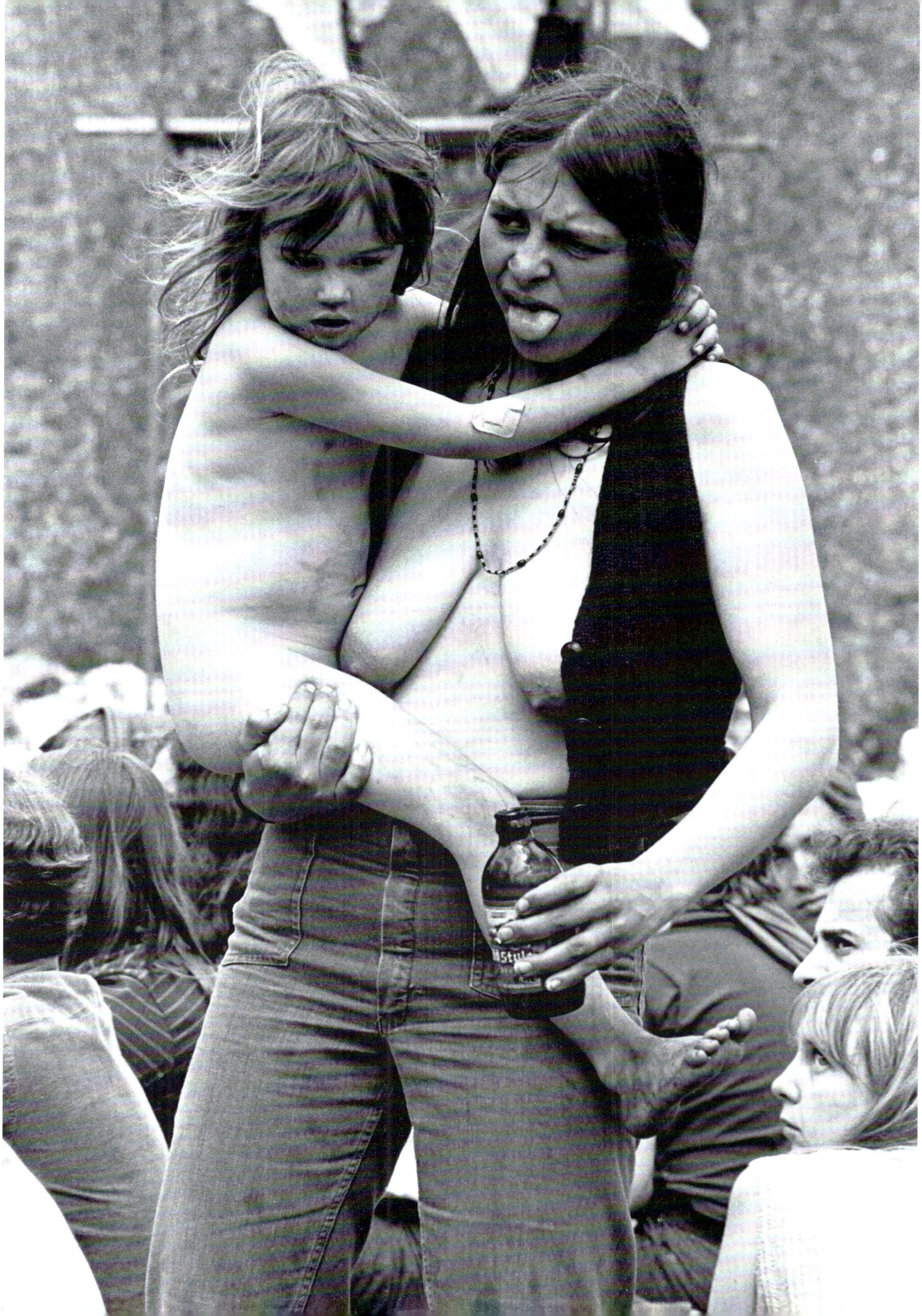

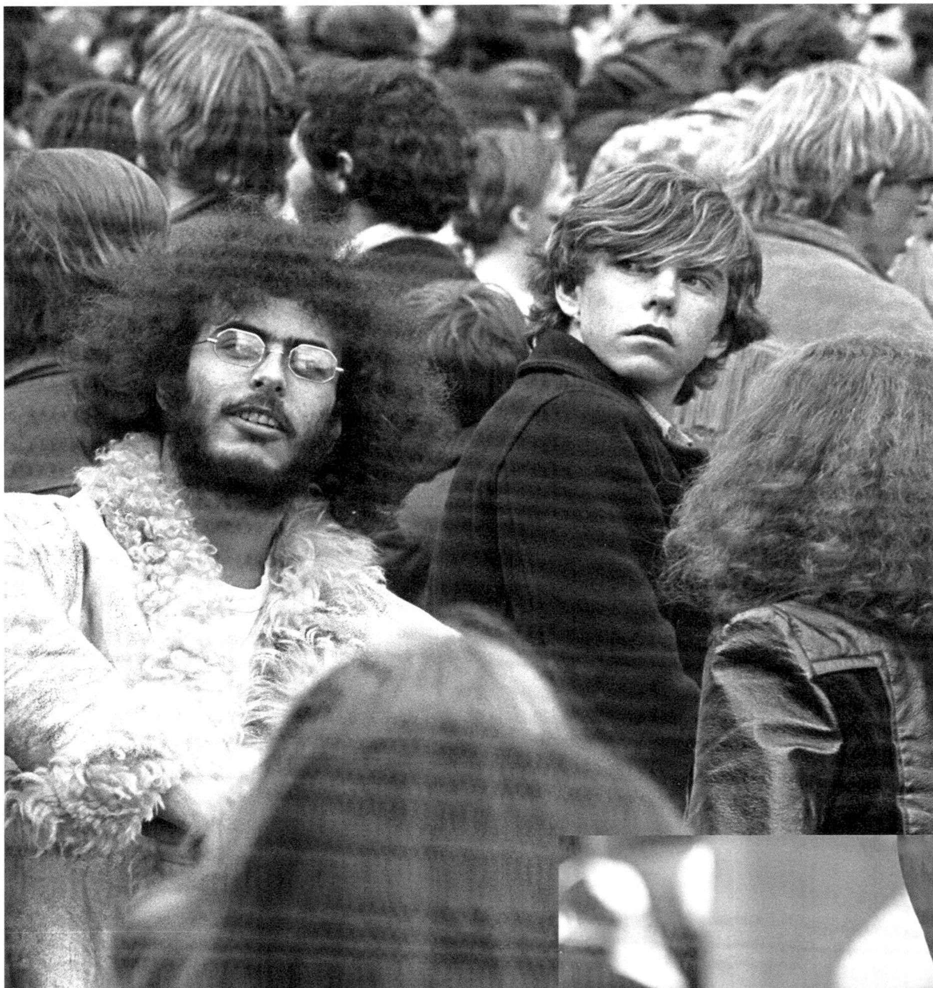

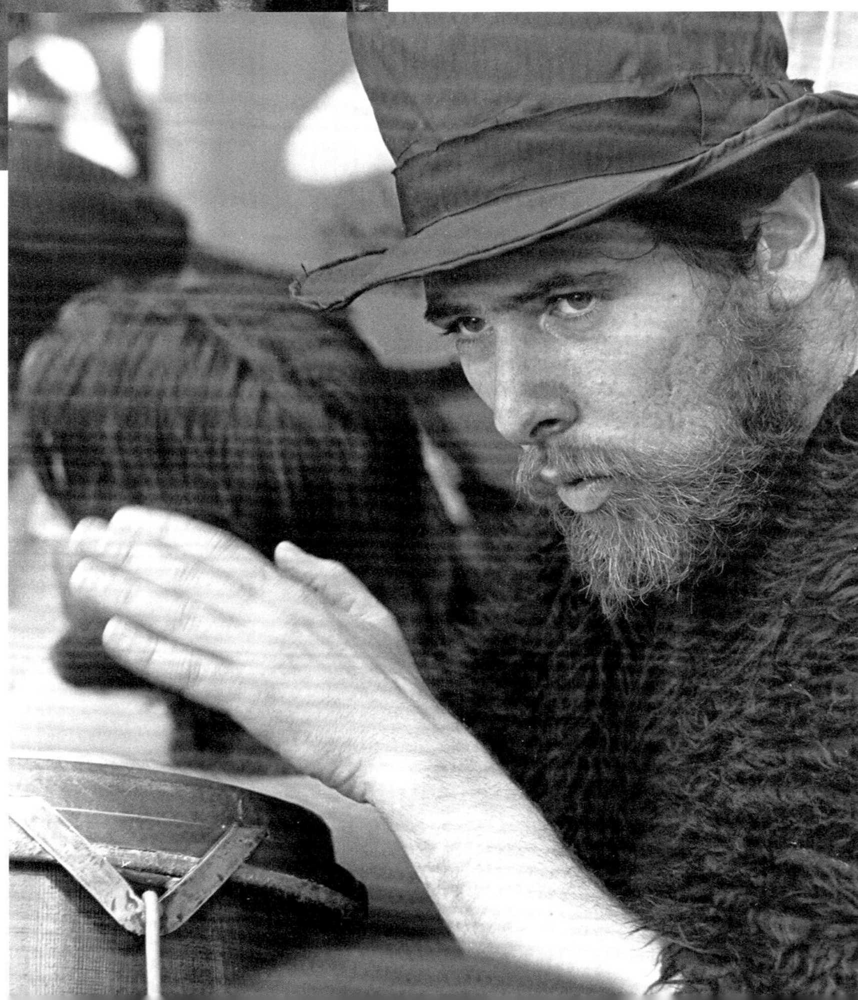

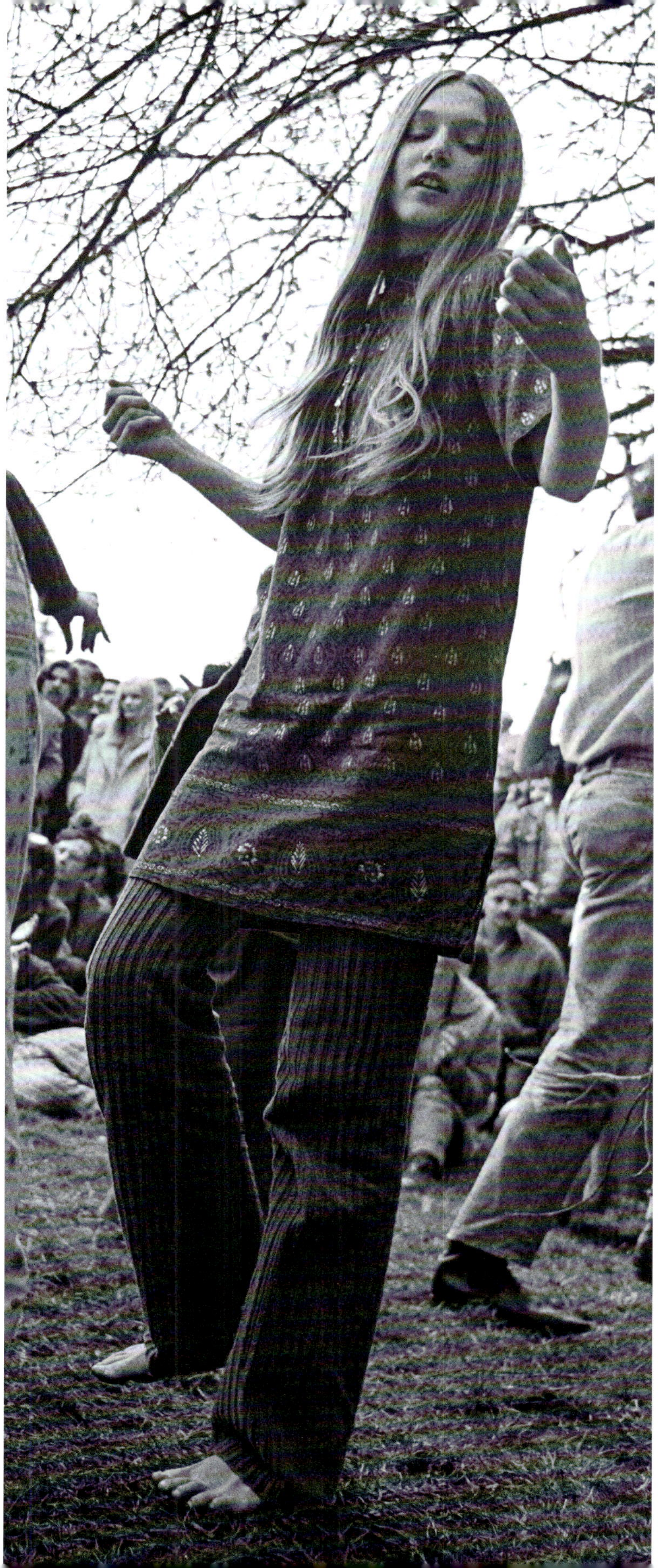

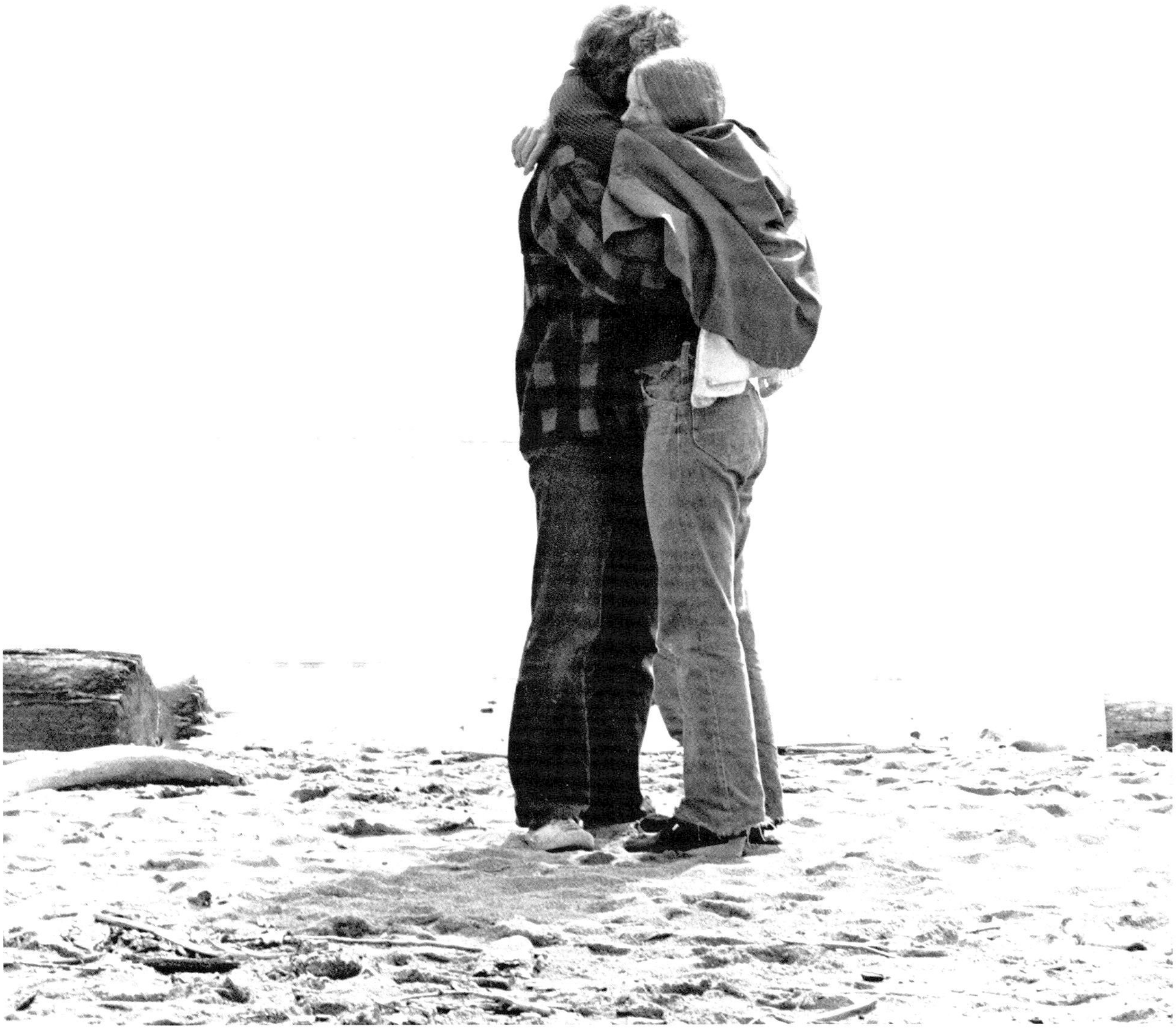

Second Beach, Stanley Park, 1970.

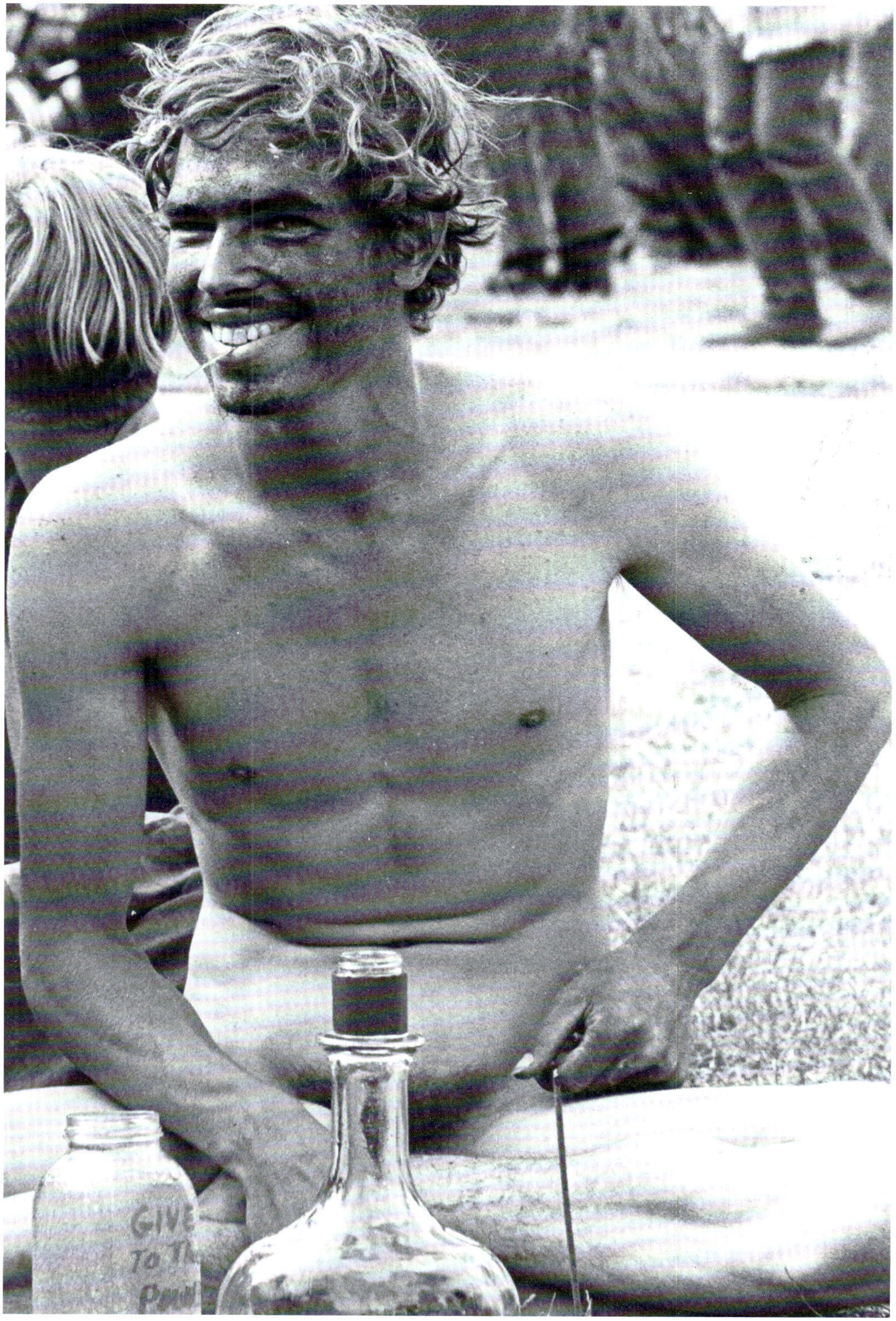

Young man enjoying the Phil Ochs free concert at Second Beach, June 28, 1970.

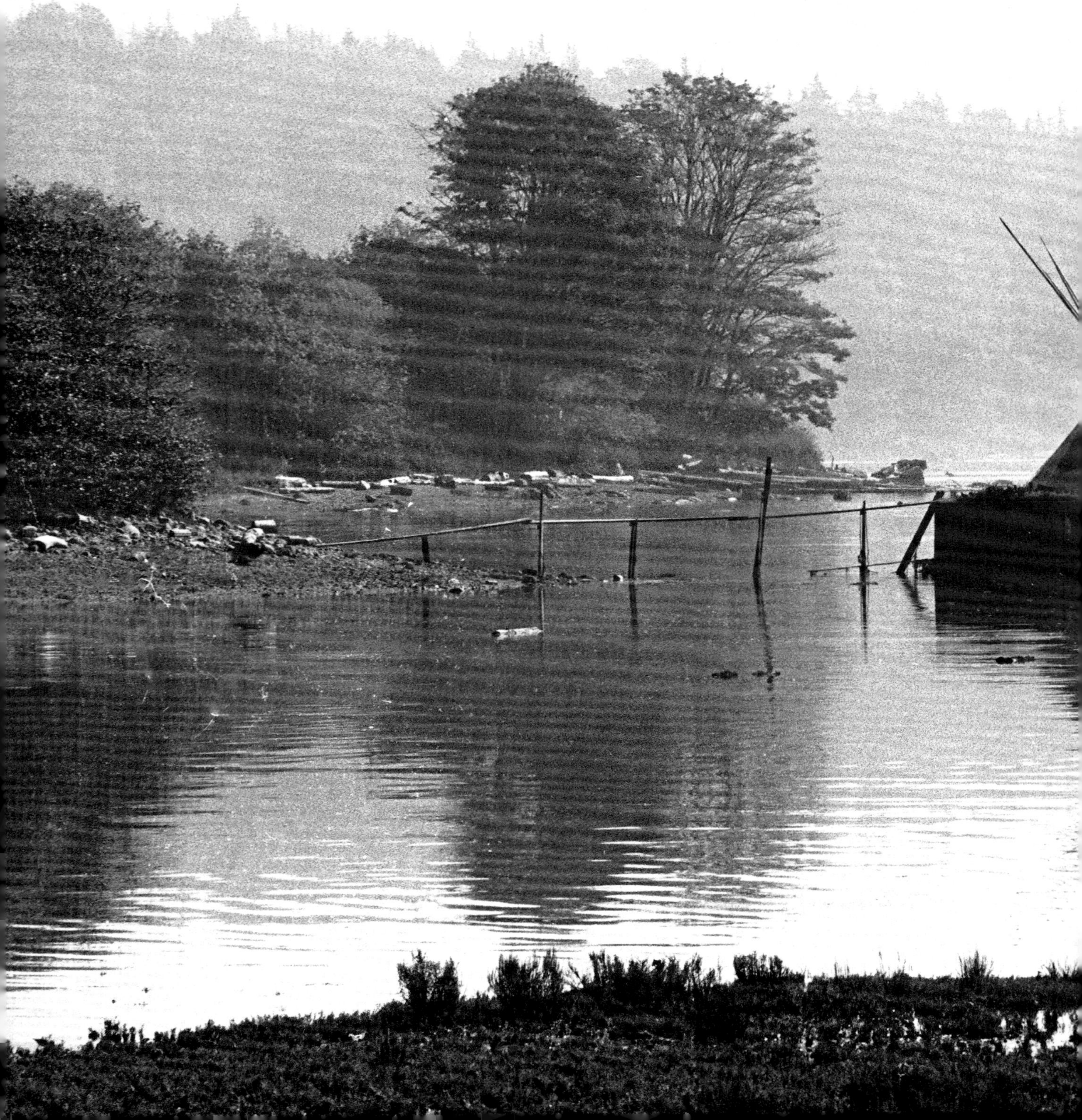

Mud Flats, North Vancouver, 1972

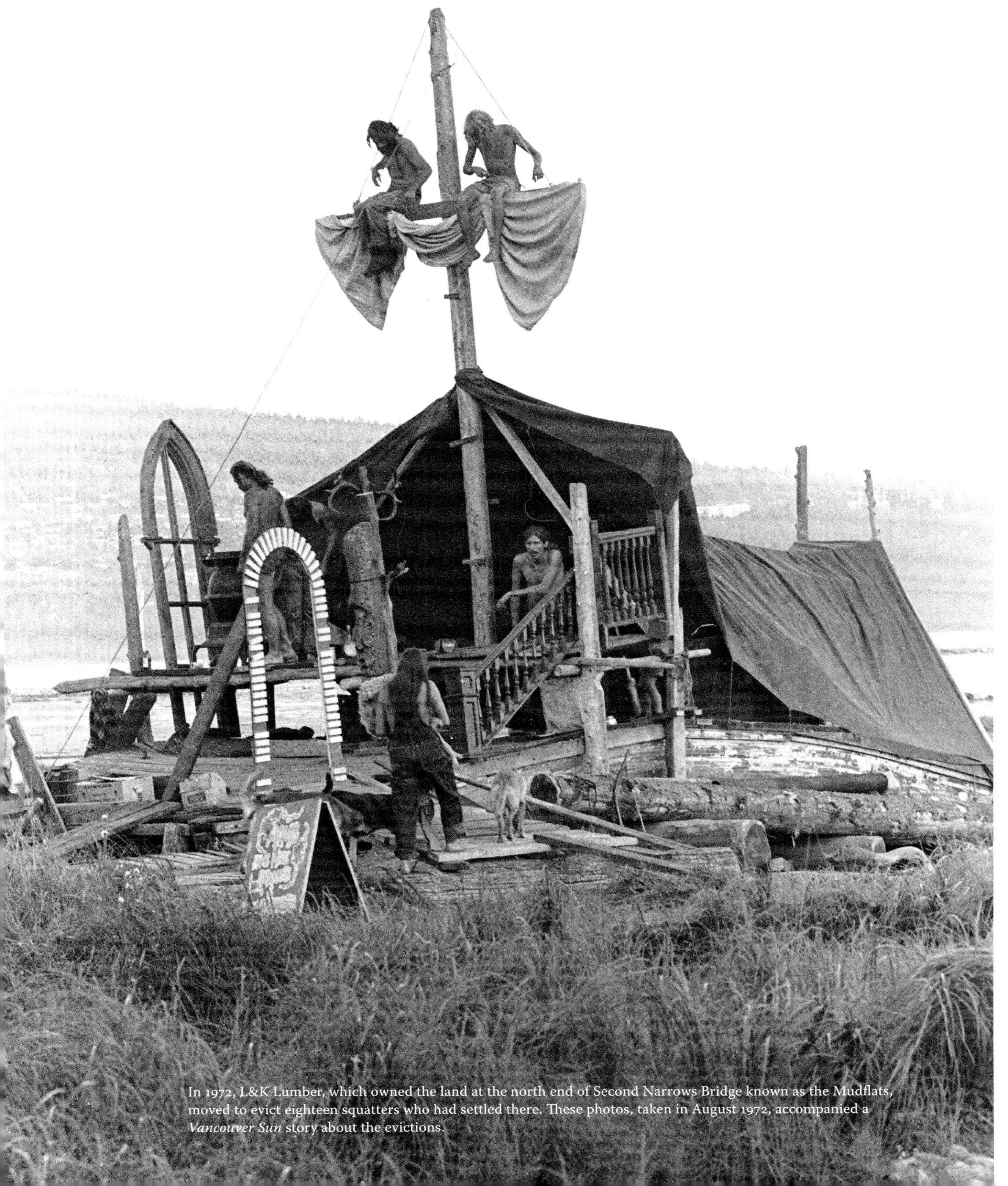

In 1972, L&K Lumber, which owned the land at the north end of Second Narrows Bridge known as the Mudflats, moved to evict eighteen squatters who had settled there. These photos, taken in August 1972, accompanied a *Vancouver Sun* story about the evictions.

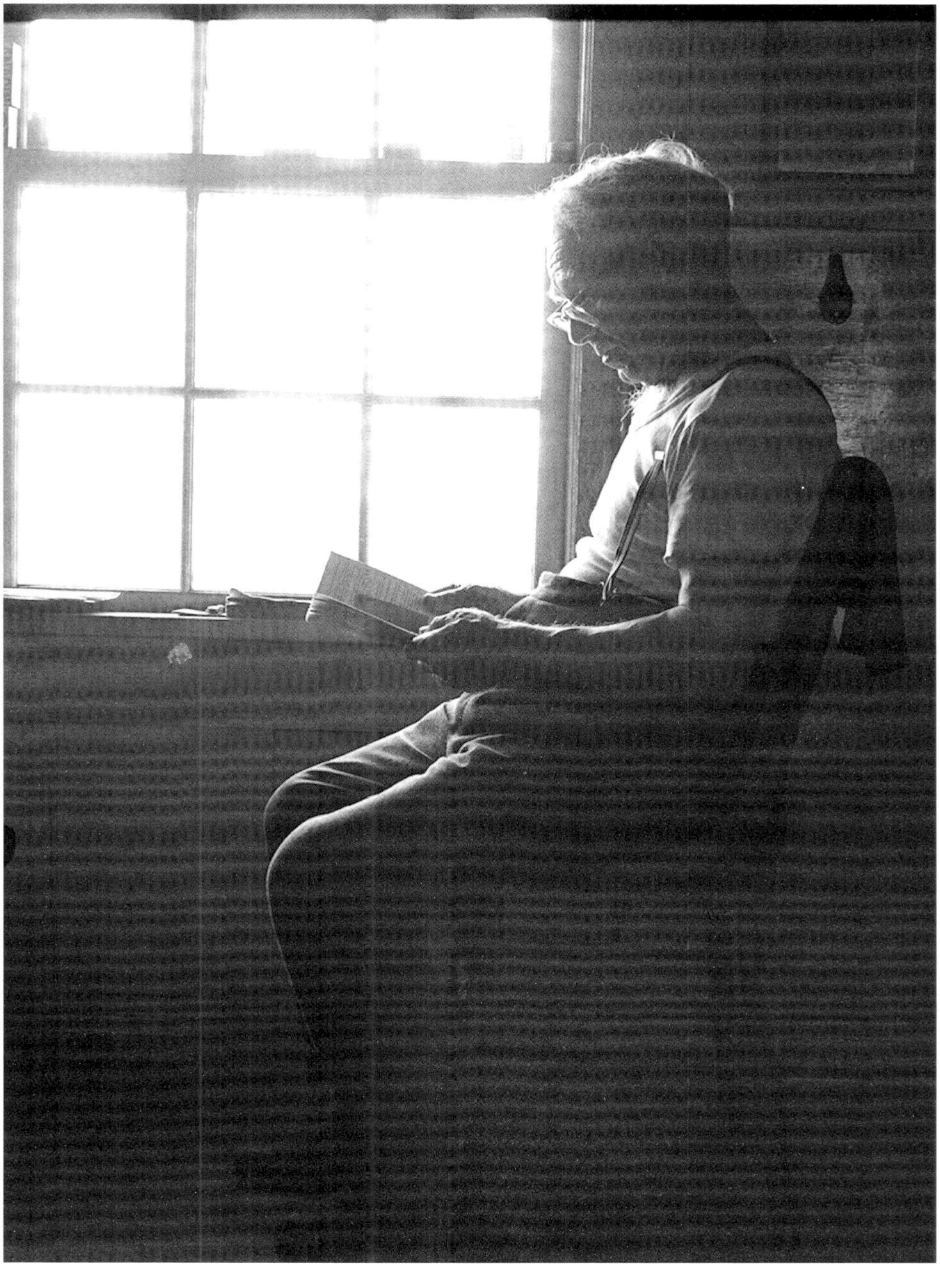

Mike Bowser, one of the long-term residents of the Mudflats who was evicted from his home in 1972.

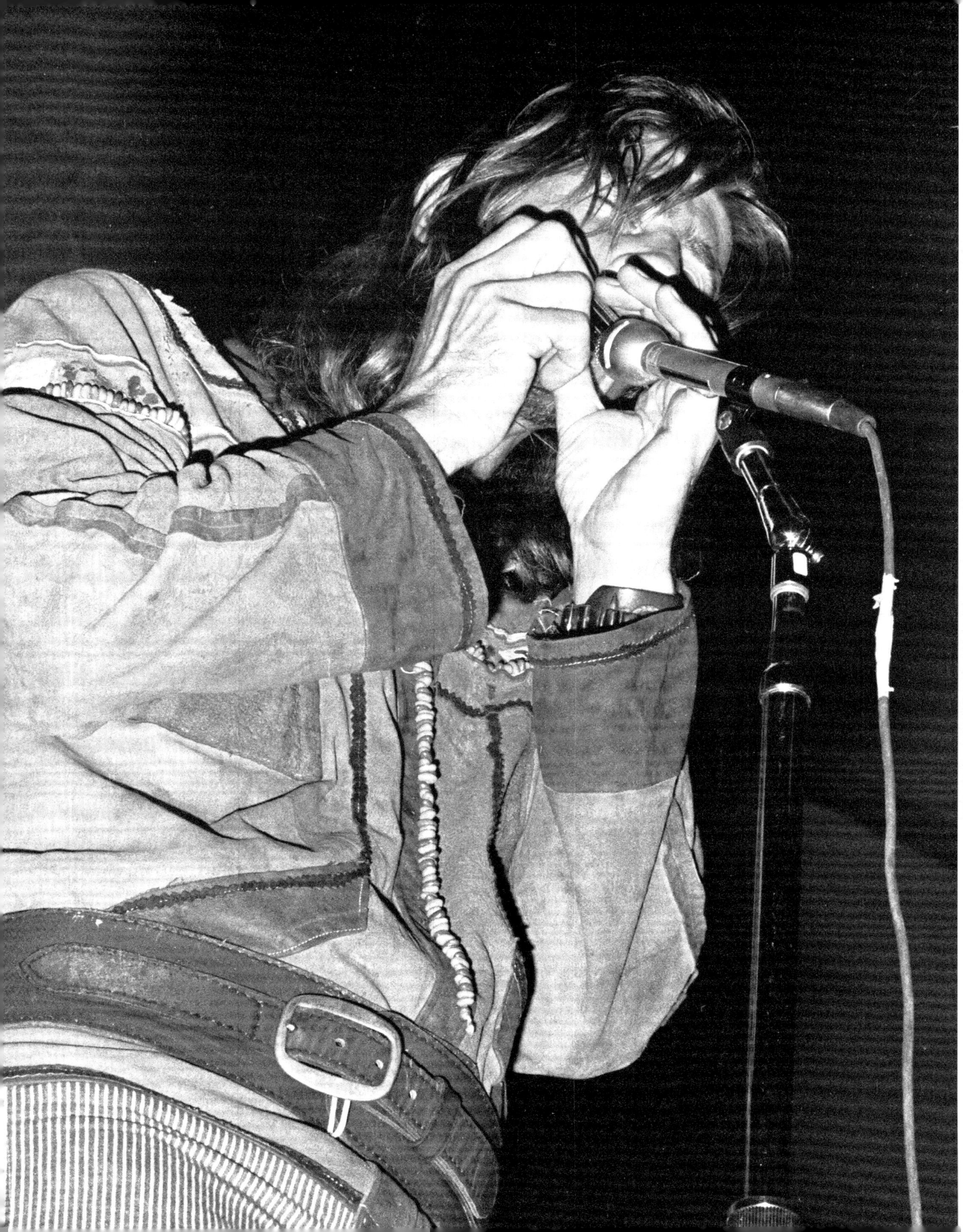

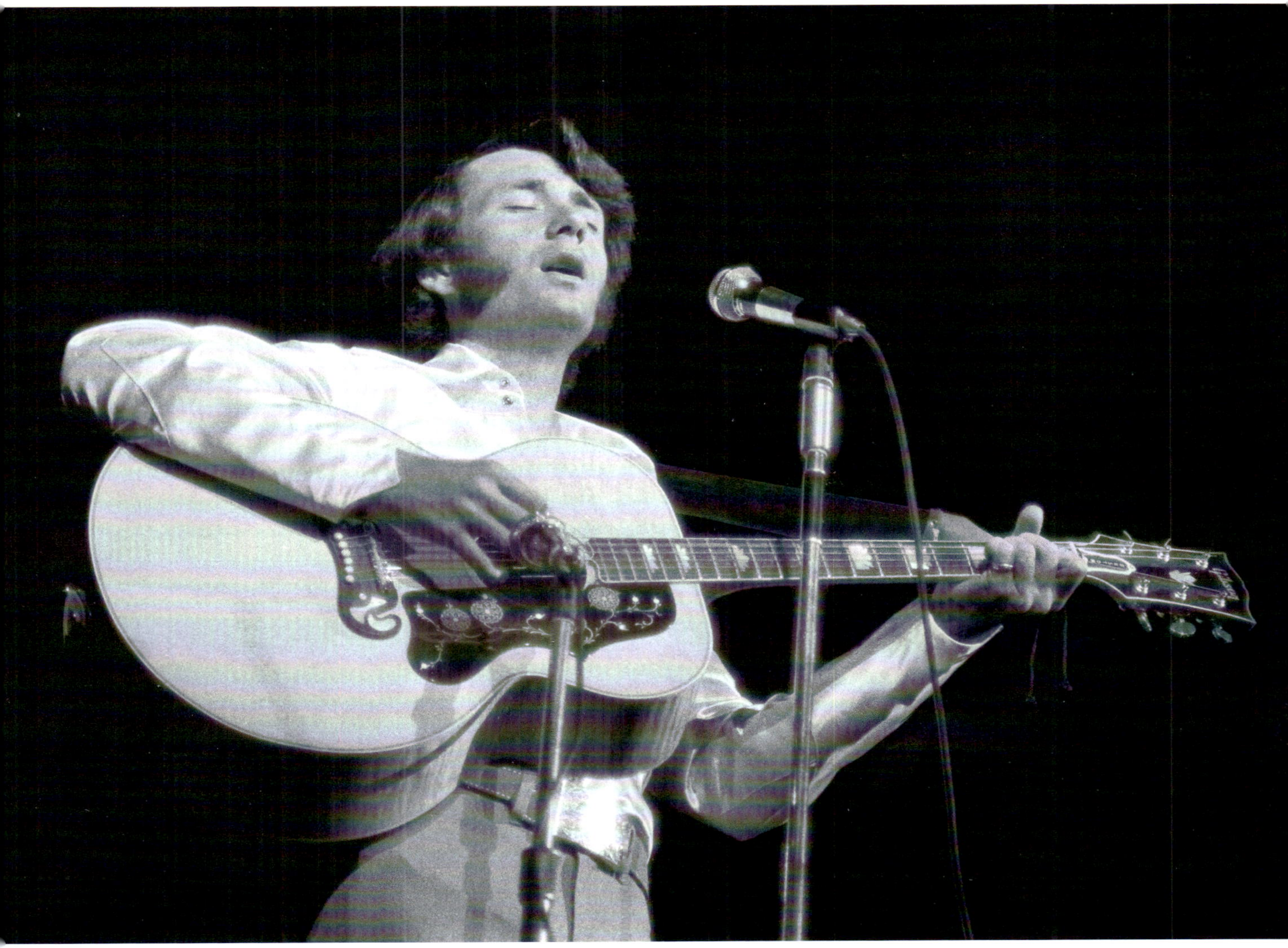

John Mayall, PNE Agrodome, 1969.

Mike Nesmith of The Monkees, Pacific Coliseum, March 1969.

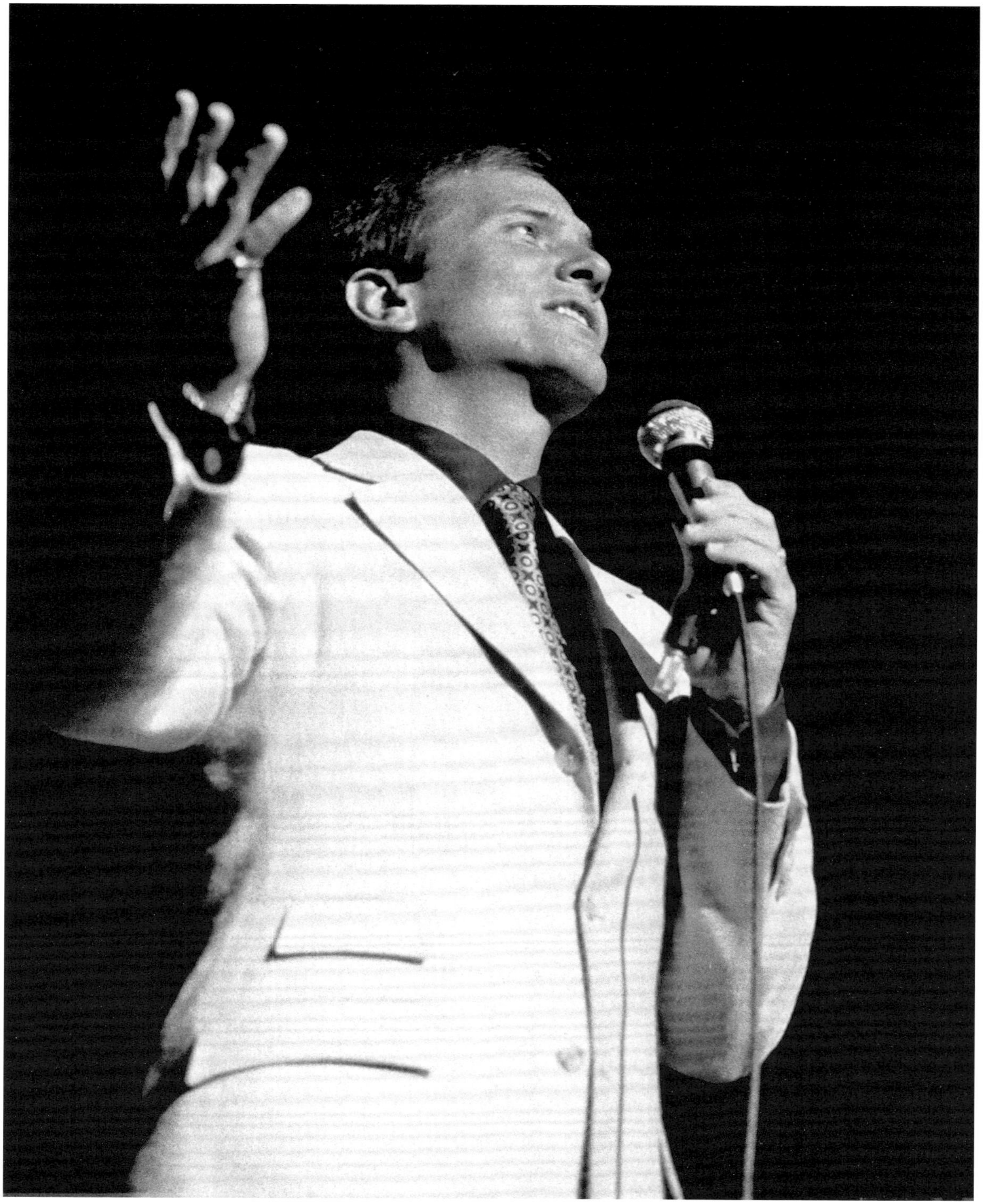

Pat Boone, PNE Agrodome, 1969.

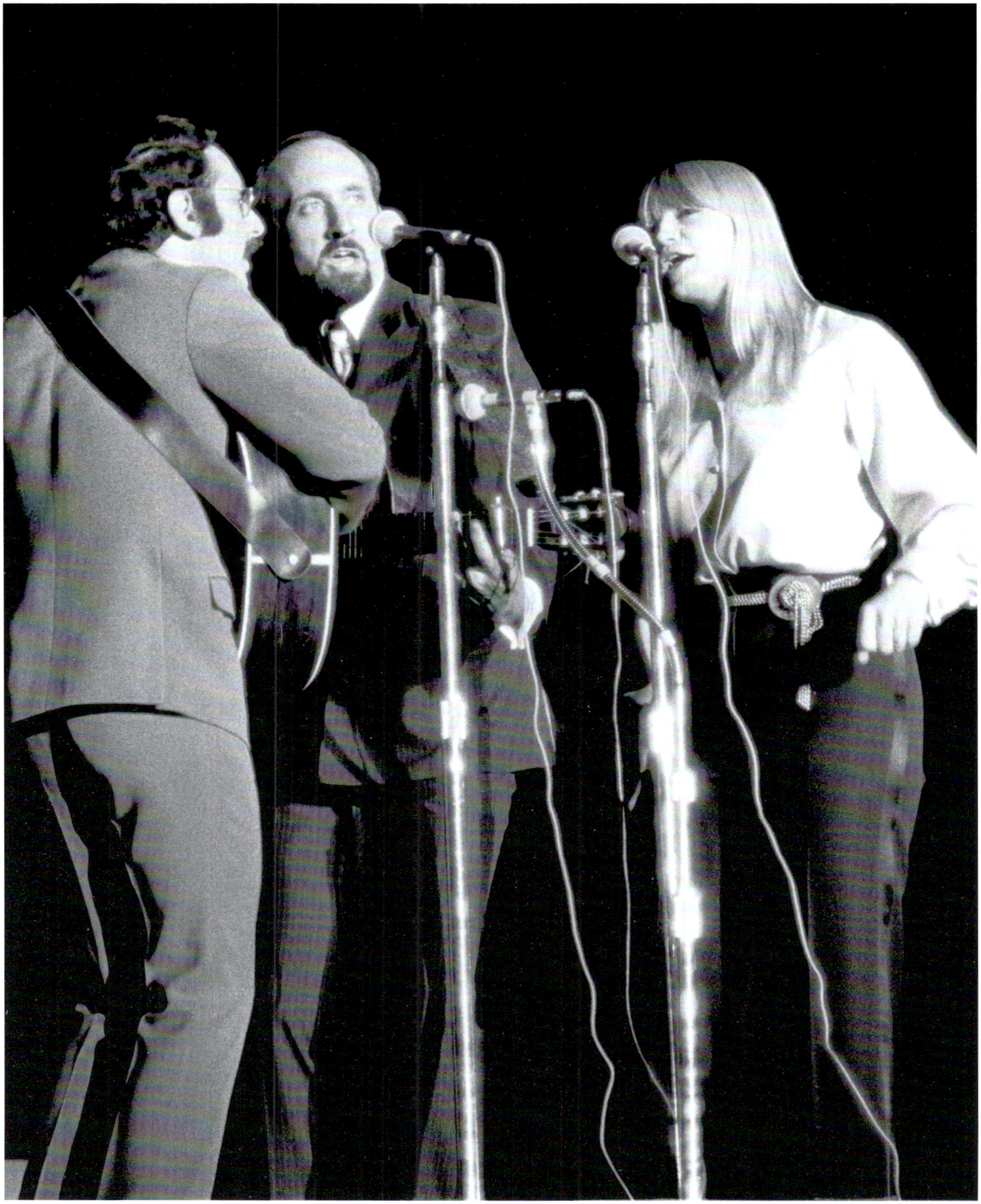

Peter, Paul and Mary, PNE Agrodome, 1969.

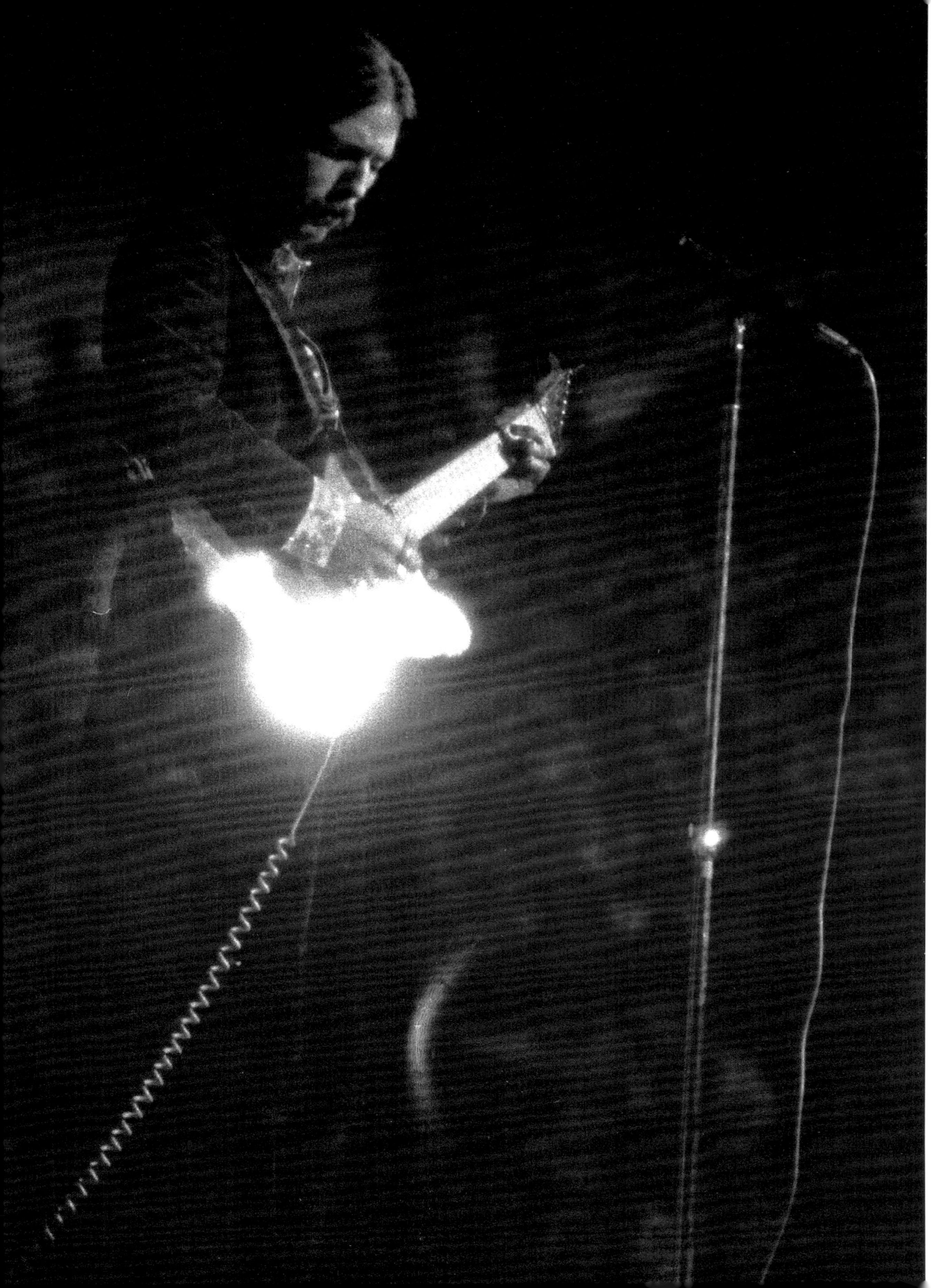

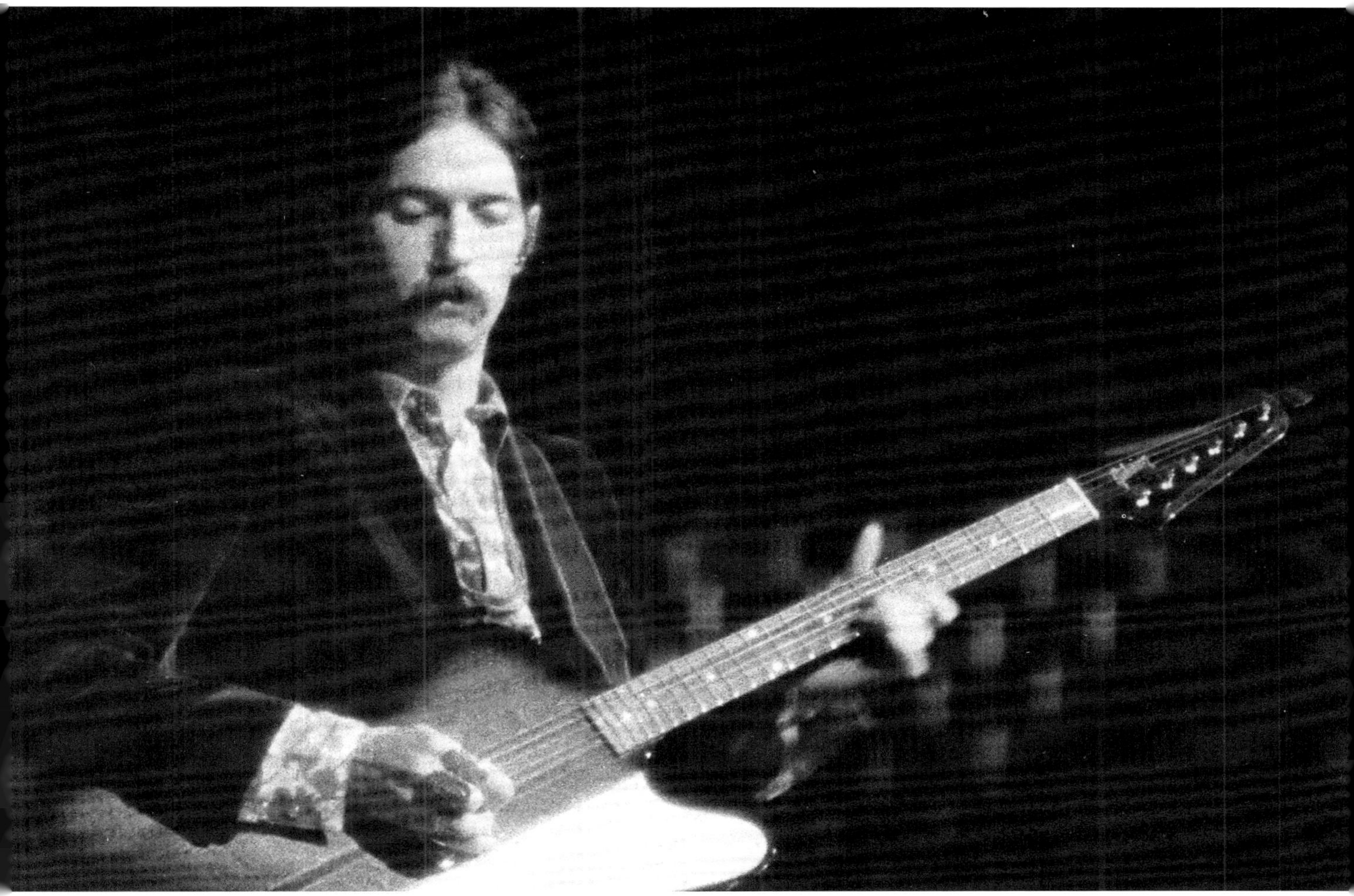

Eric Clapton of The Cream, Pacific Coliseum, June 1968.

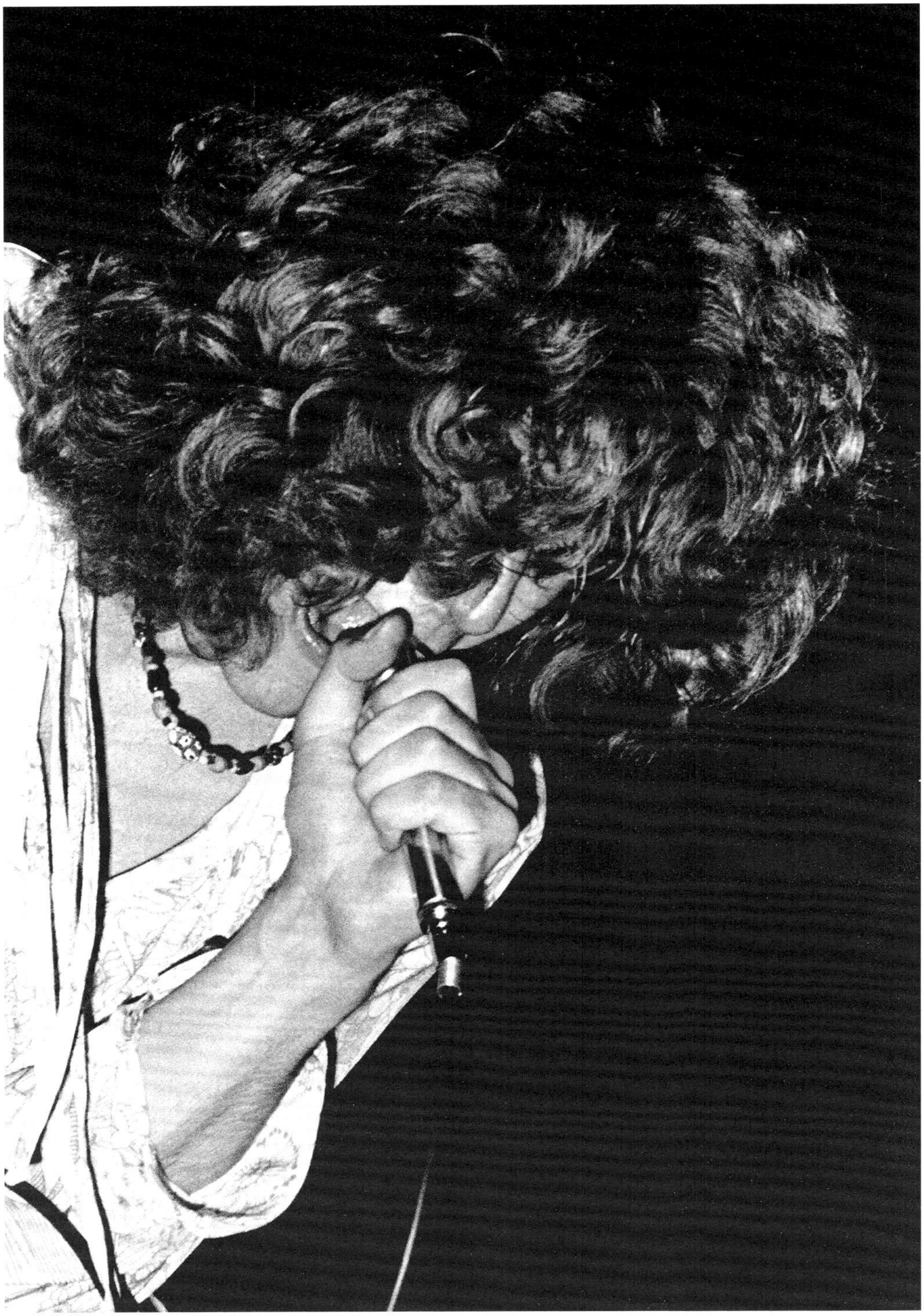

Robert Plant of Led Zeppelin, Agrodome, May 1969.

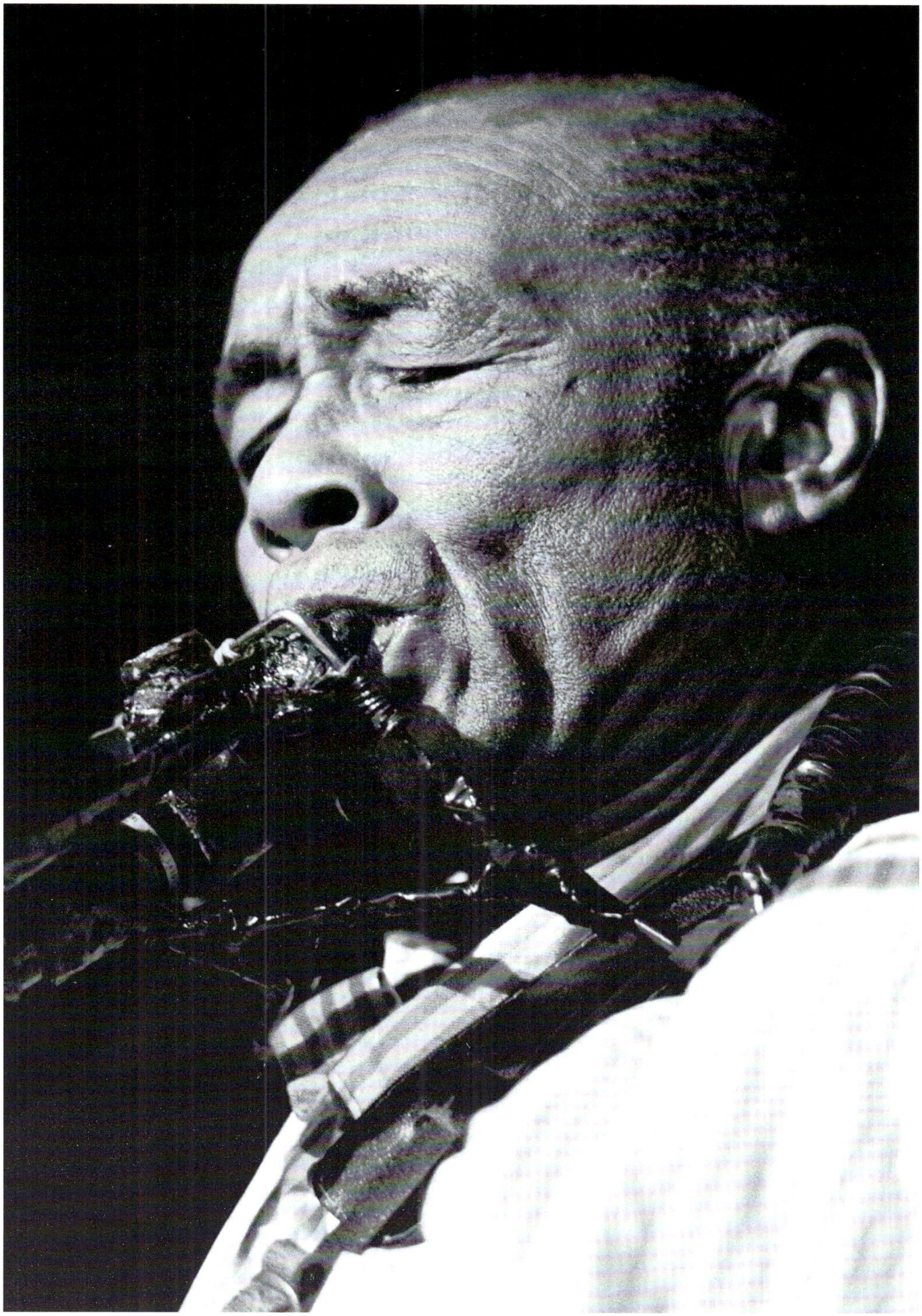

Jesse "Lone Cat" Fuller, Ronnie's River Queen on Davie Street, 1969.

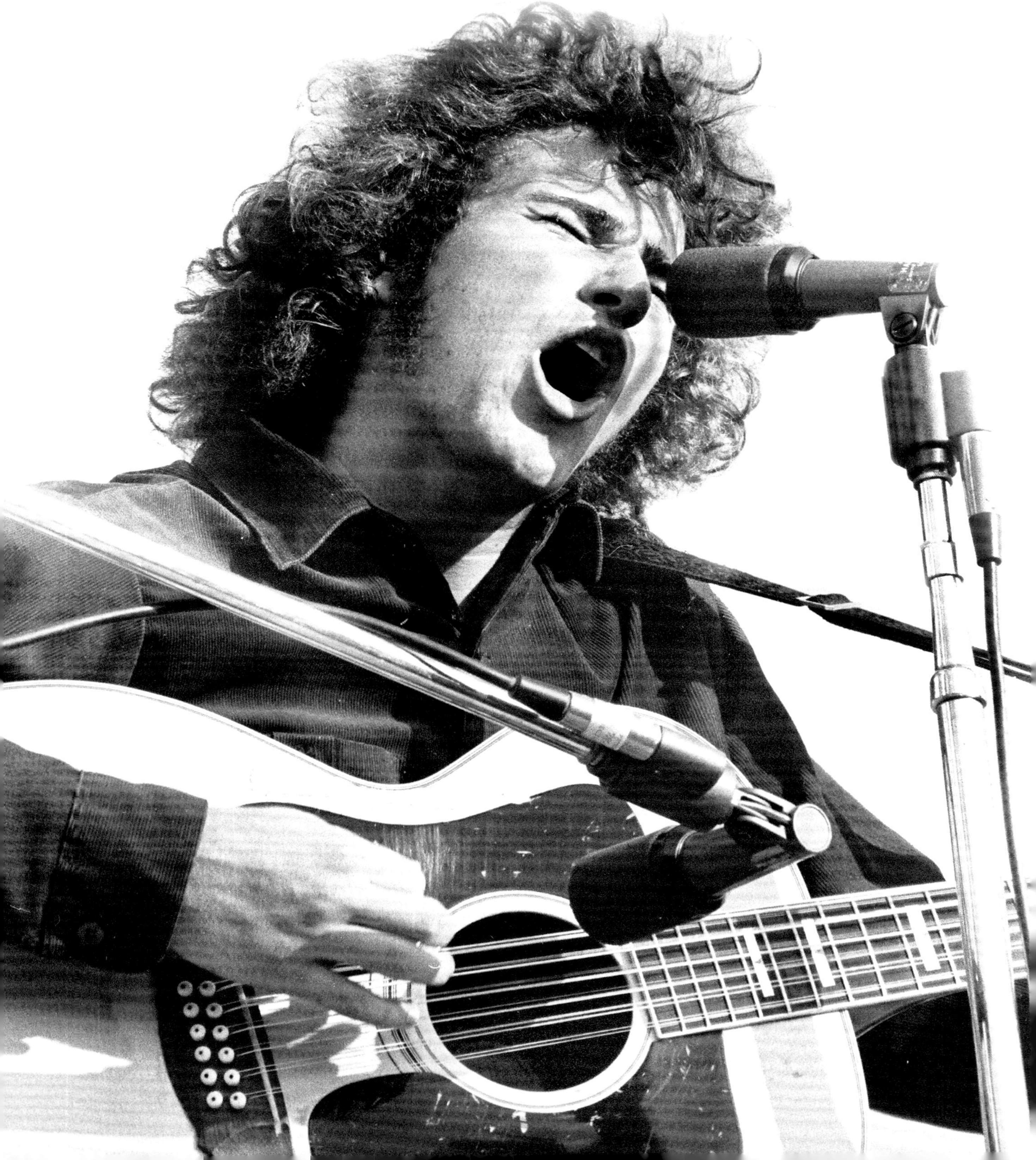

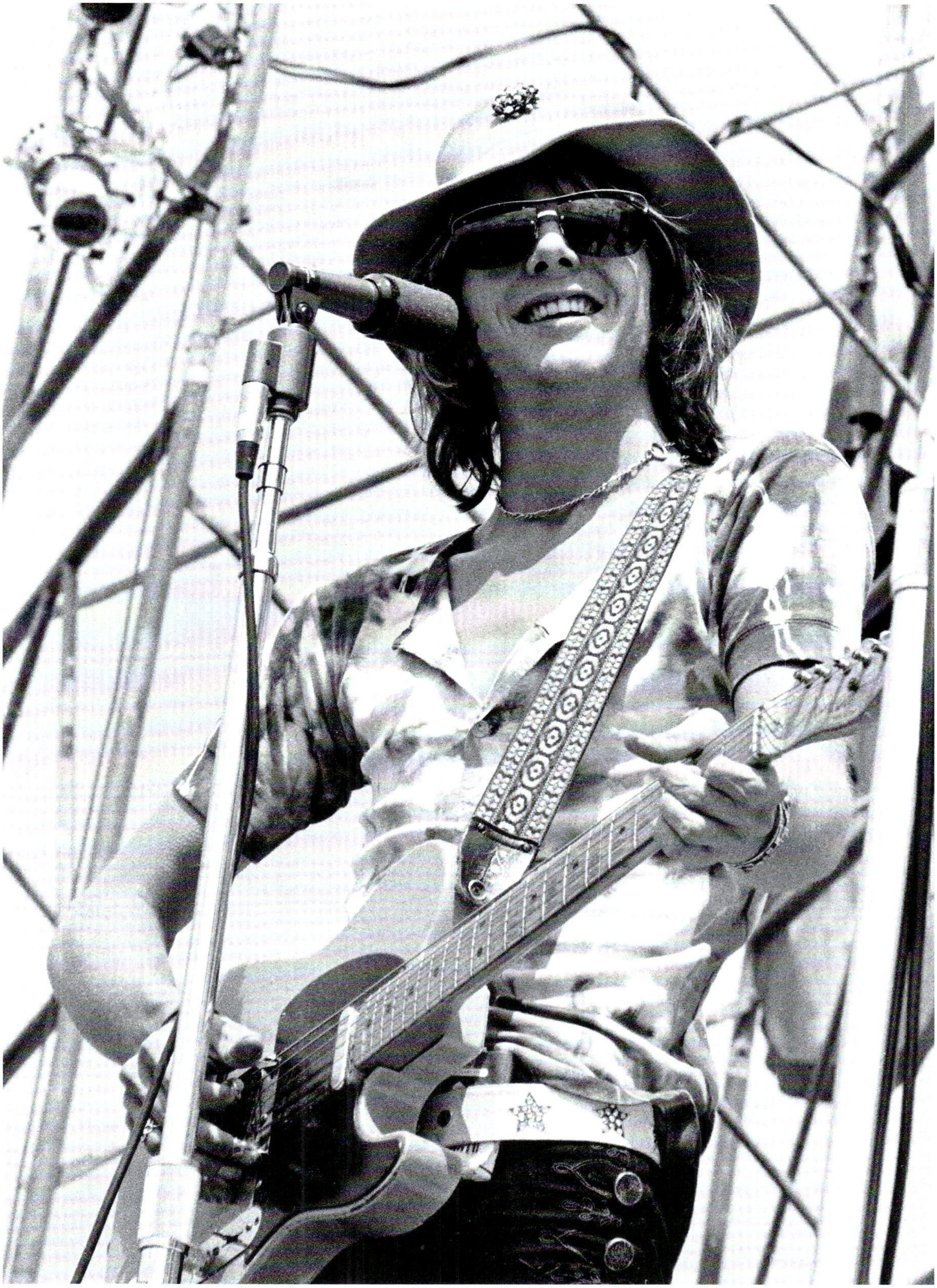

Tim Buckley, Seattle Pop Festival, July 1969.

Gram Parsons of The Flying Burrito Brothers, Seattle Pop Festival, in Woodinville, Washington, July 1969.

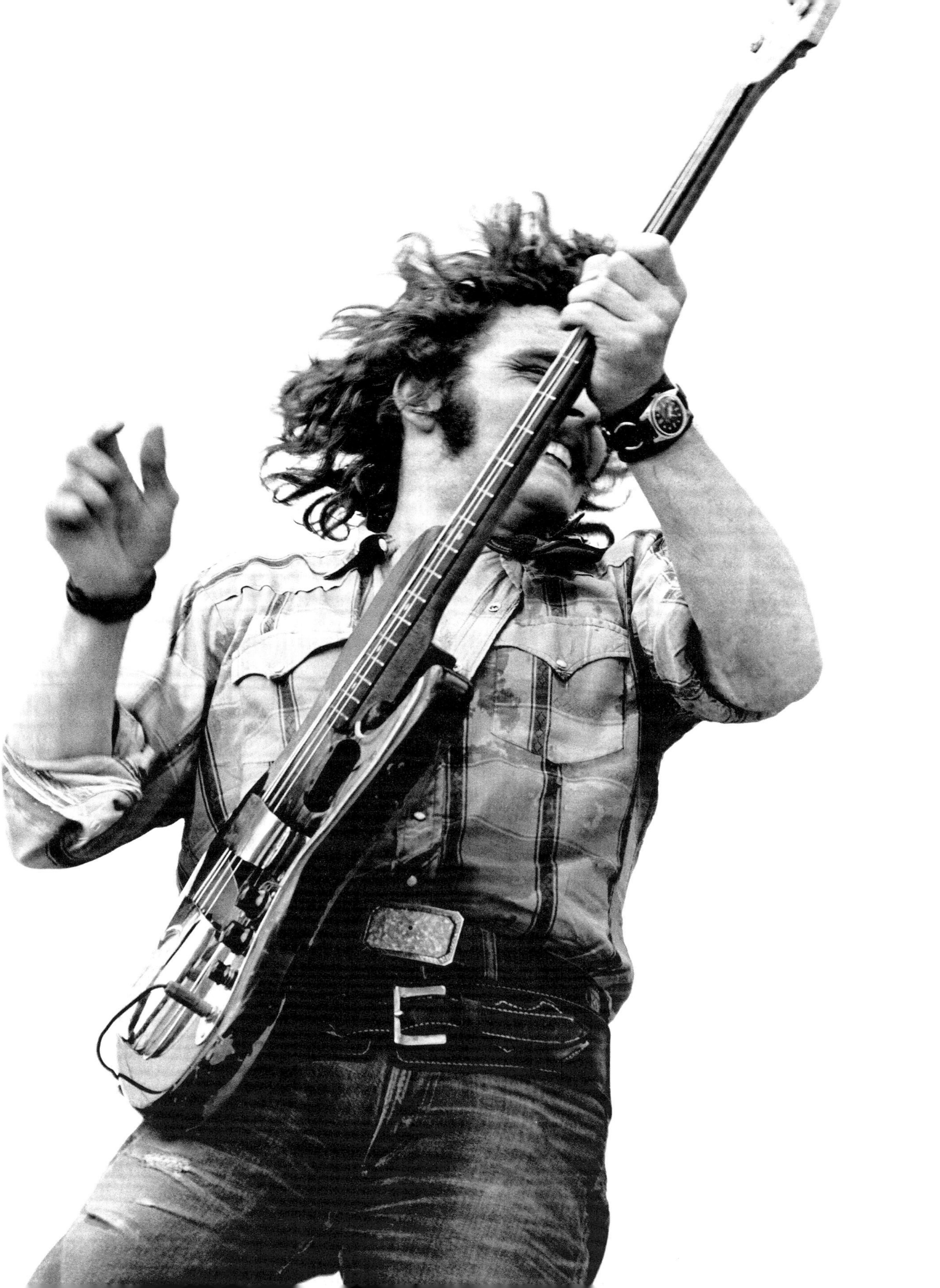

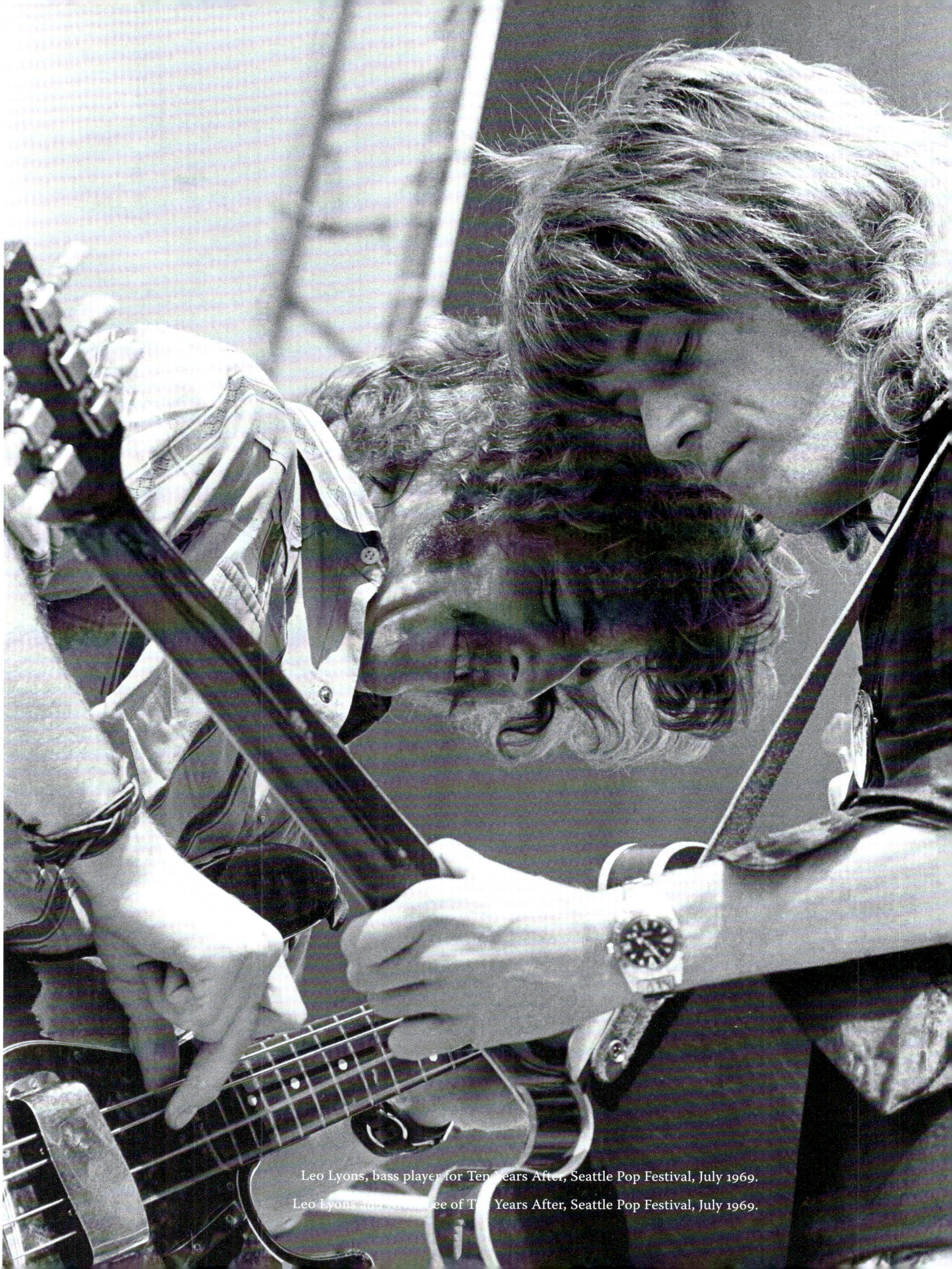

Leo Lyons, bass player for Ten Years After, Seattle Pop Festival, July 1969.

Leo Lyons and Alvin Lee of Ten Years After, Seattle Pop Festival, July 1969.

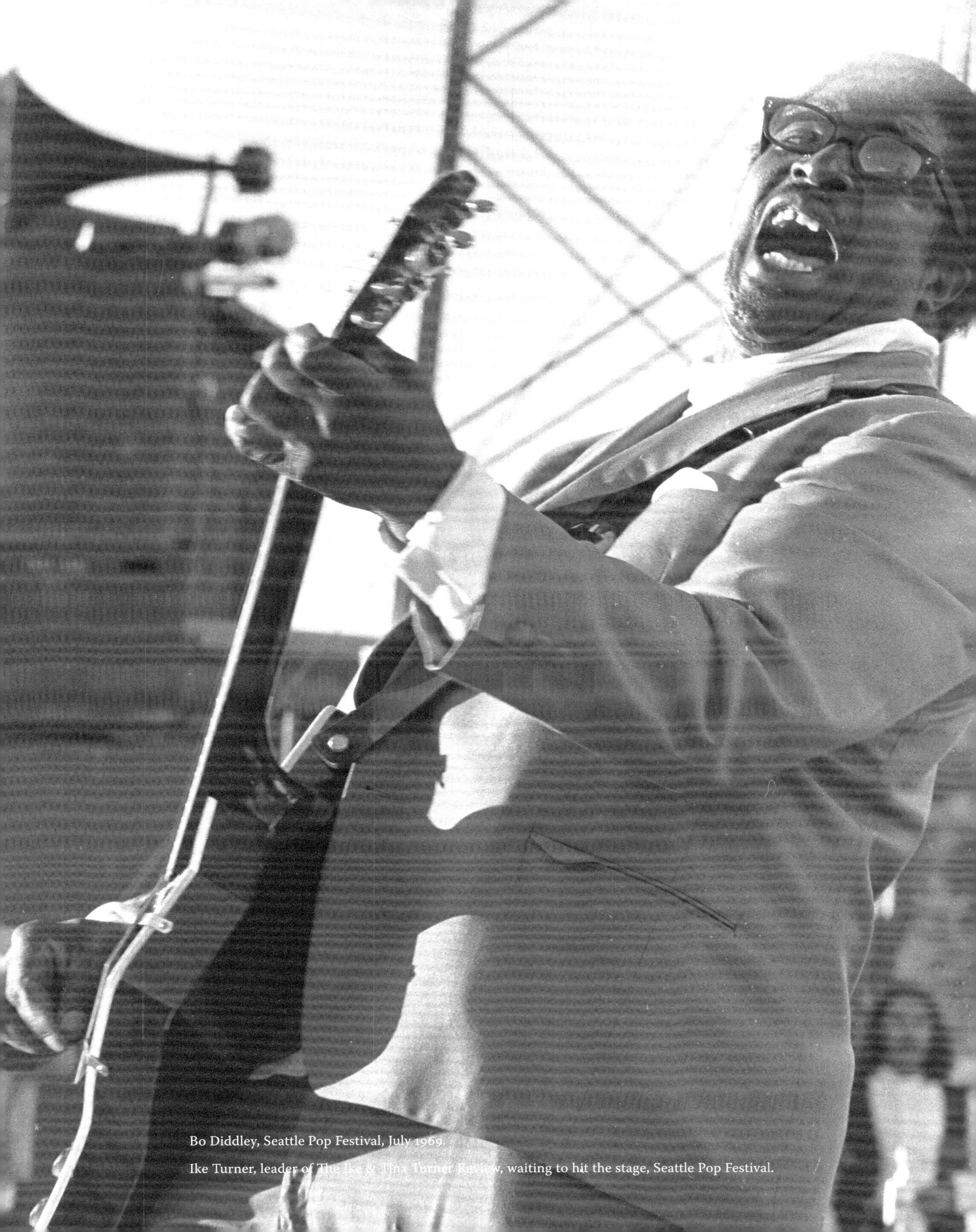

Bo Diddley, Seattle Pop Festival, July 1969.

Ike Turner, leader of The Ike & Tina Turner Review, waiting to hit the stage, Seattle Pop Festival.

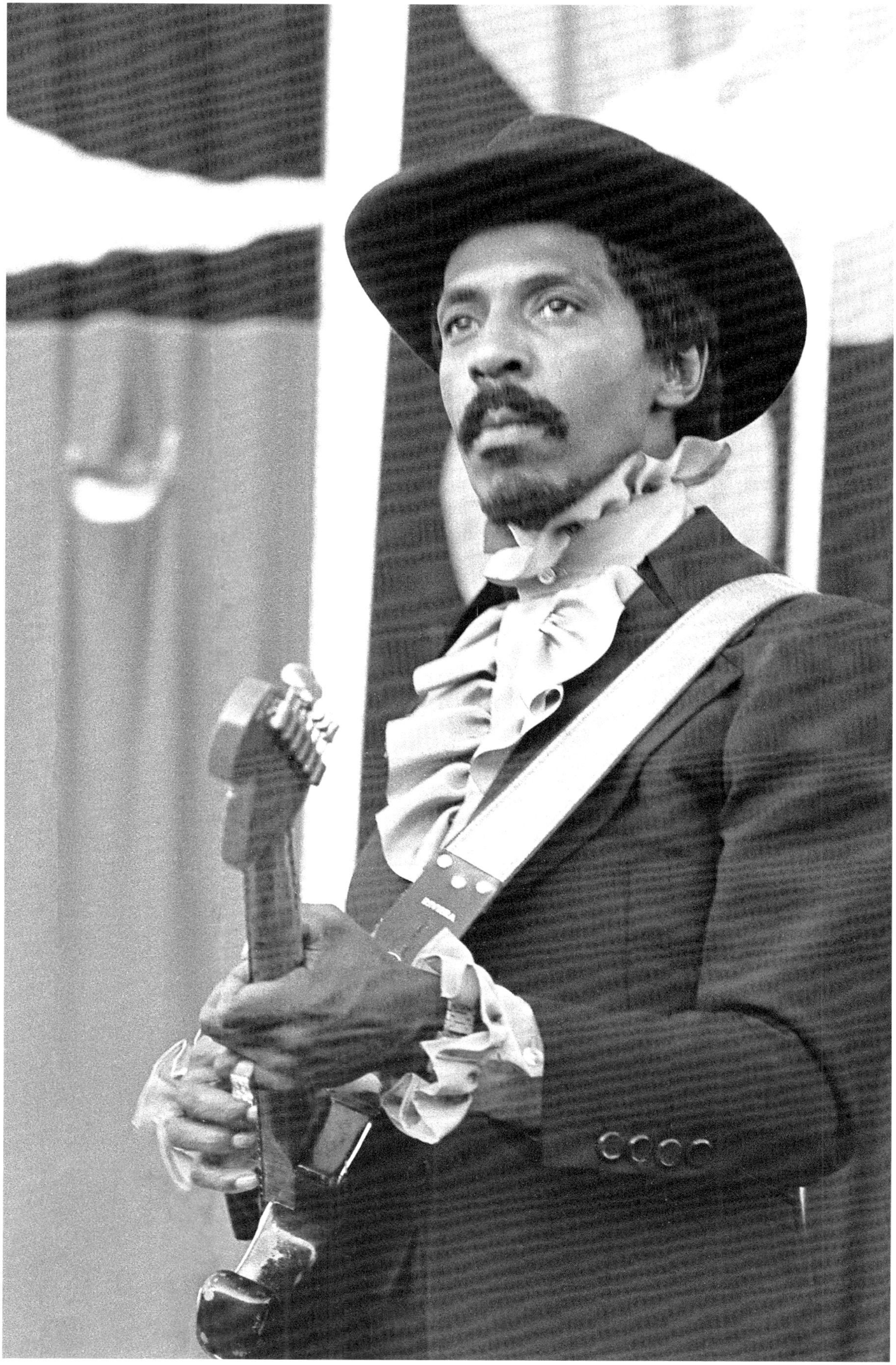

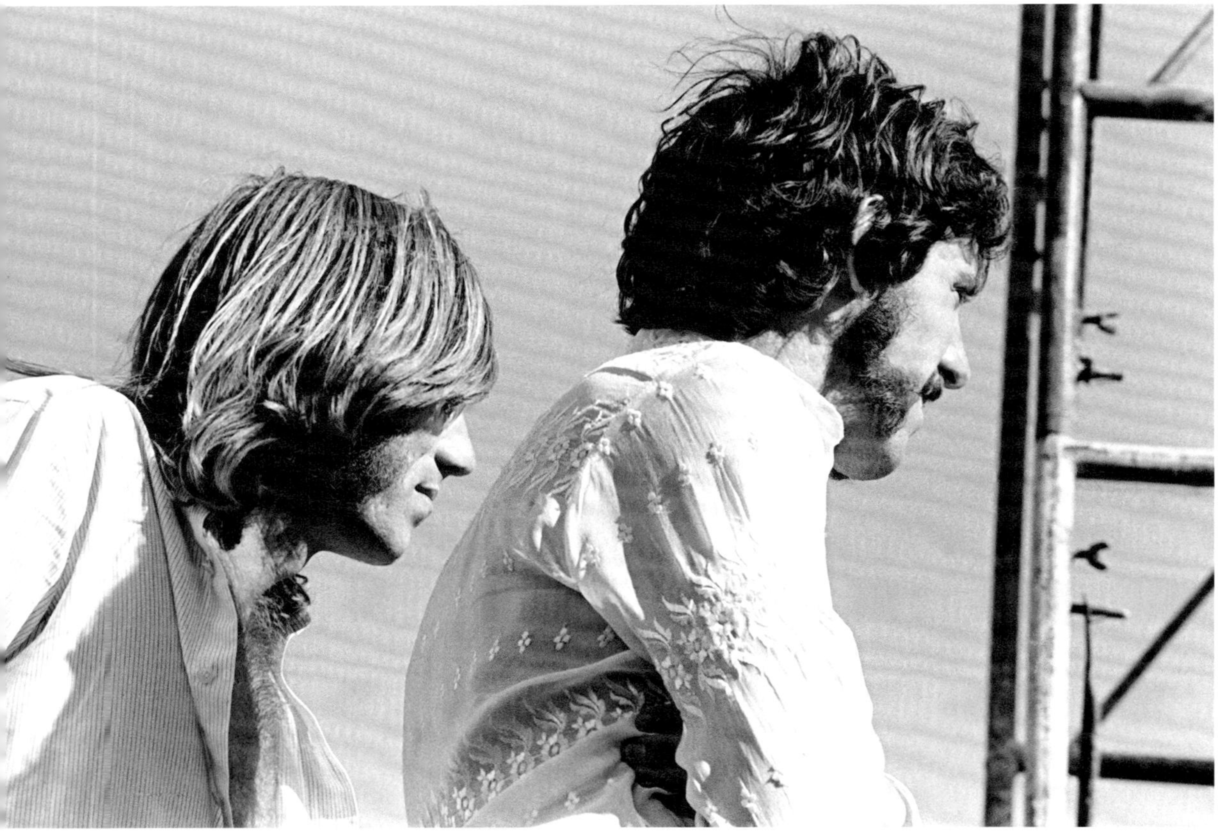

Ray Manzarek and Robby Krieger of The Doors, Seattle Pop Festival, July 27, 1969.

Jim Morrison, in the helicopter that flew him out of the Seattle Pop Festival at the end of the Doors' show on July 27, 1969.

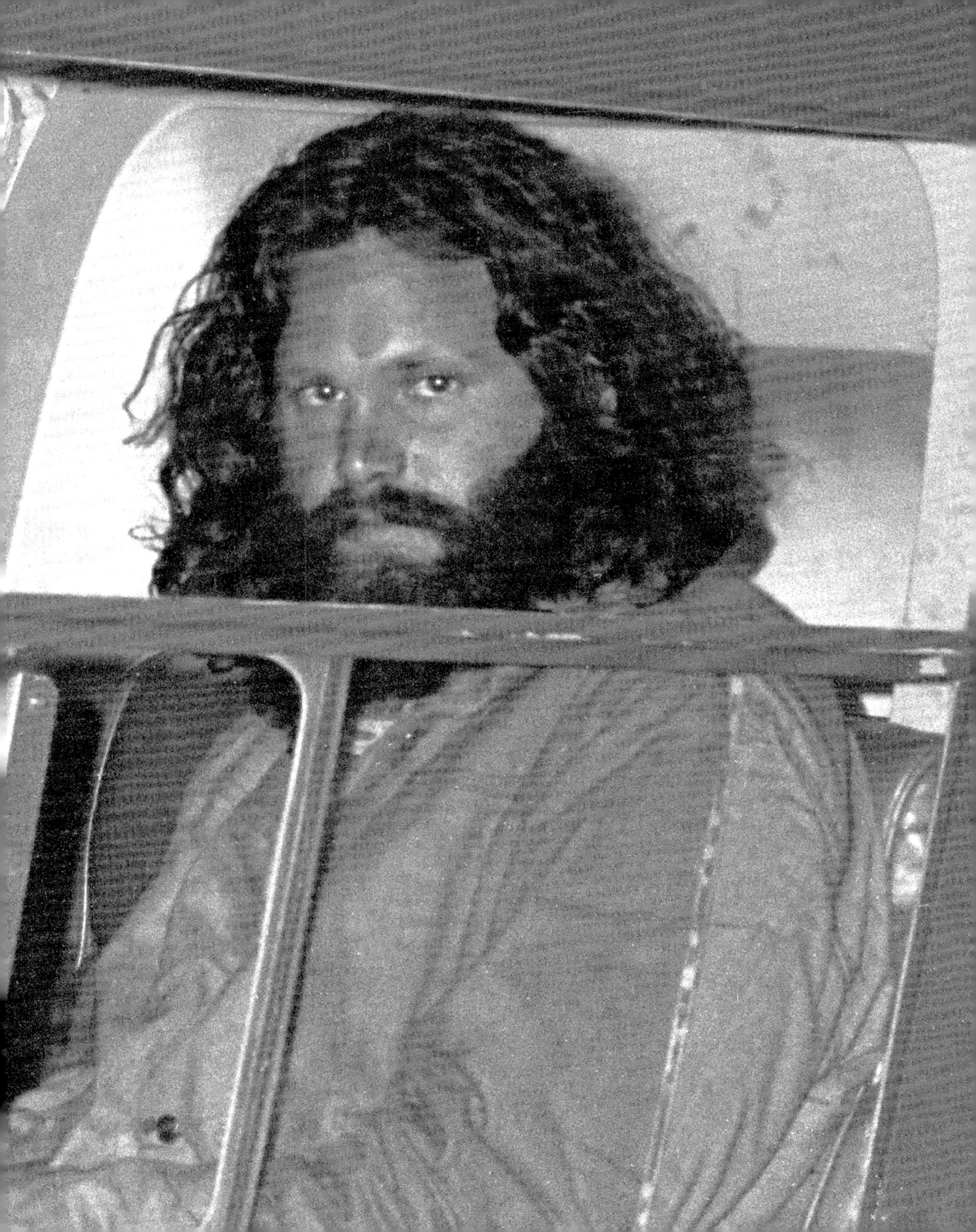

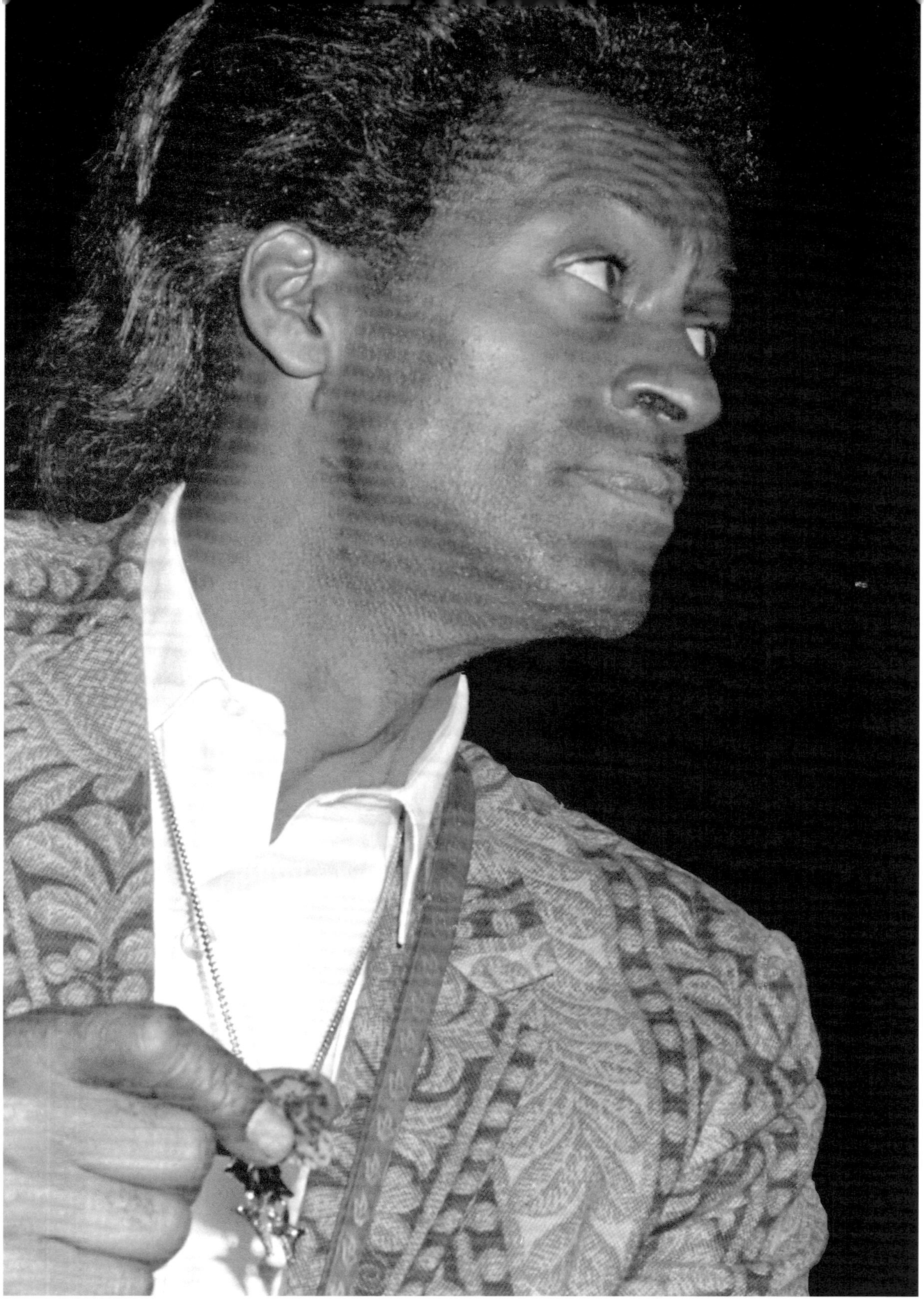

Chuck Berry, Seattle Pop Festival, July 27, 1969.

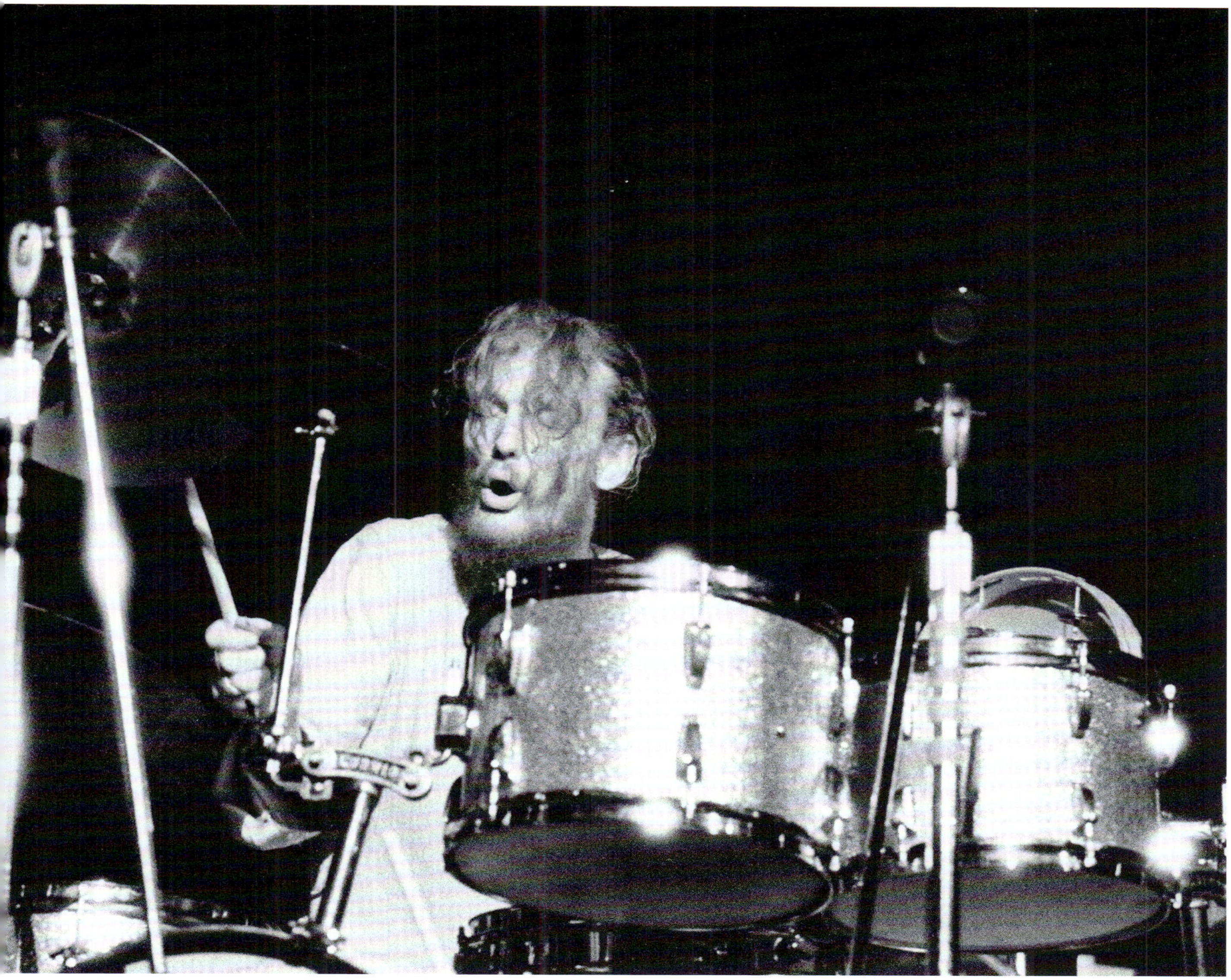

Ginger Baker of Blind Faith, Pacific Coliseum, August 9, 1969.

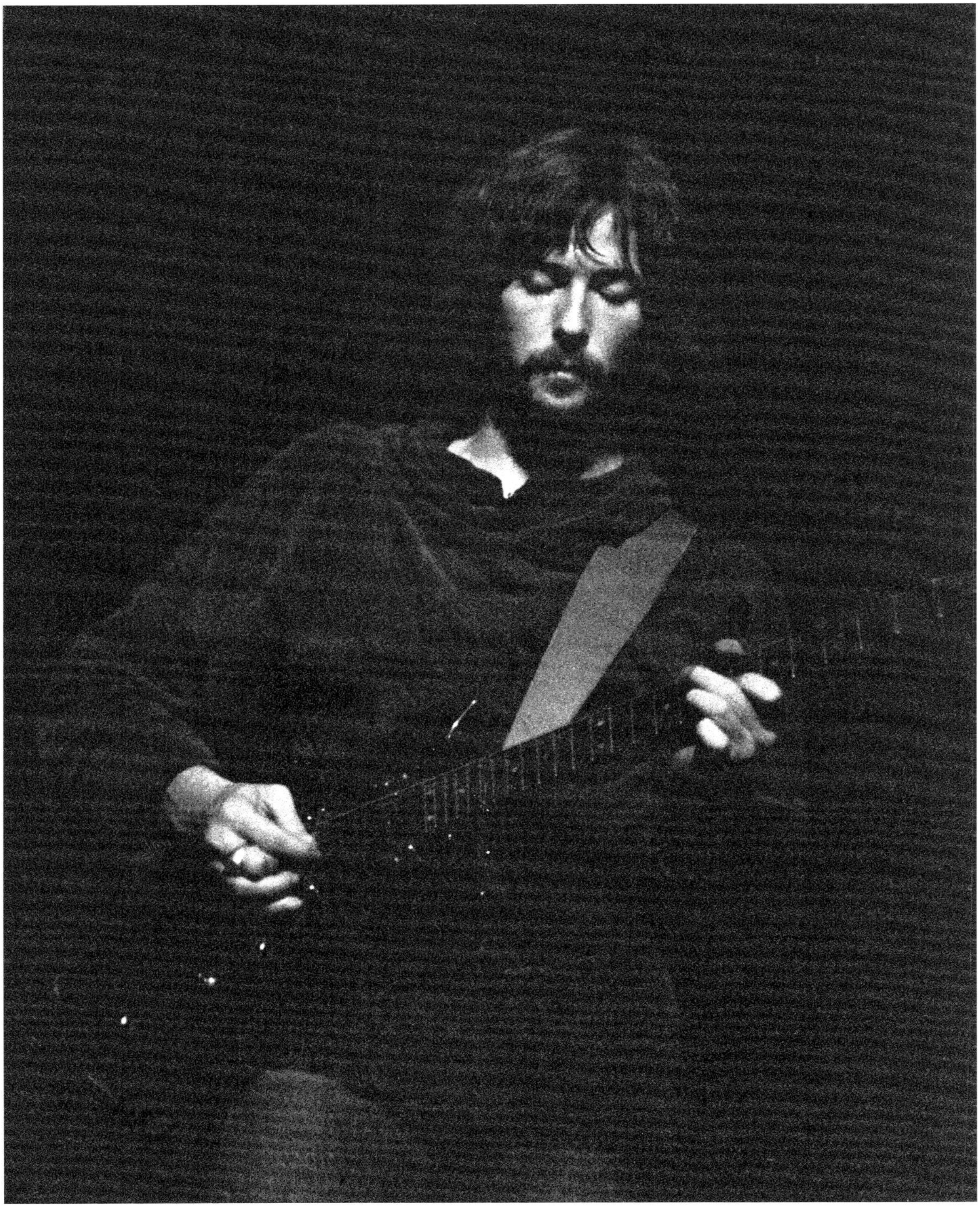

Eric Clapton of Blind Faith, Pacific Coliseum, August 9, 1969.

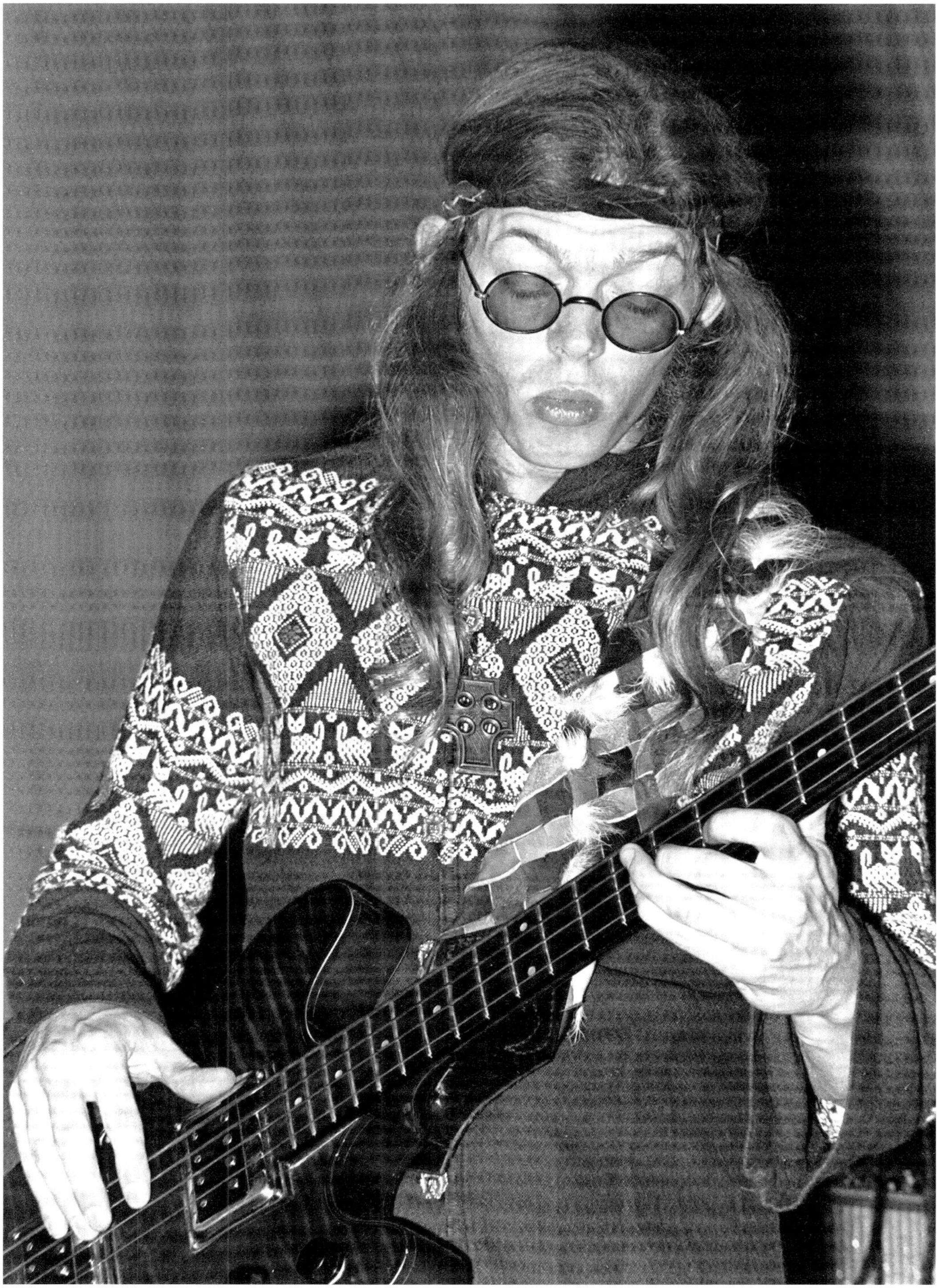

Jack Casady of Jefferson Airplane, PNE Agrodome, October 10, 1969.

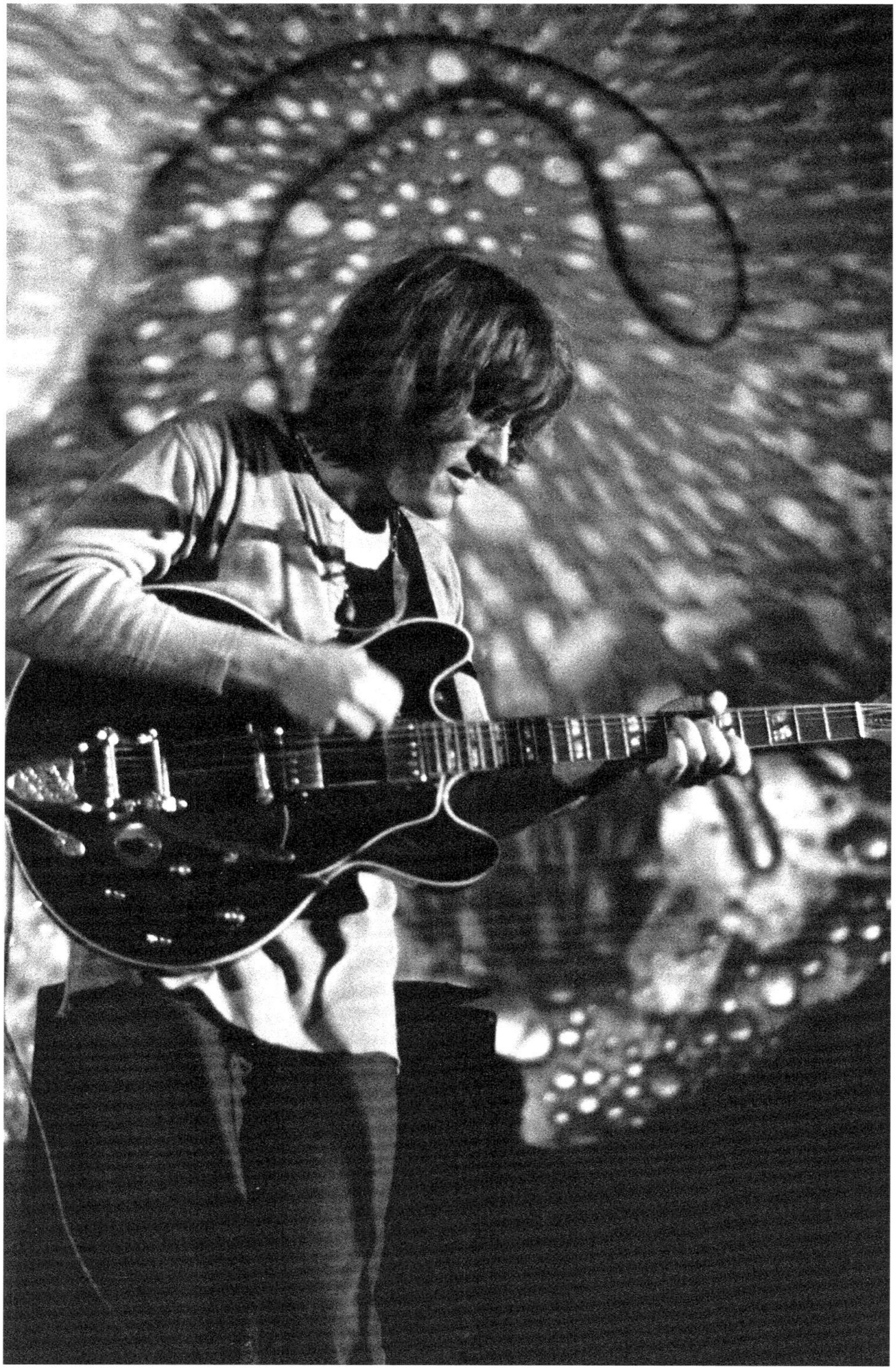

Paul Kantner of Jefferson Airplane, PNE Agrodome, October 10, 1969.

Marty Balin of Jefferson Airplane, PNE Agrodome, October 10, 1969.

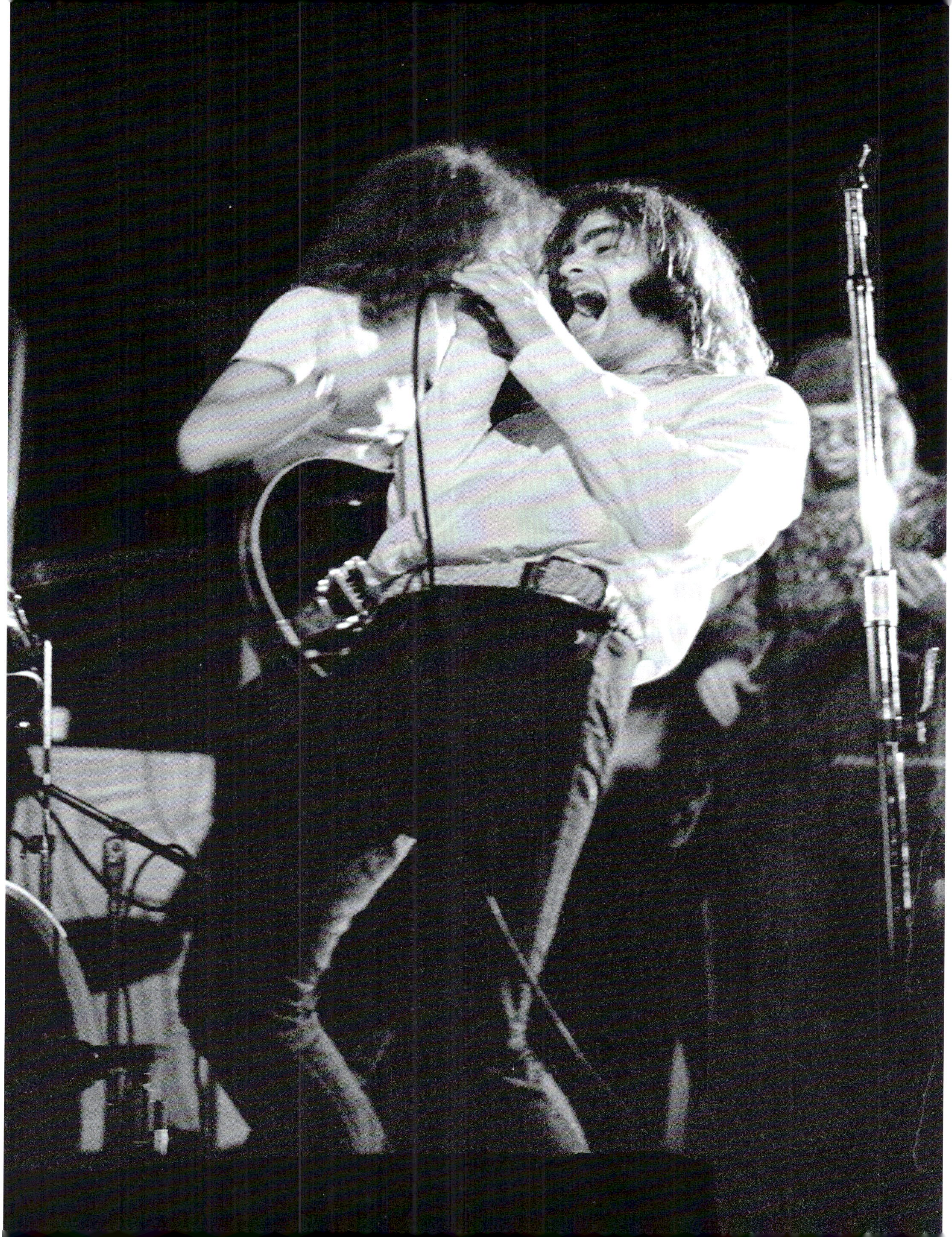

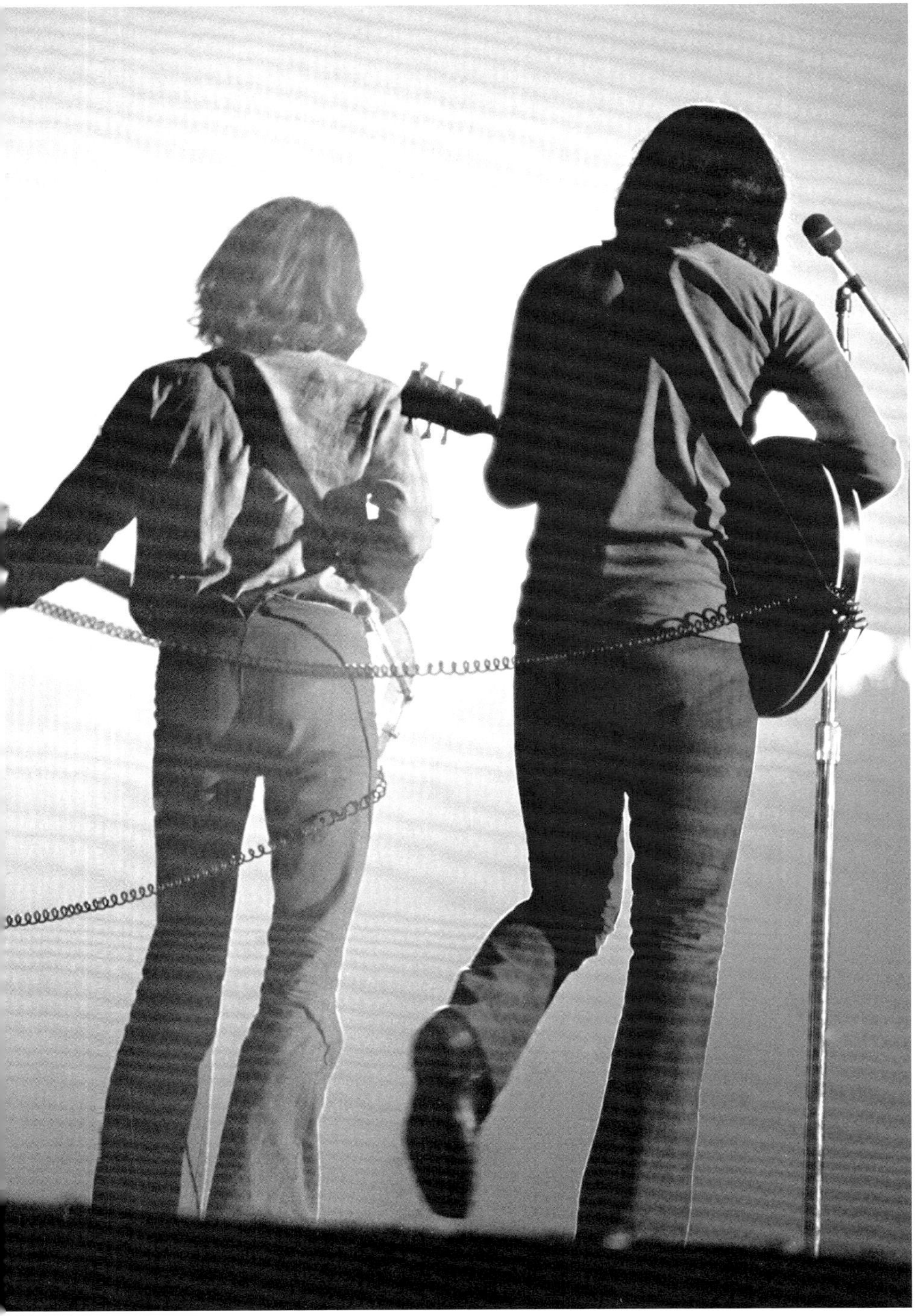

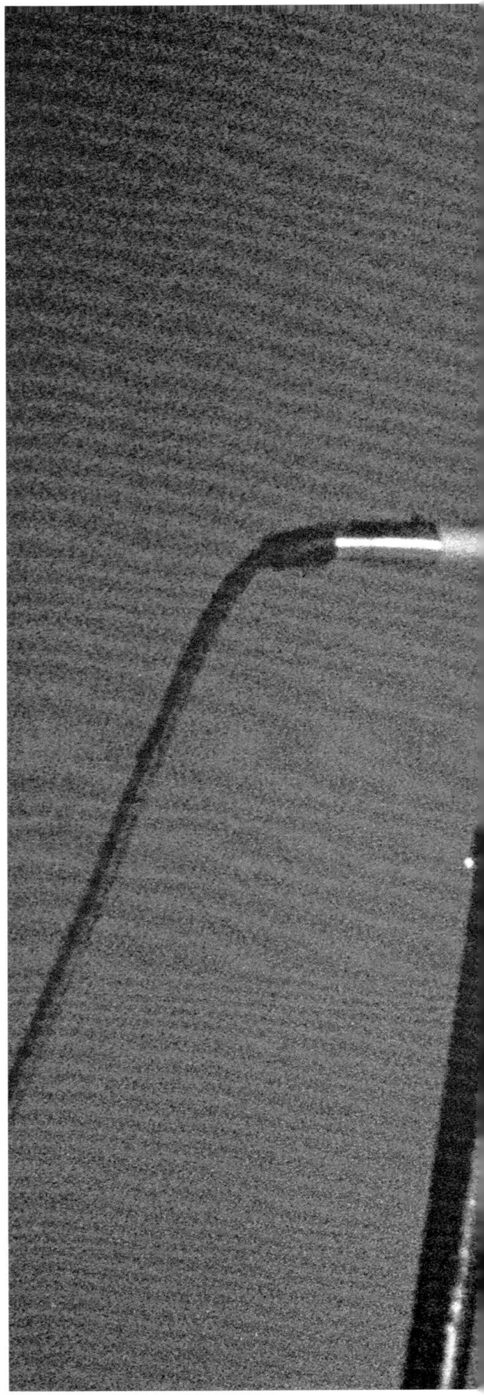

Steppenwolf, PNE Agrodome, Fall 1969.

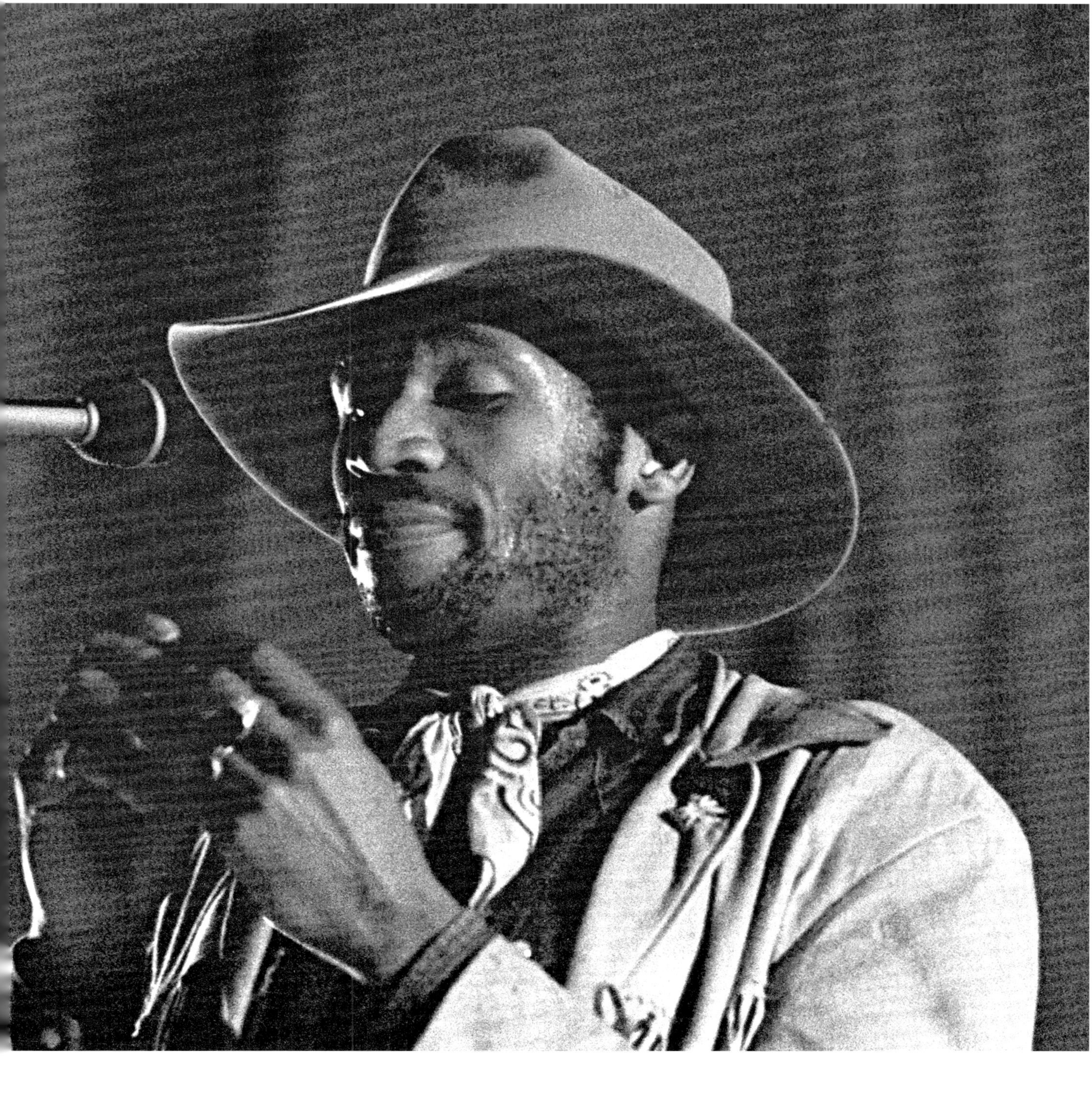

Taj Mahal, PNE Gardens Auditorium, November 16, 1969.

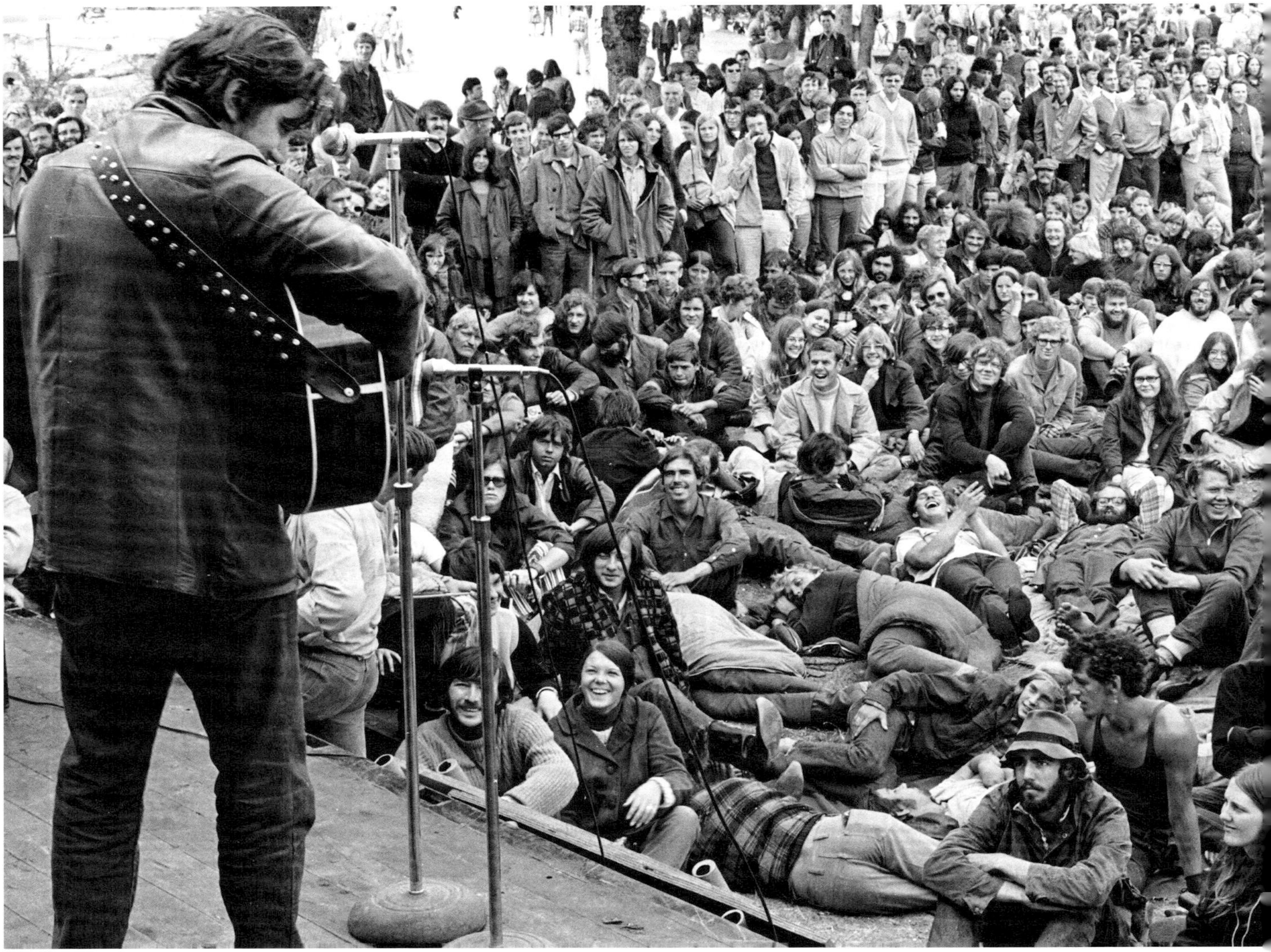

Phil Ochs performs at an illegal, free outdoor festival at Second Beach, June 28, 1970, organized by the Vancouver Liberation Front.

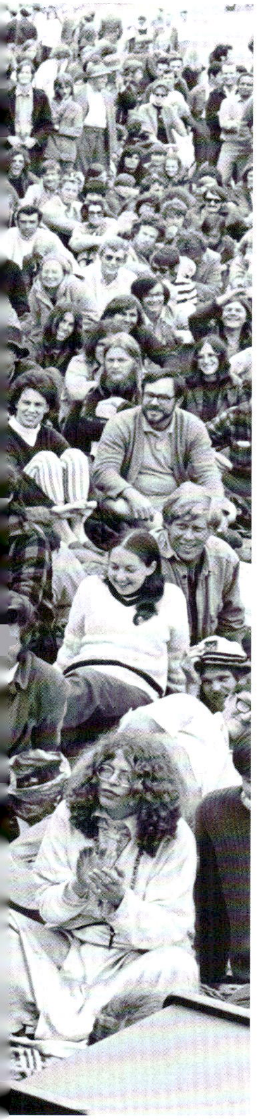

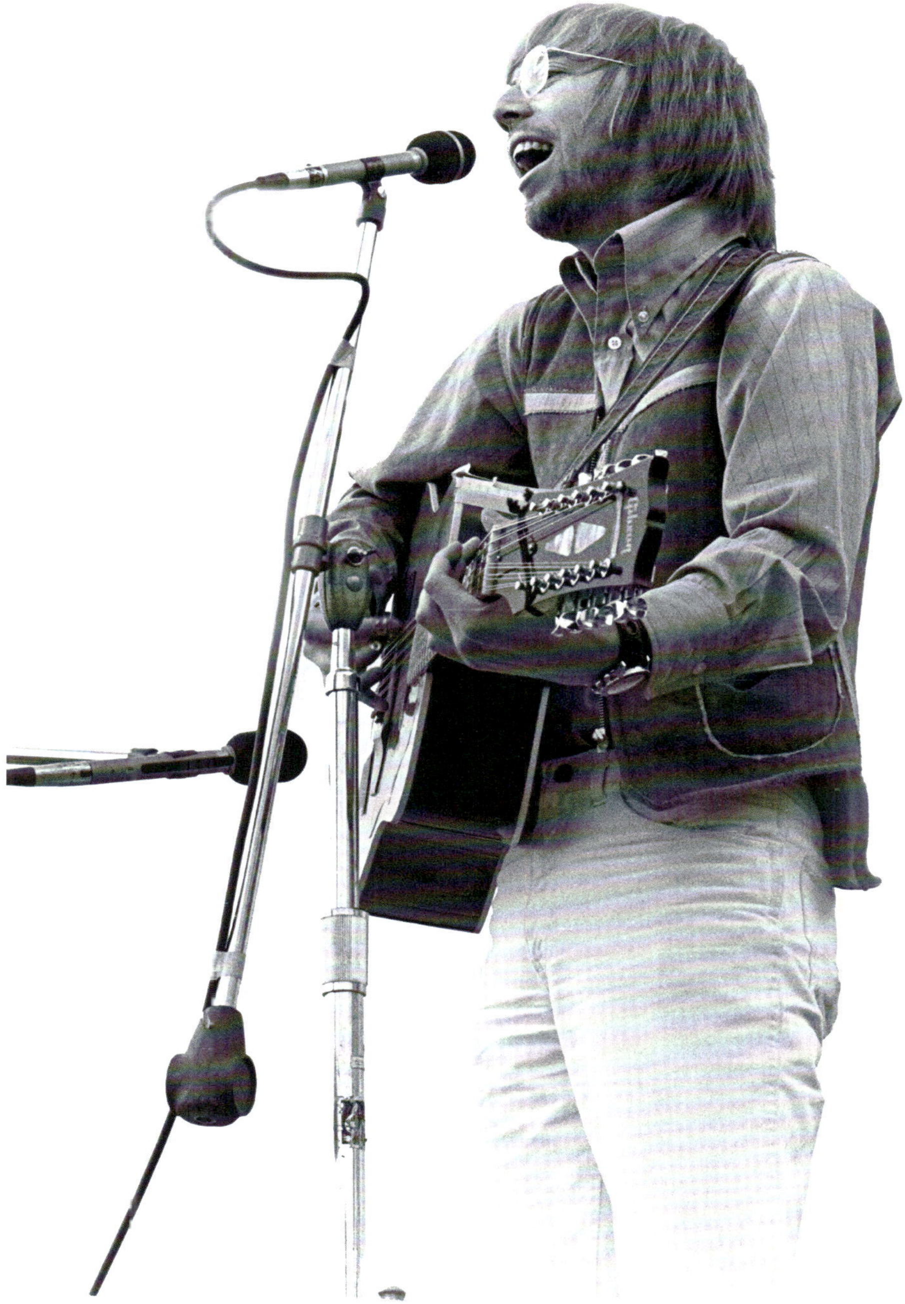

Fearing chaos and anarchy at the VLF's free festival, the City of Vancouver hoped to draw people away from that event with its own free counter-festival on False Creek featuring local folkie Tom Northcott.

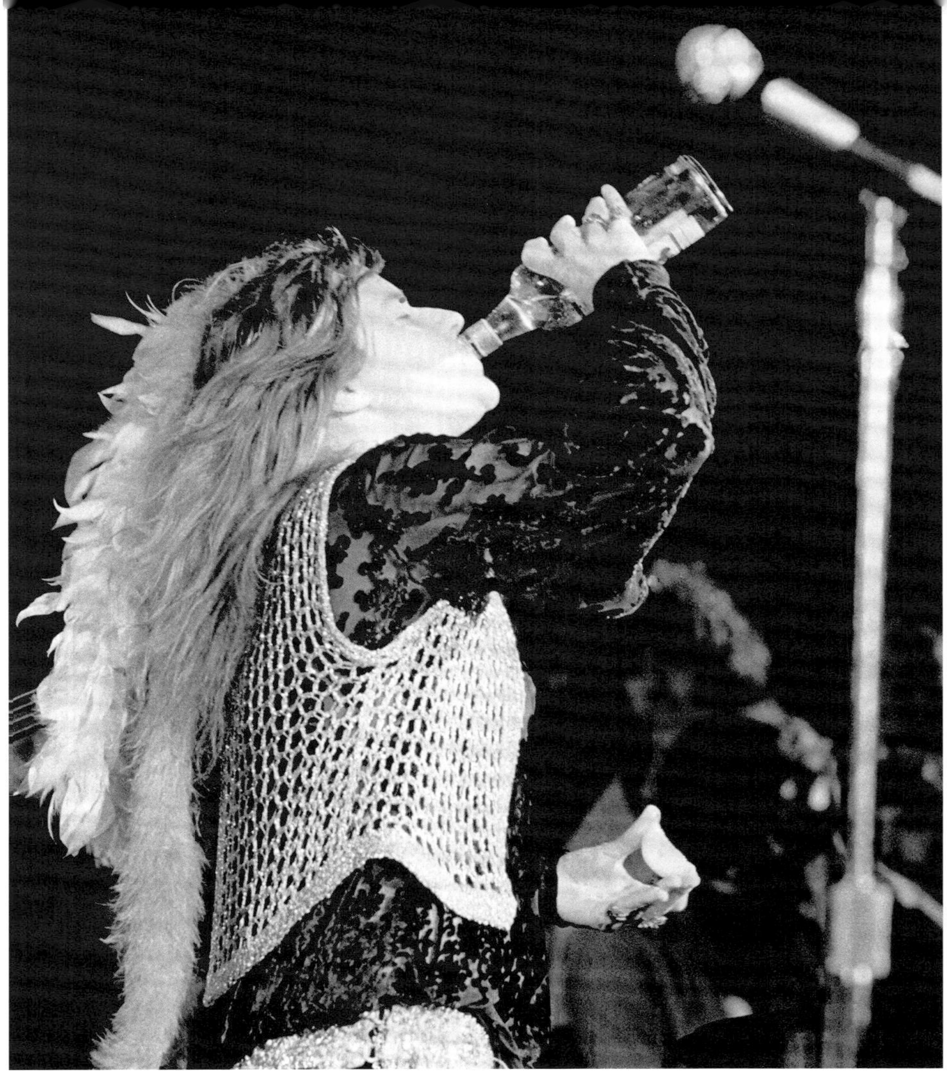

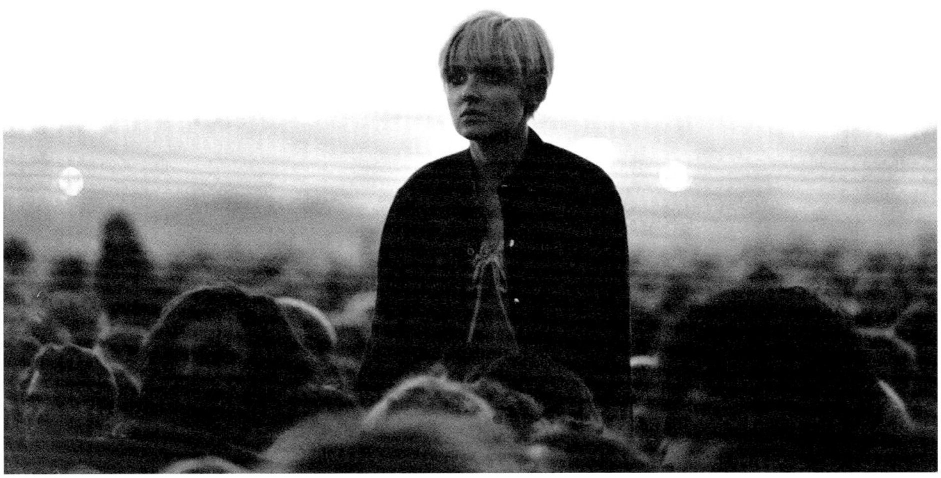

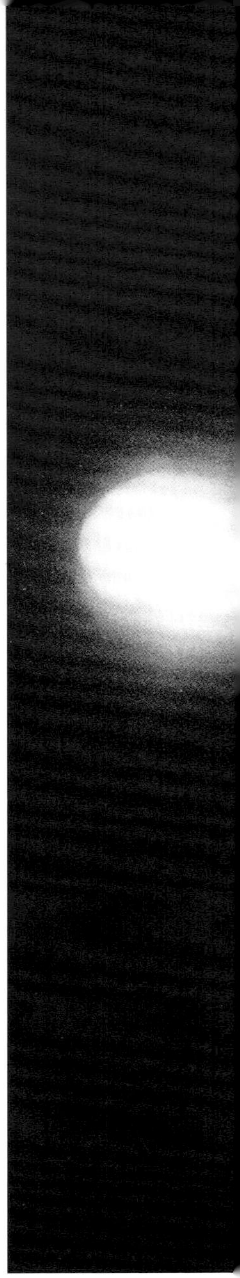

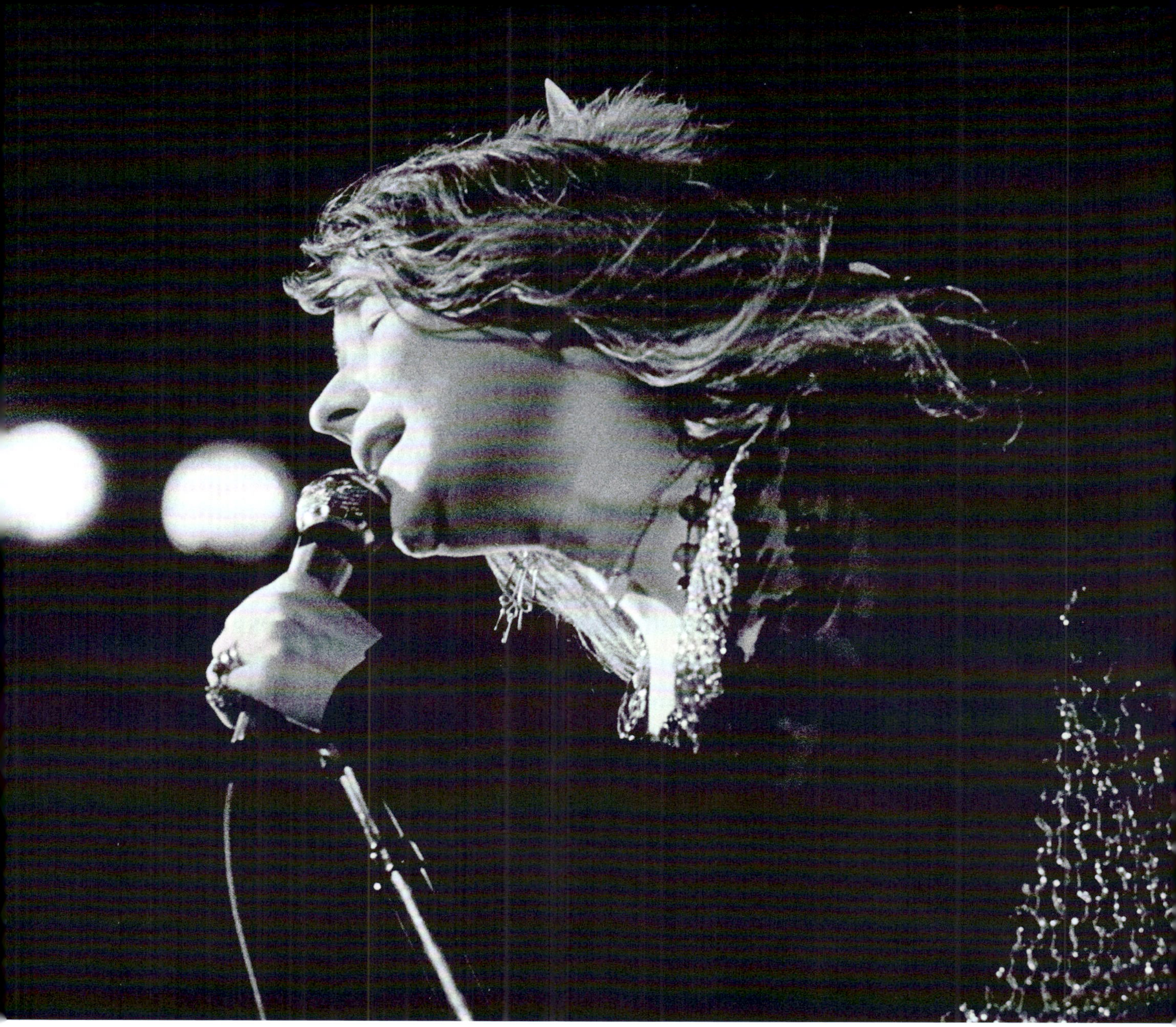

Janis Joplin, McMahon Stadium in Calgary in early July, 1970, part of the Festival Express tour.

Member of Janis's audience at McMahon Stadium.

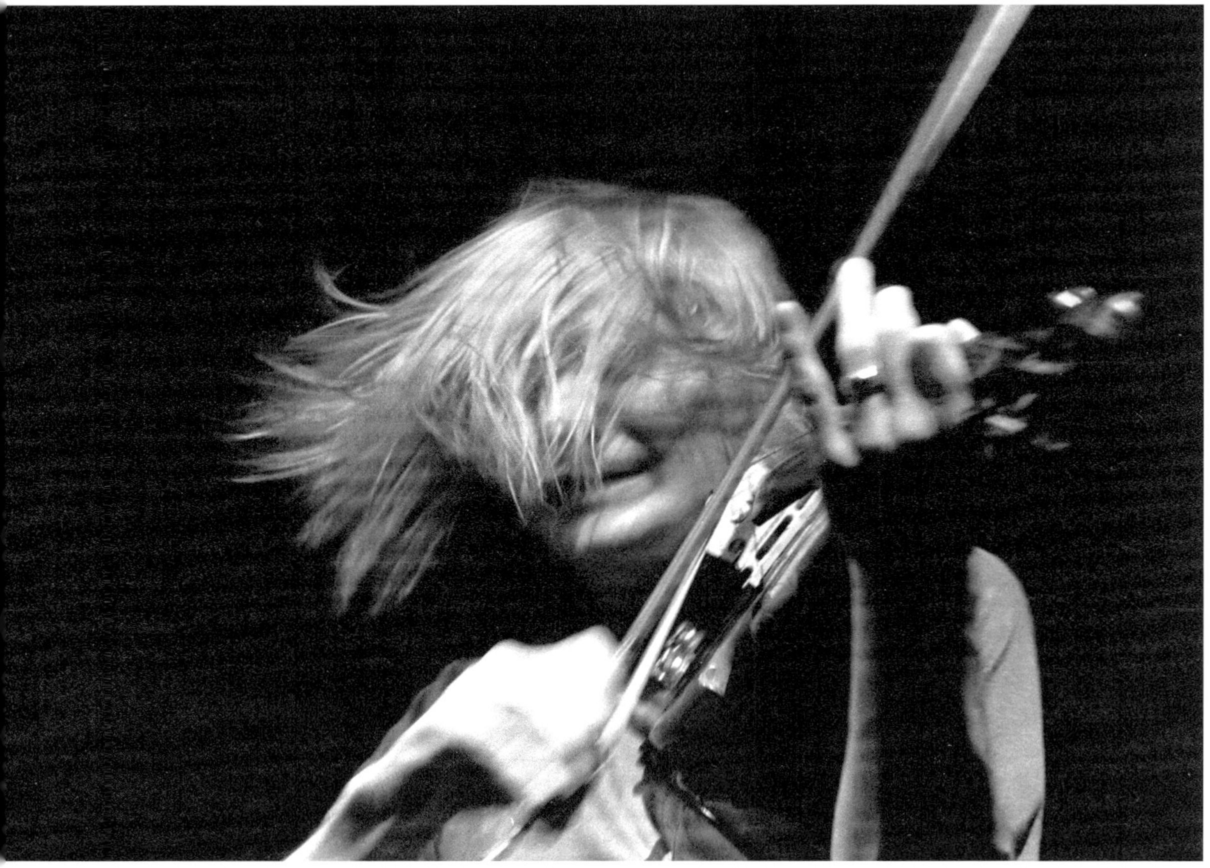

David LaFlamme of It's A Beautiful Day, Pacific Coliseum, September 19, 1970.

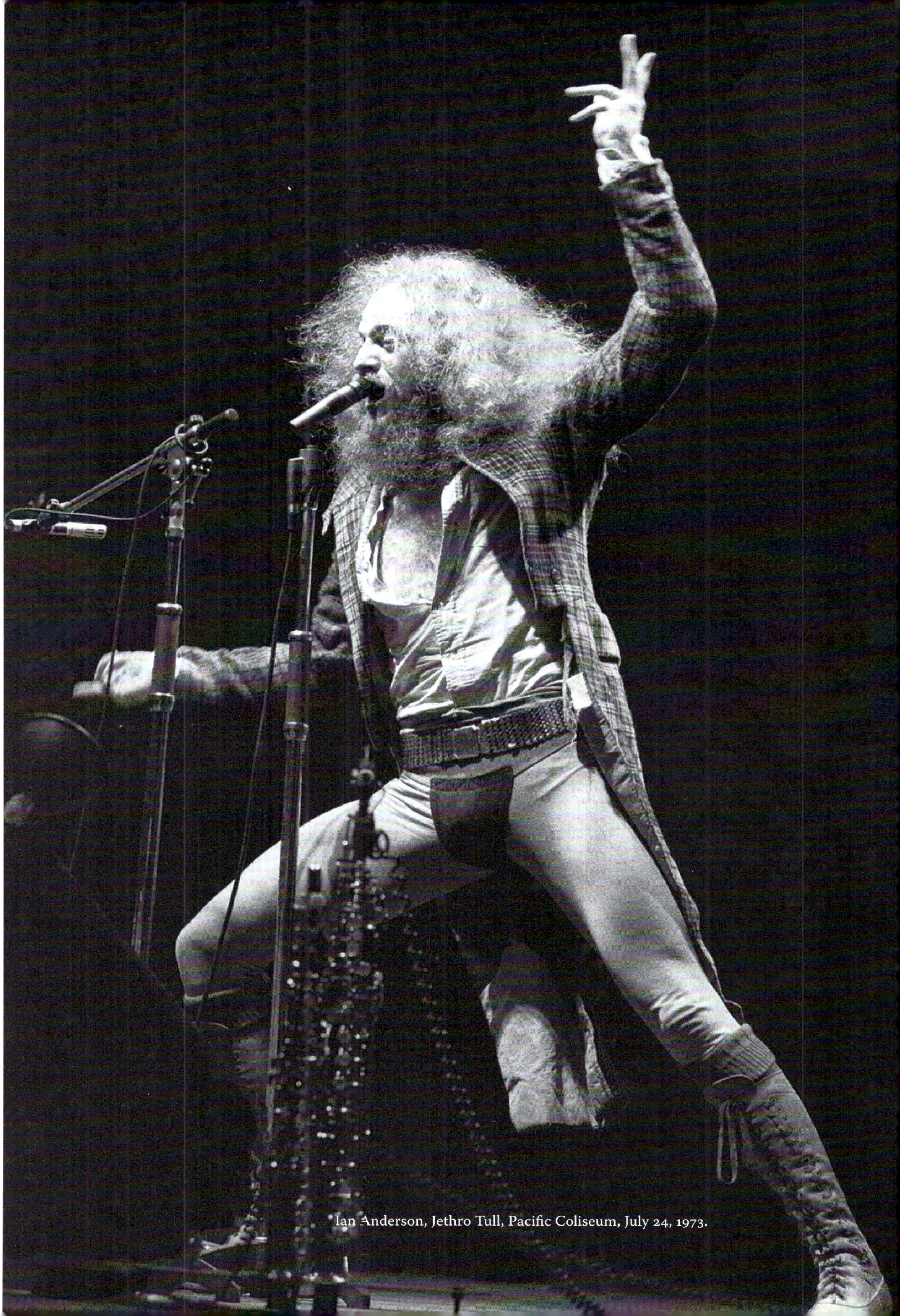

Ian Anderson, Jethro Tull, Pacific Coliseum, July 24, 1973.

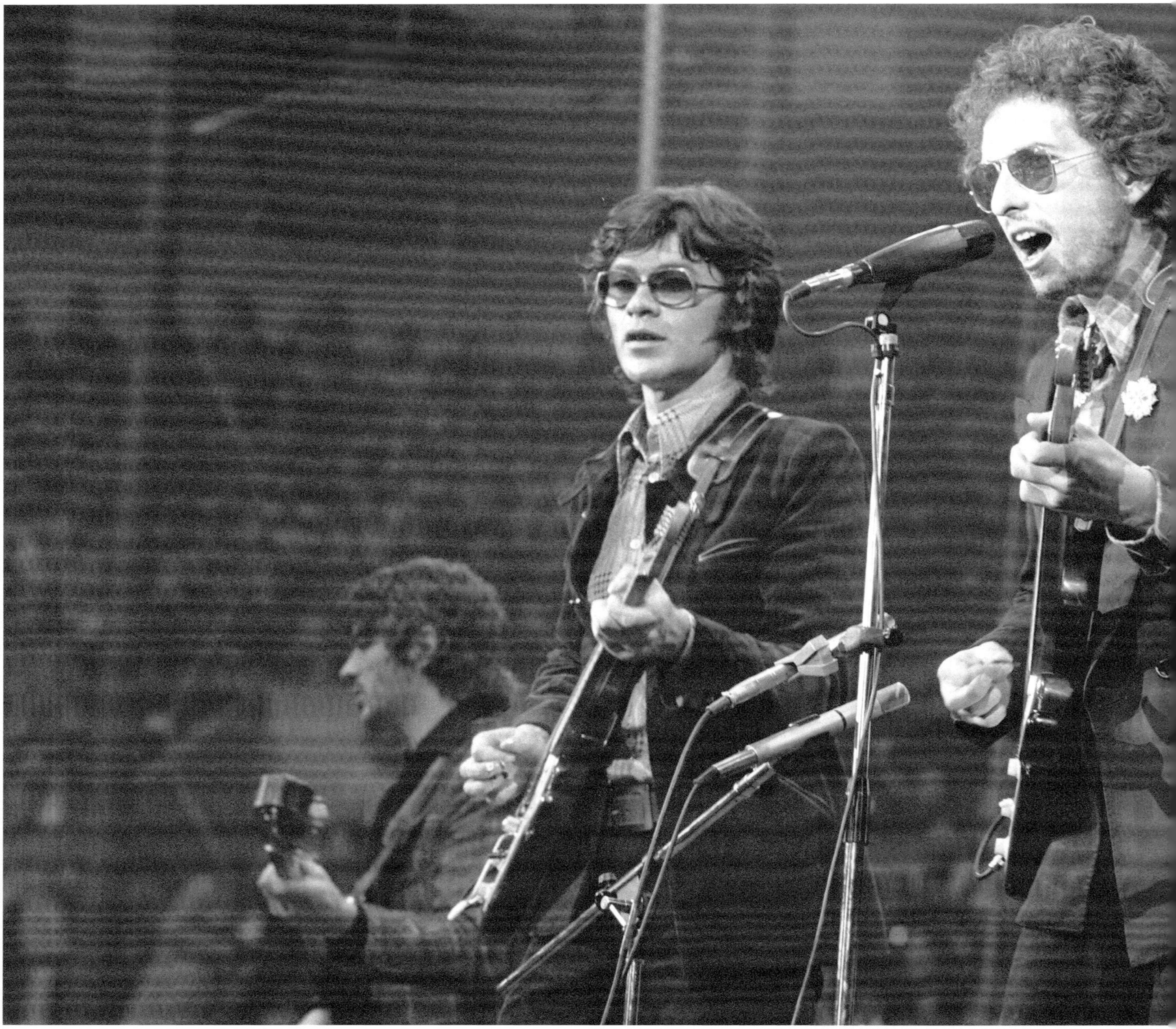

Rich Danko, Robbie Robertson, and Bob Dylan, Seattle Center Coliseum, February 9, 1974.

Bob Dylan, Seattle Center Coliseum, February 9, 1974.

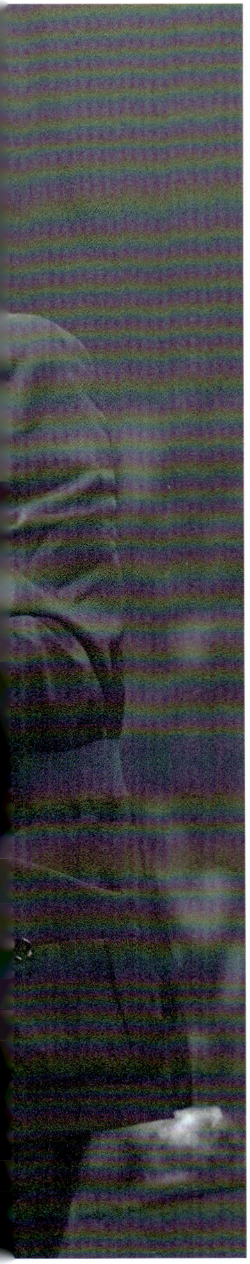

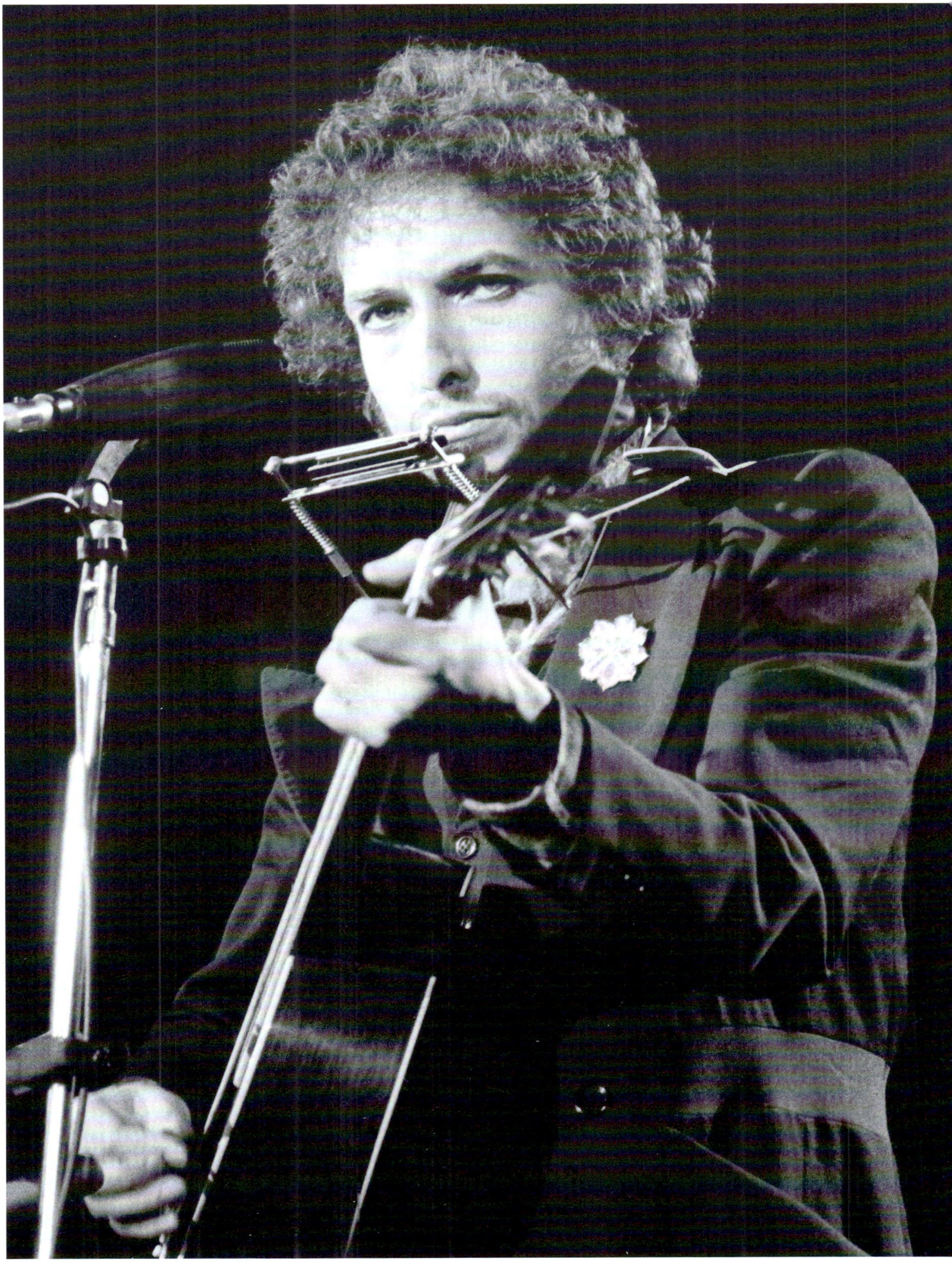

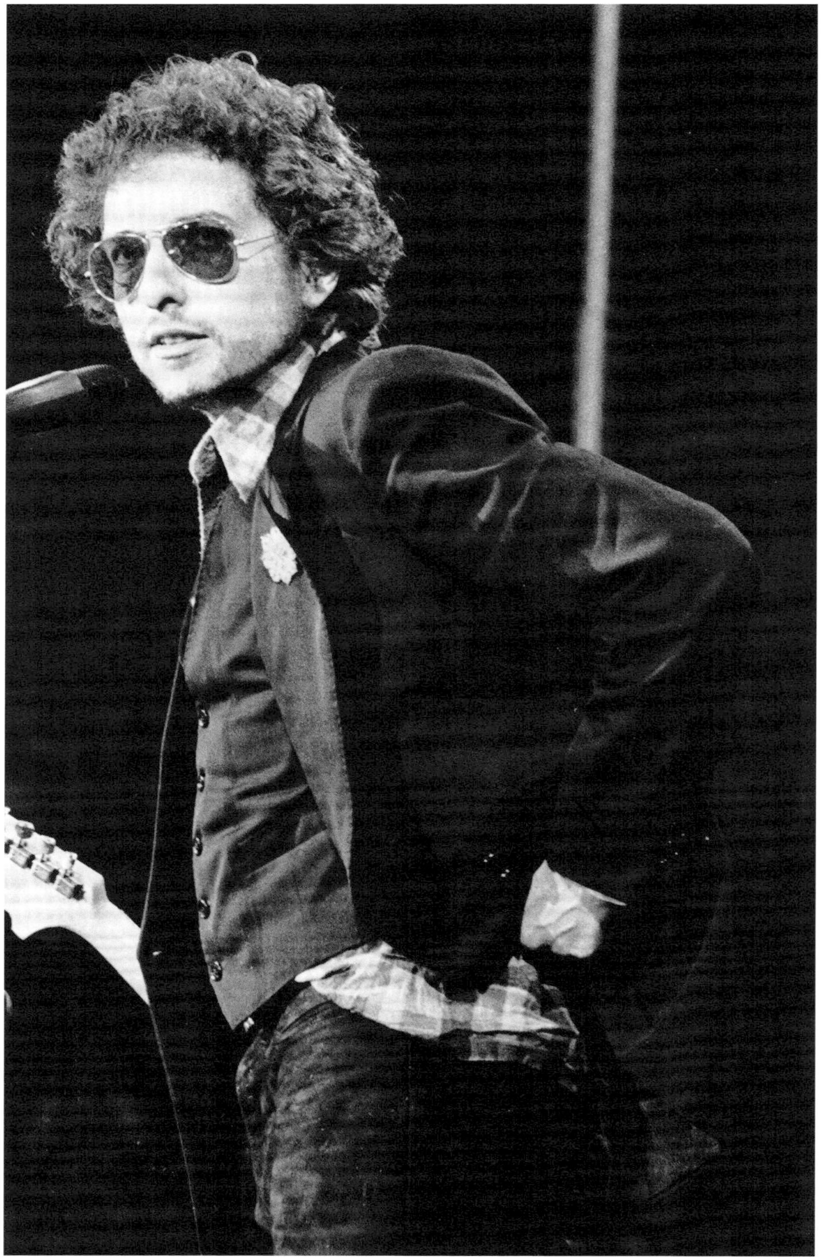

Afterword

by Jamie Reid

ON MARCH 26, 1966, BOB DYLAN led his band into Vancouver for a concert in front of a full house of 5,000 fans at the Agrodome, the city's largest concert venue at the time. It was the last show he would perform in North America for eight long years. For a new generation of youthful believers, Dylan had already been canonized by the media as a singing troubadour of their aspirations to an all-encompassing social revolution. Young people throughout the world were listening raptly to his recordings, as if they were the holy writ of their own social and political awakening, and conducting exercises in exegesis to decipher the esoteric code of their new religion.

On that grey and drizzling March evening, five of us — self-styled poets and artists all — were driving east along Hastings Street in Peter Auxier's beat-up dark blue Chevy. The goal of our pilgrimage was Dylan's concert later that night. Fervent anticipation beat in our hearts. We regarded ourselves as precocious veteran cognoscenti of the counter-culture revolution which had first sprung into existence in the late 1950s, nourished on the example of American cultural phenomena, including modern jazz and the literary florescence of the Beat generation. It's no exaggeration to say that we all saw ourselves as situated close to the very centre — perhaps even at the vanguard — of a worldwide counter-cultural movement, and had done so since the earliest days of Dylan's growing celebrity. Like thousands of other teenagers and young adults, we saw Dylan as our exalted comrade, a poet-herald of the future in the cultural war we all believed in, and dreamed we were waging against the dark, conformist past that even Eisenhower had warned against as he stepped down from the American presidency: the military industrial complex, colloquially known as The Man. A significant portion of our generation was steaming up to full rebellion against the established public order, which in our eyes threatened the future of the entire planet with atomic wars to perpetuate its world of permanent social and racial inequality. We admired Dylan as a poet and an avatar of a new world — as one of us.

Dylan, born in 1941, seemed a worthy and above all legitimate follower of the poet Allen Ginsberg and activist folk singers Woody Guthrie and Pete Seeger. My companions on that day had been part of the Vancouver counter-culture movement from the very beginning of the sixties. It was a phenomenon still little known to the wider public, yet increasingly popular at the time to the minority communities advocating public cultural action in the city. Peter Auxier, then a poet, was driving the car. He was later to become one of the forgotten founders of the *Georgia Straight*, the main media organ of the Vancouver underground when it was founded a year later. Mitzi Gibbs, a wise and sparkling personality, was also in the car with us, as was bill bissett, founder of the underground blewointment press, and now one of Canada's most revered poets and artists.

It was bissett who first spotted and pointed out Dylan sitting in the silver-grey Buick sliding up beside us at the stoplight in the centre lane. "There's Dylan!" he yelled. All our faces turned eagerly toward the window. And there the icon was, right beside us.

Two large bearded men wearing garish shirts were in the front seat. Dylan was behind them in the centre of the back seat, sitting upright, prim and alert. We were astonished to see his face so clearly and so close to us. He was sporting a gorgeous Afro like a nimbus around his head, each ash-blonde curl perfectly teased and in place. He looked like a cameo of a hip Victorian dandy, not at all like the ragged and indifferently-dressed beatnik bohemians we were. We expected that, like any normal celebrity, he would nod and smile at us with at least a polite pretense of friendly recognition. Instead, he greeted us with a cold, withering and unmoving stare of disdain.

It was not merely an indifferent snub. It was a frigid look of outright loathing and contempt — as if we were only insects splattered on his windshield. This wasn't "Mr. Tambourine Man" with his happy wandering Beatle-boot heels that we saw next to us, but the vacuum in the eyes of the mystery tramp in "Like a Rolling Stone."

At the time, he was in the midst of completing some inspiring but difficult sessions in Nashville, assembling his masterpiece double album, *Blonde on Blonde*. It's been reported since that he was taking a lot of hard drugs in those days, mostly amphetamines, to overcome the exhausting demands of his touring and studio commitments.

In that long moment, Dylan appeared to me as a sick, unhappy goblin. All of us in the car felt stunned and wounded by his attitude. Yet we overcame the moment by quickly inventing the self-assuring consensus that there was nothing the matter with us. The problem was with "Bobby," who was probably feeling sick and unhappy, we decided, forgiving him as we forgave ourselves. After all, we thought, despite being an exalted and brilliant poet hero, he was also — like all of us — a single individual in a global movement that was on its way to changing the world.

A few minutes later, Peter Auxier met up with Dylan's bodyguards while buying coffee in the arena before the show. "Your boy doesn't look too happy," Peter said to them with his usual disarming candour, always diplomatic and engaging. As Peter told the story later, Dylan's watchmen responded in kind. They were big men, and tough looking, Peter said, and they told Auxier that they were being driven crazy with the effort to keep their eye on Dylan every second. He was looking for a way to break away from them, they said, to escape from the coils of celebrity that had recently fallen upon him, turning his life into a nightmare of encounters with worshipful fans, so that he no longer recognized either himself or his fans. "There's too much money riding on this guy," they told Peter. "We can't let him get away from us."

For the record, Dylan took to the stage that night like the great professional showman he has always been. He sang a sparkling concert that aroused and enthralled the crowd. His normal slightly wry and sarcastic self, he showed no sign at all that he hated his audience, as he hated his own new life as a celebrity.

Dylan, like Eric Clapton, appears three times in this collection, more than any other musician, but the photos of him were taken eight years later — in 1974 in Seattle, Washington, not in Vancouver, BC in 1966. As I began to write this afterword about Vladimir Keremidschieff's photographs of 1960s Vancouver, I thought of Dylan's countenance that night in 1966 and wondered what might have happened had one of us had a camera and the wit and alacrity to record that shocking envenomed countenance on film.

It has been pointed out many times of late that we live in a world mediated by images. It's often said that the collective memory and world view of the public, as much as those can be said to exist, are put together from these same ubiquitous images mixed together with words. What would have happened had we somehow found the means to publish that shocking image, with appropriate captions? We had thought of ourselves as equals, brothers and sisters of Bob Dylan within a joint cultural project defined by the solidarity of its actors, but here it was suddenly revealed that we were mere nobodies beside the stars like Dylan and the other cultural heroes created, sustained and promoted in the images of the contemporary media.

Vladimir's arrangement of his photographs implicitly recognizes and pays tribute to this hierarchy of performers as stars and viewers as consumers, not through any misapprehension or volition of his own, but through the structure of social reality itself as revealed by his images.

My Back Pages, the original working title of Vladimir's project, was drawn from an early Bob Dylan song. The book documents in that "old" black and white some of the more important moments in the narrative echo of the final years of the youth rebellion as it broke out in Vancouver, then and now recognized as a Canadian centre of radical political and cultural dissent.

When Vladimir bought his first Pentax in the late 1960s, Vancouver was a growing city of 600,000 souls on the coastal edge — on the very fringe of the heartland of the American empire. Its economy and politics, like any another Canadian city, were heavily dominated by the power of corporations controlled outside the country, mainly from the United States, which in large part supplanted or marginalized whatever indigenous fringe or underground cultural movement of dissent existed in our city.

Vancouver was also an attractive destination for itinerant middle class youth, who, uniquely at that time, enjoyed the freedom, the resources, the means and the leisure to travel. They were labelled by the media as the baby boomers, the groundswell of population growth resulting from the economic boom that followed World War II. Impelled by the introduction of mass credit buying and publicized by the newly powerful advertising-funded mass medium of television, the booming economy engendered degrees and kinds of desire for consumption and pleasure that had no precedence. The baby boom cohort under the age of 25 constituted, by the mid-sixties, a vast market that became the target of a media blitz that mass-produced, packaged and sold them the goods of the cultural rebellion as the accoutrements of a consumable lifestyle.

Vancouver's attractions spoke to the enlightenment seekers of the sixties, itinerant followers of Jack Kerouac's vision in *On the Road*, the first bible and instruction manual of the counter-culture movement. The mild summer weather, the maritime atmosphere, the beaches, the parks, the mountains, the sparkling beauty of the city in the sunshine, the easy availability of full or part time employment: all enticements to those hitting the road without visible means of support, inspired by Kerouac's message of the rejection of social conformity, the embrace of sexual freedom, and a new culture of caring and sharing.

To those of us who had been at the centre of the earlier movement of cultural dissent, it seemed at first that the explosive new trend among the baby boom generation was a validation of our own earlier, smaller and more circumscribed effort. The new hippie movement, with its wide popular appeal, gave us hope that it might actually help to bring about the awakening of consciousness and transformation of society that we had all aspired to. It would be wrong to say that the youth of our generation knew where any of this would end. All the signs pointed to the fact that the young were aware of a challenging necessity for social change and were sincerely and innocently ready to put their young bodies and well-being on the line to play a role in moving our entire society forward.

Vladimir pays laudatory tribute to Dylan in his introduction, where he exults that "Listening to those early Dylan recordings was having a dump truck explode in your head. He could make the blind see, the deaf hear and the righteous weep." This "dump truck explosion" manifested itself in intense and complicated ways during those euphoric early days. Bob Dylan and the Beatles, with their unprecedented socially-critical pop lyrics, seemed to be putting words and images to the feelings and aspirations and inchoate thoughts that we all shared, but had been unable to fully articulate for ourselves. The first time I heard and felt that I had grasped Dylan's lyrics it seemed I had suddenly been initiated into a light-strewn mission, full of poetic inspiration and exaltation, a sense of belonging to an awakening generation with a new and more enlightened outlook than the past.

A kind of euphoric trance descended upon our much-expanded community of revolutionaries, and we began to entertain the possibility that anything was possible. The feeling was enhanced by the fact that the mainstream media seemed to recognize our sudden special power, pointing out that the boomers constituted more than 50 percent of the population. Collectively, we thought we could influence progressive change in North American democracies. We still believed in those democracies, and we still believed that we could give them a new direction, now that we thought we knew what the future really held.

Of course, the widespread use of drugs, mostly marijuana and LSD, played a significant role in this widespread feeling of euphoria. There were not a few who believed that the drugs themselves were the chief agency of the new consciousness, and were a kind of high road to social transformation, once the population at large had been converted to their use.

It's not as if the years that preceded the rebellious outbreak in the middle of the decade had been chock full of joy and light. A rebuffed American invasion of Cuba inaugurated the sixties in 1961, followed by the Cuban missile crisis, the most frightening of all nuclear confrontations between the two opposed superpowers of the United States and the Soviet Union. The assassination of John F. Kennedy in 1963 sent shock waves throughout the entire world. And all of this was taking place against the background of the ever-present threat of nuclear holocaust. Dark and frightening times indeed.

In Vancouver, the forces of the counter-culture movement created several venues where they could listen to their own new music and celebrate their new-found solidarity. In July 1966, Sam Perry, a filmmaker with wide local connections, organized a Vancouver version of the first San Francisco Trips Festival, a multi-media event that featured the acid-rock bands of San Francisco: The Grateful Dead, Jefferson Airplane, and Big Brother and the Holding Company backing Janis Joplin, then barely known outside California. In March of the following year, I acted as the front man for the first Vancouver Easter Human Be-In (it wasn't really necessary to "organize" anything in those days of heady collective spontaneity), in imitation of the January event of the same name in San Francisco and featuring some of the same bands, as well as star appearances by Allen Ginsberg and psychedelic drug guru Timothy Leary. To headline the event, local music promoter Jerry Kruz brought Country Joe and the Fish, one of the most outspoken of all political bands.

The local authorities wanted to stop the Be-In from taking place in Stanley Park, to which we simply replied that the impetus for the event was already underway, and that nobody could stop it now from happening. It took place regardless of the civic ban, and even continued annually for another eight or nine years. At the time of the first Be-In, the spirits of the counter-culture movement in Vancouver were still flying high in a sky of blue — but dark clouds were on their way.

My own disenchantment with the "peace and love" flower-child contingent of the counter-culture began with a pilgrimage to San Francisco in January of 1968, only six months after the highly publicised "Summer of Love." There the cracks and decay within the economics and politics of the counter-culture were starkly apparent. The Haight–Ashbury district had already dissolved into a cesspool of drug-taking, needle-induced disease, rampant venereal disease, grinding poverty, drug-profit exploitation, and drug-induced psychosis. It was enough to make me understand that the idealism and the drugs of the love and peace generation alone were never going to be enough to bring serious changes to the world.

During my pilgrimage to San Francisco there was a newspaper strike in the city that shut down all the mainstream papers, leaving the streets open to the vendors of the *San Francisco Oracle*, who proudly displayed their own dissident headline: "Guess who's winning in Vietnam?" This in the midst of the furious Tet Offensive, which for the first time raised the spectre of a humiliating American defeat — a positive outcome in the minds of the counter-cultural elements like myself and others who had taken the side of the national liberation forces in Vietnam. The joyous anticipation of this possibility, however, merely emphasized the darkness of the events taking place on the home front.

On April 4, 1968, Martin Luther King, the celebrated advocate of non-violent resistance, was assassinated in Memphis. Riots in Washington, Baltimore and other American cities were a reprise of earlier riots expressing the rage of Afro-Americans at the inequality and brutality they were still suffering in so-called democratic America. The Civil Rights movement was struggling toward light and apparent victory amidst ongoing murders and bombings and brutality against Afro-American people in the United States. The mood had been dark until the Johnson administration moved forward with its Civil Rights agenda, driven by the Civil Rights Act of July, 1964, a victory for the forces of racial equality. It had seemed as if the new youth movement was acting as the catalyst for peace and social equality, but the assassination of King lent credence to the claims of armed self-defence advocates like the Black Panthers — that the violence of the American state could not be successfully countered or overcome by peaceful means. The US was seething and collapsing into racial and ideological civil war.

On June 5, 1968, Robert Kennedy was shot after winning the Democratic presidential primary in California and died the following day. Kenneth T. Walsh quotes the American sociologist Todd Gitlin: "To think about the enormous repercussions of the assassinations of 1968, we need to backtrack to the imagery and mood of a more general Armageddon, for which the triggering moment is the assassination of 1963. Kennedy, King, Kennedy: they sometimes felt like stations in one protracted murder of hope."

Traumatic events at the Democratic Party convention held in Chicago August 26 to 29, 1968, demonstrated to the surging forces of dissent that they could not count on the support of the mainstream American political parties to fulfill their aims in seeking peace. Chicago mayor Richard Daley, also a supporter of the Vietnam war, sent out thousands of police and National Guardsmen to attack the demonstrators — the 10,000 or so mainly youth and students who came out to protest the direction the American government was taking. They were beaten with truncheons, tear-gassed, handcuffed and hauled off to jails in what a later investigation called a "police riot." Meanwhile, on the convention floor itself, Daley's hired security thugs even attacked members of the mainstream press, including Dan Rather. The message to the youth was that no mainstream party in the United States would support their efforts to end the war in Vietnam. The youth movement of the entire world was calling for peace and an end to the imperial policy of the U.S. in Vietnam, and was being countered with outright violence by the American state against its own citizens. The outcome of these traumatic events was the election of Richard Nixon, on a pro-war and law-and-order platform, as president of the United States.

The photographs in *Seize the Time* from this period are missing the jubilant spirit that animated the earlier years of the youth rebellion — a mood that had turned more sombre and reflective. This is not to say that the youth movement was ever monolithic. It represented, instead, a potpourri of concerns ranging from the seriously political and the exotically spiritual, to the hedonism suggested by the omnipresent slogans of "sex, drugs and rock'n'roll" and "do your own thing," to the outright abandonment of any serious agenda for the human future, like Timothy Leary's exhortation to "turn on, tune in, drop out." In direct contradiction to the early ambitions of the counter-culture movement, all of these slogans were open appeals for non-participation in public discourse and action.

Bob Dylan's optimistic earlier political anthems like "Blowin' in the Wind" and "The Times They are a-Changin'" gradually gave way to the overt cynicism of *Highway 61 Revisited*, with its dark humour and bitter social satire, followed by bleak veiled allegories of depression and apocalypse like "Desolation Row" and "All Along the Watchtower." The organized political youth were dismayed when both the Beatles and Dylan seemed to abandon them: the Beatles released "Revolution," which openly condemned the anger within the youth movement, and Mick Jagger has said of the 1968 Rolling Stones release, "Sympathy For the Devil," that "I wrote it as kind of a Bob Dylan song."

The images in this book are thus appropriately in black and white, reflecting more accurately the increasingly sombre mood of the times rather than the psychedelic colour of the earlier sixties. One feels the dominance of brown and grey — of damp Vancouver skies rather than summer sunshine. Those who never witnessed and experienced the events recorded by Vladimir's Pentax will probably see them as a kind of sepia representation of their parents' history and life. Those who were present will be seeking tokens of remembrance and might pore over them closely, as I did, for the sight of familiar faces, including their own. As the culture critic John Berger has parenthetically pointed out in his essay "Understanding a Photograph," "The most popular use of the photograph is as a memento of the absent."

The varied and powerful social movements documented in Vladimir's photographs are still being played out and still have their effect on contemporary reality. The peace movement is still alive, the movement for the preservation of the natural environment is active and stronger than ever before, the movement for women's equality continues. A candidate in the next Canadian federal election, whose father's image appears in this book, has recently declared that he would legalize the use of marijuana, the harmless drug that fueled many a fantasy of revolution in the sixties. The mills of the gods grind slowly, for sure — the most unimportant issue of those days works its way toward resolution, while on the important issues, the achievement of world peace and social equality, mainstream politics remains stalled on the same dangerous yet familiar pathways of money and power.

The survivors of the sixties protest movements whose youthful enthusiasms are recorded in this book might well now be asking how much their idealism, effort and sacrifice has actually accomplished in terms of effecting positive social change over the past half-century.

Vladimir's photographs can be divided into three distinct categories: the city and its people, the music, and the protests. Appreciating the value of the book requires the recognition that above all it is a book about people and human social activity. It is not about the architecture of the city that frames their actions, nor is it about the rich and famous of the city, or the local political elites who exercise their power in the city. It is not even so much about the majority of the people of the city, although their visible presence always remains suggestively in the background. More than anything else, the book is about the dissident youthful minority and their musical heroes and idols, their models of the time, misguided or otherwise.

According to Vladimir's introduction, he made his living by taking photographs of the counter-culture entertainers who performed in Vancouver and selling them to the mainstream press: within the context of the times, an honourable and probably badly underpaid occupation. His photographs of the protests are more like an unpaid genuine labour of love, not money, and all the more valuable on that account. Their ideological message is obvious and sharply contrary to the prevailing powers of the time.

The demonstrators appear in the main in a positive and happy light. Vladimir wants to present his subjects as people with an honest mission, worthy of attention and affection. He is on their side, and not on the side of authority. *Seize the Time* is openly, avowedly and transparently a book of visual polemics, aimed at assisting the process of making changes in a society that Vladimir obviously sees and presents as unjust and inhumanely organized, requiring change. The named musical heroes and the unnamed faces in the crowds of demonstrators are presented as the agents of the demand for that change.

The photographic argument begins with the old BC Hydro building, the unquestionably necessary electrical centre of the industrial, and therefore the economic life of the city and the province. Every window in the building is filled with light against the darkness of the surrounding night, a symbolic image of misplaced opulence and wanton waste of a precious natural resource, a political statement in its own right. Yet despite the environmental movement and its demand to save precious energy for useful purposes, some still view this image of conspicuous consumption as a source of civic pride. In any case, a source of ongoing political contention in the city is evoked from the very first pages of the book.

A series of Vladimir's photographs from 1970 document an effort on the part of Harry Rankin, a well-known reformist Vancouver politician, to organize public discourse among sections of the population not normally consulted in civic affairs. Their neighbourhood, Gastown, a decaying district beside the now notorious Downtown Eastside, is in the process of being developed into a quaint and profitable tourist destination. The citizens represented in these images are obviously unhappy and impoverished, disempowered and disenfranchised, their hardened faces skeptical and resigned. Today, as international visitors tour Gastown directly from the cruise ships that stop over in the city, the surrounding blocks remain a centre of unrelieved and growing homelessness and ongoing civic dissension.

The opening section of the book also contains photographs of Vancouver's elder citizens of those days, reflecting their curiosity and bewilderment at novel events in their changing world — like the two senior women who are observed bemusedly watching and pointing at "Hare Krishnas singing and dancing," as we are informed by the caption.

Other images are more mysterious and harder to interpret, although they evoke immediate feelings and speculations. A photograph of two "square" middle-aged Vancouver citizens flanking a young woman is captioned only "Two men and a lady." Her hand gesture toward her mouth seems to signal uncertainty and a sense of vulnerability, but the expressions on the faces of the men, though intense, cannot be fully read or interpreted. A woman taxi driver with a face like a movie star, were it not for her blurred, sad, burdened and hardened expression, leans out of the window of her cab. The caption tells us suggestively that the photograph was "for an article on female cab drivers, a somewhat controversial occupation for women in those days." The section also contains strong portraits of young people whose dress and posture signifies their self-declared status as members of the counter-culture. Their expressions are proud and thoughtful.

Though not foregrounded, a few of the prominent politicians of the day make occasional appearances. A portrait of the then Vancouver mayor presiding over a council meeting is captioned "Tom 'Terrific' Campbell," as he was in fact sarcastically labelled by the population. A champion of the well-heeled real estate developers who transformed the city's west end during the 1960s, he once labelled hippies gathering around the steps of the Vancouver Courthouse as "scum," and carried out a hysterical and physically brutal campaign against them until a City Council committee finally declared that the mild and non-violent hippies of Vancouver were "no threat to the society." Canadian Prime Minister Pierre Elliott Trudeau appears in a Karsh-like "sensitive" portrait. A second photograph shows him, a practising Catholic, meeting in a highly casual atmosphere with a group of women talking about abortion issues. A bearded, bespectacled poet wearing a beaded necklace, at "UBC open house festivities, 1970," reads from a book called *Our Word* with a photo of an automatic rifle on its cover. Four decades later the young poet would re-emerge as the popular and well-dressed trade union leader George Heyman, recently elected as a member of the British Columbia legislature.

Seize the Time presents a series of photographs of some of the musicians who were the idols and mentors of the counter-culture, mostly in performance. They were taken, according to Vladimir's introduction, primarily for publication in newspapers, and as such are unabashed fan pics.

A few stand out as portraits — unique and especially revealing of their subjects, caught exactly at moments that really count. Janis Joplin, with a leonine mane, drinks desperately from a bottle of what looks like tequila in the middle of a performance, while the lights in the facing photograph seem to burn into Janice's emotion-filled face as she sings into a hand-held microphone. Both photographs together showcase her famous flame of passionate intensity. Chuck Berry's clear-cut facial features as he thumbs an amulet strung around his neck foreground the confident sexual intensity that rings out so hotly in his performances.

My own favourite is the candid photo of Jim Morrison of the Doors, taken perhaps by surprise through the window of the helicopter in which he sits. Morrison gazes calmly at the photographer with a look both sceptical and defensive. The young Dionysius appears flushed and slightly bloated, world weary and thoughtful, tired, older than his age. He would be dead within a year. It's an affecting reminder of the dangerous and self-destructive character of not a few of the culture heroes of the day, dogged by drugs and suicide. For me, it is one of the most iconic pictures in the book, bearing visual witness to the hubris and self-indulgent recklessness of the counter-culture — the blindness that prevented the youth movement of the time from effecting wider positive changes in the society we inherited.

Vladimir's photos of protests consist almost entirely of crowd scenes, many of them taken on the steps of Vancouver's former Courthouse, converted to become the Vancouver Art Gallery in 1983, and still today the preferred site of political demonstrations in the city. Here we view the meaning of Vladimir's's efforts, the message that the book seems designed to carry — the crowd tableaus look as if their actors are appearing on stage for a curtain call. They are carrying flags and waving placards: "U.S. Aggressors Get Out of Vietnam," "Honour Geneva Agreements," "Their Fight is our Fight," "Stop Shipment of War Materials," "Peace Now," "Escalate "People's War"; along with representations of the revolutionary leaders of the day, Ho Chi Minh, Che Guevara, Mao Tse-Tung. The people are singing and shouting and playing guitars as they march. There is a photograph of an actual fight on the steps of the Courthouse, a sign of the ideological divisions within the ranks of the dissenters of all ideological stripes, Trotskyists, anarchists, Maoists. They depict mostly but not exclusively young people. Their faces are determined and serious, but also proud.

Most of the photographs taken throughout this period by others emphasize a drama played out between dissenting demonstrators and police, the representatives of order and the status quo. But images of police are oddly missing from this collection. It's as if the photographer has made the conscious decision to leave them out in his effort to produce a positive image of his subjects as they appeared in themselves and for themselves.

Recent discourses of photography emphasize two main issues: the photograph as documentary object reflecting social and historical reality, and the photograph as art object embodying human emotion and values. In Vladimir's photographs, the two are wound together in inextricable ways. His work presented here clearly acts in both of these directions: documentary and aesthetic.

This photographer works not from the fringes of the crowds but from front and centre — less a voyeur, more a participant. Vladimir's subjects in these photos saw themselves as the moral agents of necessary change, and they need to be remembered as such. Vladimir has done them that honour.